Madame de Pompadour

Madame de Pompadour

A LIFE

EVELYNE LEVER

TRANSLATED FROM THE FRENCH
BY CATHERINE TEMERSON

FARRAR, STRAUS AND GIROUX
NEW YORK

Farrar, Straus and Giroux
19 Union Square West, New York 10003

Grateful acknowledgment is made to the following institutions for their kind permission to reproduce paintings and other images:

Le Normant de Tournehem by Louis Tocqué; *The Château d'Etiolles*; *Alexandrine Le Normant d'Etiolles* by François-Hubert Drouais; *The Cardinal de Bernis*; *The Château de Bellevue*; and *Belle Jardinière* by Louis-Michel Van Loo © RMN/Art Resource, N.Y. *Louis XV* by Maurice-Quentin de La Tour © Giraudon/Art Resource, N.Y. *Madame de Poisson* by Adélaïde Labille-Guillard and *The Marquis de Marigny* by Jean-François de Troy © Tallandier. *Louis XV* by Jean-Marc Nattier © The State Hermitage Museum, St. Petersburg. *Madame de Pompadour* by François Boucher; *The Hall of Mirrors*; the etching of the celebration of the Dauphin's marriage by Charles-Nicolas Cochin; and *The Duc de Chouiseul Stainville* by Louis-Michel Van Loo © G. Dagli Orti. The image of the secret staircase © Plon/Perrin. *Madame de Pompadour* by Maurice-Quentin de La Tour © Louvre, Paris, France/Bridgeman Art Library

Library of Congress Cataloging-in-Publication Data

Lever, Evelyne.
[Madame de Pompadour. English]
Madame de Pompadour : a life / Evelyne Lever ; translated from the French
by Catherine Temerson.
p.   cm.
Includes bibliographical references and index.
ISBN 0-374-11308-4 (hc : alk. paper)
1. Pompadour, Jeanne Antoinette Poisson, marquise de, 1721–1764.
2. Louis XV, King of France, 1710–1744—Relations with women.
3. Favorites, Royal—France—Biography.   4. France—Kings and rulers—
Mistresses—Biography.   5. France—History—Louis XV, 1715–1774.
I. Title.

DC135.P8 L4313 2002
944'.034'092—dc21
[B]

2002022811

Designed by Jonathan D. Lippincott

www.fsgbooks.com

1   3   5   7   9   10   8   6   4   2

For M. B. L.

Contents

CONTENTS

Madame
de Pompadour

One

DEATH OF A FAVORITE

The Court is in turmoil and Louis XV is in despair. In her mansion in Paris, on the rue du Bac, Madame de Châteauroux is dying. Ever since his mistress's condition has become critical, the King has avoided appearing in public. Confined to his private apartments in Versailles, he anxiously awaits every bit of news. The Duc d'Ayen,[1] the Duc de Luxembourg[2] and the Marquis de Gontaut[3] take turns giving him the latest health bulletins; the banker Pâris de Montmartel sends him four messengers a day from the patient's antechamber where he is keeping watch. Unfortunately, the messages are more and more alarming and the masses celebrated on the sovereign's orders fail to bring mercy from Above. On December 7, 1744, while Madame de Châteauroux receives the last sacraments, the King quietly leaves Versailles for the Château de La Muette, at the edge of the Bois de Boulogne. It is there, the following day, that he receives the dreaded news. He had asked to be disturbed only in an extreme emergency, and only a few intimate friends had been given the order to join him.

The King has been obsessed with death since childhood. Indeed, death had carried away all the males in the royal family prematurely and made him, a fragile two-year-old prince, the successor to the most illustrious of monarchs.[4] In 1715, when his great-grandfather, the Sun King, died, he ascended to the throne under the name of Louis XV. He was only five years old, but the anxious solicitude with which he was surrounded soon made him aware of both his omnipotence and vulnerability. At the slightest cold, people worried that his life might be in danger, and he was brought up in fear of the devil and hell. He thus became accustomed to the idea of his own death at a very early age and liked to allude to it, perhaps the better to ward it off. He would often talk about death, the dying and the punishments of the afterlife. One day, when the Duc de Luynes advised him to banish such images from his mind, he replied: "Why should I? Isn't that moment bound to come?"[5]

The sudden passing away of Madame de Châteauroux rekindled past sorrows in this intensely melancholic man. He could not fail to be reminded of the loss of Madame de Vintimille, his previous mistress, who died in childbirth on September 9, 1741. Devastated by that blow, he had refused to see anyone for an entire day, and had taken refuge at Saint-Léger, in the home of the Comtesse de Toulouse, his confidante. Now he remained listless and despondent in his La Muette retreat; he barely ate and found comfort only in the company of four or five people who had been close to Madame de Châteauroux. The days went by, weighed down with grief. However, eventually he had no choice but to end this isolation and return to Versailles. Grown pale and thin, on December 14, the sovereign took up residence, not at the château, but at Trianon, as a way of guarding against his inevitable obligations.

Still "very preoccupied by his grief,"[6] he rose at ten or ten-thirty, heard mass, and presided over the Council or conversed with his ministers until two o'clock. He then lunched with the close friends who were always by his side since Madame de Châteauroux's death. After the meal, which he ate without any appetite, they indulged in a few languid quadrilles until the King went out for a walk in the grounds adjoining his apartment. He returned at around six and worked until supper, at nine, with the same guests with whom he had had lunch. They talked until two in the morning.[7] Social intercourse required much tact, as the latest news was far from cheerful: Madame de Ventadour, who had been like a mother for the sovereign, had also just died. She was ninety-two and the King had always shown her a great deal of affection.

It wasn't until Christmas that Louis XV agreed to return to his apartments in the château. He seemed disconsolate, and the new year began as sadly as the one that had ended. In deference to their master's grief, the courtiers were elegantly bored when at Versailles, but in Paris they enjoyed themselves. Besides, the favorite's death had set tongues wagging. At first, the suddenness and violence of her illness had spread fear. As always, when there was a sudden, unexplained death, everyone spoke of poison. Some people truly believed this; others were doubtful; however, no tears were spilled over Madame de Châteauroux, for she had not been very much liked. At Court the dead are always at fault and quickly forgotten. They leave behind a position to be filled. And the position of official mistress is the most coveted of all. Being loved by the King is the greatest conceivable honor; and this particular monarch, in the full splendor of his thirty-fifth year, is considered the handsomest man in his kingdom. Adored by his subjects, who have nicknamed him the *Bien-Aimé* (Much Loved), he stirred many hearts, and wakened the wildest ambitions. The beloved of this king would not only gain glory and pleasure from her elevation, but she would also secure many advantages for herself, her family and her inevitable protégés: nominations to the most enviable positions, pensions and bonuses of various kinds. Her power might reach even further: she might hold sway over the King's mind and influence major decisions. Since the rise of a favorite brought all her relatives in tow, all the Court clans were on the alert. They each had their candidate, for the conquest of the King was impossible to achieve without a powerful lobby— a well-organized cabal, based on an alliance of noble families united in the defense of their interests.

Louis XV was not at all like Louis XIV. He did not choose his mistresses. He waited to be seduced and showed more shyness and distrust of the fair sex than might be expected. Cardinal Fleury, his tutor and later his Prime Minister, had warned him against the dangerous temptresses who lead men—particularly kings—into sin. A sensible adolescent, obedient to Fleury's wishes, he was married at fifteen to ensure the dynasty's posterity. In the beginning, he was a faithful husband to the devout Marie Leczinska. This modest Polish princess, his elder by seven years, was undivided in her love for him. She idolized him and spoke to him in a humble, submissive voice. Almost always pregnant, she gave him two sons, though only one survived—the Dauphin, Louis-Ferdinand—and eight daughters, six[8] of whom reached adulthood. However, after several years of a somewhat dull conjugal life, the King wanted to experience other pleasures. Worn out by her successive pregnancies, his wife gave herself to him only reluctantly. She even reproached him for smelling of champagne when he joined her in her bed, where she lay buried under a heap of eiderdown quilts.

Bachelier and Le Bel, the King's loyal valets, secretly brought him a few casual mistresses whose caresses he could enjoy without any commitments. But these dalliances no longer satisfied him. He was bored. His merry late-night supper companions urged him to take a favorite. The virtuous Cardinal Fleury had to accept reality. But to be certain that the sovereign (or his friends) did not choose an ambitious woman who might exert too much influence, he took it upon himself personally to find a woman he found suitable. It was he who asked Bachelier and Le Bel to go along with the scheme of putting Madame de Mailly in the King's bed. Gentle and reserved, she was not beautiful, but she was extremely elegant and knew how to exploit the advantages nature had given her. Above all, she loved the King passionately and ambition played no part in her love. She never asked him for anything, either for herself or anyone else. Their affair, which was kept secret for three years, became official in 1737 after the Queen had turned the King down and he had completely given up asking her "to do her duty."

Uninterested in intrigues, Madame de Mailly was enthralled by the sovereign, who lavished affection on her in spite of being assailed every once in a while by religious scruples. Louis XV seemed happy and Fleury was satisfied with a plan that did not hinder the course of government. He would soon be disillusioned. Madame de Mailly was the daughter of the Marquis de Nesle and she had several sisters who did not resemble her in the least. In all innocence, she gave in to the entreaties of her younger sister, Mademoiselle de Nesle, who was still in the convent. She arranged to have her come to Versailles, unaware that this proud and brazen young woman had made plans to replace her with the King, get rid of the Cardinal-Minister, and reign in the shadow of the monarch. Ambitious and intelligent, she seduced Louis XV with her biting repartees. He enjoyed himself with her. Though she was far from beautiful, he fell in love with her and made her his mistress, without ceasing to honor her older sister. When Mademoiselle de Nesle became pregnant by him, he immediately married her off to the accommodating Marquis de Vintimille. The romance had been short-lived, and the King returned to Madame de Mailly; he moved her into a secret apartment above his own and their liaison continued—but not as happily as before. Madame de Mailly was no longer able to enliven the informal suppers in the private apartment. She wept often, and so did the King. When he shared her bed, he would sometimes get up in the middle of the night to recite an act of contrition. Then he would get back into bed with her—a mistress decked out like a shrine, for she never slept without her jewels. As always, Versailles sensed the master's mood and, foreseeing the imminent end of the affair, the courtiers schemed to find a new favorite for the sovereign. "Who will hold sway over the King's mind? In whose arms will he fall? For he must fall somewhere. I don't know and this worries me,"[9] wondered the Duc de Richelieu. This great libertine nobleman, born in 1696, was the King's irreplaceable companion in pleasure. But he was not content just being the King's minister of love. He expected a lot more from the sovereign, whose weaknesses he intuitively understood. His dream was quite simply to succeed Fleury, who was going on ninety.

In September 1742, the arrival of Madame de Mailly's three other sisters revived the hopes of a restless and bored Court. Louis XV was immediately struck by the beauty of the two youngest sisters, Madame de Flavacourt and Madame de La Tournelle. But to his great surprise, neither one ventured to make overtures to him. Madame de Flavacourt had no intention of being unfaithful to a jealous husband, whereas Madame de La Tournelle, recently widowed and hence free from all marital ties, was known to be very much in love with the Duc d'Agenois. She had just been made a lady-in-waiting by the Queen and aspired to no other favor. Though he did not declare his love, the King had eyes only for her.

To satisfy his own ambitions, Richelieu had to place a woman who was devoted to him by the King's side. The ambitious and intelligent

Madame de La Tournelle, who was his relative, had, he felt, all the qualities of the ideal favorite. Hence he decided to take the matter in hand. He had to convince the King to be more forward with the young woman and put an end to her affair with the Duc d'Agenois. Louis XV followed his mentor's advice and sent the attractive young man to Languedoc. The Court was all eyes and ears for several days. Richelieu could frequently be seen leaving the King's quarters and going straight to Madame de La Tournelle and later to Madame de Mailly. Anticipating the fate that awaited her, the unhappy favorite wept all the time. Exasperated by her tears, the King was blunt with her: "I promised to speak plainly with you. I'm madly in love with Madame de La Tournelle; I haven't had her yet, but I will."[10] However, the coquette had to be coaxed. In his impatience, Richelieu spoke firmly to the King: "Given how beautiful she is, she must be conquered. Your generals will not conquer her for you. She will not be conquered unless you conquer her yourself. Your rivals have advantages, but the greatest advantages in love are being young and handsome like Your Majesty and especially being outgoing. François I, Henri IV, Louis XIV went to a lot of trouble to be loved. This should be easier for Your Majesty than for anyone else. A mistress is not a portfolio and while your ministers can bring their portfolio to your Council, I doubt they can put Madame de La Tournelle into your arms. You must make yourself attractive to her and start by telling her you are in love."[11] The King listened to his master in *libertinage*, who then arranged secret meetings for him, in disguise, with the woman he coveted. Madame de La Tournelle held out for a long time and set down her conditions. Following the example of Madame de Montespan, she wanted to be the King's *"maîtresse déclarée"* (official mistress) and insisted that he hold court in her quarters. Moreover, she demanded that the unfortunate Mailly be sent away from Versailles permanently. Louis XV gave in to all her demands and, in early December 1742, he could enjoy his new lover's prerogatives. Richelieu was triumphant. As Madame de La Tournelle did not love the King and he seemed very taken with her, her influence might be all the greater.

Louis XV's passion did not cool. In October 1743, Madame de La Tournelle received the duchy-peerage of Châteauroux, with an annual revenue of 86,000 livres. The new Duchesse was as witty as she was beautiful and gaiety returned to Versailles. The King's sadness had vanished as if by magic, and he yielded to the delights of his new love affair. His mistress presided over the suppers in the private apartment with elegance. A free and gallant circle of intimates had formed around the monarch and his favorite that included the Princesse de Conti, Mademoiselle de Charolais, Mademoiselle de La Roche-sur-Yon, Madame d'Antin and several noblemen with loose morals, led by Richelieu. "Head of the fashionable set,"[12] he still hoped to play a major role in government, even though the King had not given him Fleury's position when the latter died on January 29, 1743. His disappointment had not been too bitter, as Louis XV had decided to do without a Prime Minister and govern on his own. Richelieu consoled himself with the position of First Gentleman of the Bedchamber, which put him in charge of organizing all the Court festivities and spectacles.

When she became a duchess, Madame de Châteauroux adopted superior airs that made her insufferable, particularly to the Queen. She liked splendor and sought jewels and clothes that would make her more glamorous. The King, who gave in to all her whims, called her *Princesse.* The only fly in the ointment was that she had to put up with her royal lover's weakness for one of her sisters, the stout Madame de Lauraguais who seemed not to have anything particularly seductive about her. But the King was as he was, and his caprices had to be endured without complaint.

Madame de Châteauroux dreamed of glory for the sovereign and started to meddle in politics. She had become attached to two ministers, Philibert Orry, Comptroller General in charge of Finances, and the Comte d'Argenson, Minister of War. She soon persuaded the monarch to lead the armies himself in the next campaign. This decision earned Louis XV considerable popularity. However, after his departure, she devised a thousand stratagems to join him, along with Madame de Lauraguais, the Princesse de Conti, the Duchesse de Chartres and several other ladies, who were delighted to get away from the Court now that its master and all the most dashing gentlemen were away. These charming women were a subject of scandal wherever they went, but the unexpected reunions delighted Louis XV, who shared his time between Mars and Venus.

He was enjoying the perfect love affair when he suddenly fell sick with a malignant fever in Metz, in the beginning of August 1744. Alarmed, the physicians gave him up for lost, and the Church authorities decided he should receive the last rites. But the Bishop of Soissons, Monseigneur de Fitz-James, demanded that the sovereign make a public declaration of repentance after first dismissing Mesdames de Châteauroux and de Lauraguais, who had not left his bedroom since the beginning of his illness. The monarch had no choice but to comply. After the two women had driven through the city in a sealed carriage, to the crowd's catcalls, the sovereign made a speech of public repentance for his past conduct. He begged forgiveness of the Queen, who had rushed to his side, for the sorrow his scandalous private life might have caused her. The clergy and the *dévots* (the religious faction) had gained the upper hand. Louis XV was still too physically weak to realize it.

All of France was distressed over the sovereign's illness. Couriers were stopped for the latest news. They were kissed when the news was good and greeted with silence when it was bad. People crowded into churches, recited novenas and marched in processions, praying for the *Bien-Aimé* to recover his health. The great scene of repentance moved many to tears. The King was forgiven for everything. Public condemnation focused on his mistress, as though she were wholly responsible for his dangerous state of health. After several days of anguish, the fever died down. The King was out of danger. Three weeks later, he joined the army again, before returning in triumph to the capital.

Humiliated by the "scenes of Metz," which he would never forget, the King wished to summon his favorite whom he had been forced to repudiate. More appalled by the affront she had endured than anguished at losing her lover, Madame de Châteauroux had written vehement letters to Richelieu freely expressing her wrath. She hid in her Paris residence, with Madame de Lauraguais, concocting plans of revenge against those persons who had forced the King to send her away. When she received the sovereign's letter asking her to return to her duties, she had just enough time to write a few notes to friends informing them of her reinstatement. Several hours later, she fell violently ill with a high fever and headache. She never recovered.

The King, therefore, had to be given a new mistress. Some people wagered that the stout Lauraguais—up to now a secondary favorite—would be raised to the rank of sultana. She had an advantage over all the others in being already in place. Since the King had been unusually faithful to the same family, Richelieu and the King's intimates thought that Madame de Flavacourt, the only Nesle sister not to have succumbed to the sovereign's charm, would now finally yield to him. "Is choosing an entire family being unfaithful or true?" the lyrics of a song went. However, most of the great noble families in the kingdom sought to depose the Nesle sisters, who had benefited disproportionately from His Majesty's favors. The Princesse de Rohan—tall, beautiful and shapely—hoped to attract the King's attention. With this prospect in mind, she sacrificed the Duc de Richelieu, her unfaithful lover, as well as her young attentive escort, the Marquis de Valfons. The latter predicted that she might end up outsmarted, "for the King's friends did not want her."[13] However, nothing could "divert her from the desire prompted by ambition to see the universe at her feet."[14] As d'Argenson wickedly put it, women who want to become the King's mistress "think they'll find glory in a whoredom that is part of History." The ravishing Duchesse de Rochechouart, widowed for a year, and who had once lived in Rambouillet on familiar terms with the young sovereign, also put herself in the running—but without luck. She was compared to the horses in the small stable—always presented but never accepted. Hopes ran very high for the aspirants to royal favor. It was a sign of the times that bourgeois women and the wives of financiers—among them, Présidente Portail and Madame de La Poplinière—were presumptuous enough to aspire to the honor of being chosen. Their pretensions made the Court smile, for it was known that sharing the royal bed was an aristocratic privilege. Circumstances could not have been more favorable for capturing this highly coveted heart. The King, whose spirits had improved, was preparing, with Richelieu, the festivities for the marriage of his only son, the Dauphin, to the Spanish Infanta, Marie-Thérèse Raphaëlle.

Two

M A D A M E   D ' E T I O L L E S

Among all the women who sought to conquer the King, there was one who dared not believe her luck. She had just turned twenty-four and was radiantly beautiful. Tall, slim and well proportioned, she was very graceful in her movements. Her face was shaped in a perfect oval, her hair was light brown, and she still had a fresh and unaffected quality, especially when she smiled and revealed her flawless white teeth and dimpled cheeks. No one could remain impervious to the bewitching, tender, insistent gaze of her gray eyes, which burned at times with an incandescent light. "Any man would have gladly had for a mistress"[1] Madame Le Normant d'Etiolles, whom Louis XV was secretly seeing in his private apartment. No one, or almost no one, knew their secret yet. Was it a passing infatuation or the beginning of a great love? Even the two lovers did not yet know.

This ravishing young woman, who was almost unknown at Versailles, was one of the most glamorous socialites in Paris. She had bedazzled Président Hénault, one of the Queen's faithful friends. He had met her at the Opera three years earlier, and had not concealed his admiration for her from Madame du Deffand: "I have met one of the prettiest women I have ever seen. She knows music to perfection, she sings with the greatest gaiety and taste, knows a hundred songs, and acts in plays at Etiolles in a theater as lovely as the Opera house, with stage machinery and scene-changing equipment. Paris is marvelous for its diverse social circles and its countless amusements."[2]

Endowed with every talent, Madame d'Etiolles, born Jeanne-Antoinette Poisson, had behaved very sensibly till then. Married to a financier with excellent prospects and mother to a little girl, Alexandrine,[3] she was reserved with her many admirers. She repeatedly said, with a laugh, that she would never betray her husband, except with the King. Belonging by birth and marriage to the world of finance—a world very much looked down upon by the Court—her chances of being admitted into the King's intimacy were very slim, even though she, like so many others, dreamed of being loved by the young, handsome, seductive monarch whom everyone revered like a demigod. Her mother's insinuations and the predictions of a fortune-teller had nevertheless encouraged her wildest wishes. Her mother had always been intent on persuading her that she was *fit for a king*, and the fortune-teller had told her that she would become the sovereign's mistress. The story is not just a legend: some twenty years later, when Jeanne-Antoinette felt that her final hour was near, she left the soothsayer a six-hundred-livre bequest to thank her for her happy prediction.[4] While she waited for this improbable good fortune to come to pass, Madame d'Etiolles quite naturally kept informed of the latest Court news. Luck smiled down on her. She succeeded in attracting the King's attention while he was hunting in the forest of Sénart, not far from her small château of Etiolles. On the days when he was in the vicinity, she always found a way of crossing his path; and either she wore a light blue dress and rode in a pink phaeton, or she wore a pink dress and rode in a blue carriage. One day, when he had hunted on her property, Louis XV had thoughtfully arranged to have a large quantity of game delivered to her house. The sovereign's sudden interest in the beautiful chatelaine had alarmed Madame de Châteauroux. She claimed that "people wanted to give him the young d'Etiolles woman."

The Duchesse was not completely wrong. The young woman was indeed encouraged in her fantasies by her protectors, the three Pâris brothers, who were the most powerful financiers in the kingdom. Pâris de Montmartel—who, in some quarters, was believed to be her father—was the Court banker. The promotion of a woman from their milieu to the rank of royal mistress would have signaled the irreversible ascension of the social group to which they belonged, and opened up an invaluable source of profit. It would allow them to aspire to a certain control on government. But as long as Madame de Châteauroux—with whom they maintained an excellent relationship—was alive, it was unthinkable to try to put Madame d'Etiolles in the King's bed. It would have been a dreadful blunder. Now, after the favorite's death, the young Etiolles could try her luck.

However, it is not known exactly how the Sénart forest nymph first fell into the King's arms. The two lovers carefully guarded the secret of their first meetings. The Dauphin's *valet de chambre*, Binet de Marchais, seems to have been the go-between. A cousin of Madame d'Etiolles and acquainted with the Pâris brothers, he recommended Jeanne-Antoinette to the King. Louis XV needed to be consoled, yet feared falling into the traps set by ladies at Court. He was weary of their machinations and determined not to be taken in under any circumstances. He therefore listened attentively to Binet when he offered to make him meet a woman who was different from all the women he knew and who, he claimed, had always loved him. The King accepted his proposal, and this was undoubtedly how Madame d'Etiolles first came discreetly to his quarters.

In that month of February 1745, the final preparations were being made for the Dauphin's wedding. As always in such circumstances, elaborate festivities were planned in Versailles and in Paris. The King invited the pride of the French nobility to his son's nuptials, as well as the representatives of the Paris bourgeoisie. For its part, the city of Paris invited the royal family and the Court to sumptuous entertainments in which the common people were allowed to take part. The Duc de Richelieu had already sent out invitations, in the King's name, to the costume ball that was to take place at five in the evening on the twenty-fourth, the day after the princely marriage. The ladies were told to wear "their hair in formal curls."[5] Madame d'Etiolles received an invitation and casually told Président Hénault that Binet had arranged for her accommodations at Versailles.

It had been a long time since the drapers' shops, milliners and wig-makers had had so much business. All the pretty women required their services in trying to outshine one another and dazzle the monarch.

And the monarch himself had never seemed so relaxed. To the Queen's great surprise, on February 7, he insisted on a ball being held in his daughters' apartments, though the princesses did not like this kind of entertainment. "At their age, everyone likes to dance," he said gaily. And the very serious Duc de Luynes, to whom we owe this piece of information, tells us that several days earlier, the monarch had gone, incognito, to a masked ball in the city of Versailles with a mysterious stranger. "People speculated that a love affair may be in the offing," he wrote, and prudently added that this was "a rash and not very probable suspicion."[6] Louis XV took liberties that Louis XIV would never have allowed himself to take. On the night of the eleventh, after his official *coucher*, he left the château and returned only in the early hours of the morning; the following night, again, he went to a masked ball in the city of Versailles and returned to his bedroom at six in the morning. On the fourteenth, disguised as a peasant, he was seen at yet another ball, this time in his daughters' apartments.

However, the Infanta was approaching Versailles, in small stages. The royal family, followed by part of the Court, went to meet her at Sceaux, and the King welcomed her at Mondésir, just beyond Etampes. But people were much more interested in where the sovereign's gaze was directed than in the looks of the new bride, who, let it be said, dazzled no one. A redhead with an unattractive face, she looked haughty and unkind, though this hardly prevented the Dauphin, a clumsy, overweight, hypocritical dullard, to find her very much to his liking. On the twenty-third, the day of the wedding, the King—who quite unintentionally eclipsed the young couple—led the princely procession through the brilliantly lit Hall of Mirrors, in the midst of a silent and respectful crowd. In the evening, there was a performance of *La Princesse de Navarre*, a comic opera by Voltaire, with music by Rameau, in the Salle du Manège, which had been decorated by the Slodtz brothers in 1737, and which was used for large-scale royal entertainments before the construction of the Opera. The spectacle did not meet with universal approval. Bad acoustics detracted from the music and the singers. Some members of the audience considered the subject somewhat tactless, for greater homage was paid to France than to

Spain. Furthermore, the stage set seemed ridiculous; the Pyrénées Mountains had to be lowered to make way for the Temple of Love. After the supper, where the entire royal family was present, the guests proceeded, as tradition required, to the *coucher* of the newlyweds.

Madame d'Etiolles attended the formal ball the following evening, but went unnoticed, for it was an official event where the King personally picked out the dancers, all princes and princesses of royal blood and members of the oldest aristocracy. Everyone waited impatiently for the masked balls at Court and in the city, where they really expected to have a good time and strike up a romance.

On the evening of February 25, the facade of the château on the courtyard side was illuminated by thousands of glowing, constantly replenished candles in earthenware vessels. By eleven-thirty, hundreds of coaches were streaming into the avenue de Paris. The King and the royal family, who had had a formal State dinner, retired as soon as the first guests arrived. Since invitation cards had not been sent, anyone wearing a mask was admitted into the Salon d'Hercule. The crush was such that the ushers were soon overwhelmed. Fifteen hundred people crammed into the room, and stood or sat on the floor. While they waited for the merrymaking to start, people looked at the huge buffets spread with fish (as the Lent diet required) and sweets between pyramids of oranges.

Finally, the doors to the royal apartment were thrown open and the Queen appeared, in formal court attire, escorted by the Dauphin and Dauphine, dressed as shepherd and shepherdess. People wondered where the King could be when suddenly eight yew trees, shaped like the ones in the park outside, burst into the hall. There was no doubt that one of the trees was the sovereign, but who could recognize him? A swarm of pretty girls surrounded the mysterious shapes. Présidente Portail felt faint when one of the shrubs bowed and led her away from the crowd. She thought she was the lucky winner. Her illusions would be shattered a short time later, after she had bestowed her ultimate favors on the person she had mistaken for Louis XV. . . . Cochin, the Court engraver, immortalized the scene, showing a yew tree wooing a beautiful huntress, a clear homage to the sovereign and the woman whose star now shone so brightly.[7] For the present, people remained cautiously watchful; those who uttered Madame d'Etiolles's name in an undertone thought the King was merely indulging in a whim.

On the following days, the young woman was not seen at the many other fetes that took place at Versailles, but the King was radiant with happiness. Life smiled on him again and he even seemed to have several irons in the fire. The Abbé de Bernis alludes to another charming young woman whom the monarch had noticed at the ball of the yew trees.[8] Not in the least "disgusted" to find out that this unmarried girl's relatives belonged to the world of finance, he arranged to meet her at the ball of the Hôtel de Ville, on February 28. Eager not to miss any opportunity to have fun, he had also gone to the small masked ball called "*le bal d'un écu*"[9] in Versailles. He awaited the Paris soirée with unconcealed impatience.

On that evening, *dimanche gras*, Louis XV let the Dauphin set off alone for the reception given in his honor at the Hôtel de Ville. Clad in a black domino, he left Versailles shortly after midnight with the Duc d'Ayen and a few intimate friends. At the Sèvres tollgate, he passed by his son's coach as it was returning to the château. Now that he knew that the Prince had left Paris, the King could be confident that he was no longer expected there. In order to pass completely incognito, he exchanged his coach for a hackney and was driven to the ball like a simple bourgeois.

However, the area around the Hôtel de Ville was so congested that he had to put off his plan. He went to the ball at the Opera, where he paid his entrance ticket. There he danced for several hours without being recognized. Once he had exhausted the delights of that gala, he returned to the Hôtel de Ville, though he knew the financier's pretty daughter would not be there. Her parents, briefly bedazzled by the marvelous prospects offered by such a meeting, had finally wanted her fate to be more in keeping with conventional morals. The beautiful young lady was barred from going out.[10] But at the Hôtel de Ville, the King would join Madame d'Etiolles, who had been waiting for him all evening. Panicked by the masks that had nearly smothered her, she had asked the Provost of Merchants, Monsieur de Bernage, for help. He had led her into a small drawing room, where the Marquis de Valfons had already secluded himself with a female companion. Madame d'Etiolles "was wearing a black domino, but was very disheveled because she had been pushed around by the crowd over and over again like so many others," he recalled. "A minute later, two masks, also wearing black dominos, crossed the same room; I recognized one by his height and the other by his voice: they were Monsieur d'Ayen and the King. Madame d'Etiolles followed them out."[11] The King decided quite simply to spend the remainder of the night at his mistress's house, on the rue Croix-des-Petits Champs. He knew he was in no danger of facing a jealous husband. Most opportunely, Monsieur Le Normant d'Etiolles had left on a trip several weeks earlier.

But as King, Louis was ignorant of the fact that it would not be easy to cross the capital in a hackney on a night of celebrations. All of Paris was still in the streets and the carriage could only inch its way through the jubilant crowd. Louis XV was not used to being confronted with such trivial matters. No matter. He would give the coachman a huge tip. The Duc d'Ayen had to stop him: so large an amount would arouse the driver's suspicions. One écu would do perfectly. And so, a short time later, Madame d'Etiolles was welcoming her lover into her bedroom. The King returned to Versailles only at nine in the morning. Before going to bed, he gave the order to be awakened at five. For the King and his favorite, that thrilling night would remain one of their most exciting memories.

With the wedding celebrations over, tongues began to wag. People were only mildly interested in the Dauphin and his difficulty in consummating his union; what really interested them was the King's new love affair. The entire Court now went on about a Madame d'Etiolles who had been spotted at Versailles on several occasions. "People say that, for some time now, she's been in *ce pays-ci* [this country, i.e., the Court] and that the King made the decision," the Duc de Luynes wrote. "If that's true," he adds, incredulous, "chances are she is merely a passing dalliance and not a mistress."[12] For this aristocrat, that the monarch should choose a favorite from the Paris bourgeoisie seemed so incongruous that he could not see it as anything but flirtation. Yet soon the Duc de Luynes and his friends had to accept reality: Madame d'Etiolles was spending more and more time with the monarch.

On April 1, to the Court's astonishment, she appeared, very elegantly dressed, at the theater in the evening, in a small box near the two royal boxes, the King's and the Queen's. Opera glasses were pointed at Louis XV, his wife and the newcomer. Newcomer or intruder? No one knew yet. This uncertainty tempered the venom in people's conversation. Yet with every passing day, the Duc de Luynes's apprehensions seemed increasingly confirmed. On April 7, he deplored that Madame de Lauraguais, who "looked very distinguished," did not occupy Madame de Châteauroux's apartment during an excursion by the King to Choisy. And he seemed to be nursing resentment against his master for falling into the arms of a bourgeoise when he wrote that the King's conversation had become "much too free."[13] Such lapses could only be due to his spending time with a "chatterbox."

Clearly, the King was quite taken by this woman; he supped alone with her in his private apartment, "or some other place that is not known."[14] The Duc de Luynes still tried to ignore the evidence and cheer himself by taking note of the small attentions the sovereign paid to Madame de Lauraguais. But these were mere token gestures of politeness. It was well known that Madame de Lauraguais was no longer on intimate terms with the King. The Court was vigilant and people sought information by any means. Countless rumors went around concerning Binet's involvement. Madame de Luynes tried to make him talk, but he denied responsibility; all these calumnies about him "were dreadful and completely unfounded."[15] The Church party was indignant. Unable to contain himself, Monseigneur Boyer, Bishop of Mirepoix and former tutor to the Dauphin, summoned Binet. Boasting of his continued influence on the young Prince, he ordered the valet to tell him everything he knew about the King's liaison. Binet claimed that Madame d'Etiolles had come to see His Majesty to solicit a position of *Fermier général* (collector of indirect taxes) for her husband. As soon as the position was granted, she would leave Versailles. This explanation could hardly satisfy a prelate who was thoroughly familiar with the ways of the Court. He knew the King was not directly involved in such appointments. Incensed, Monseigneur Boyer cut the meeting short and threatened the valet with dismissal if his story turned out to be untrue.

The King could not care less that he had plunged the Court into a state of anxiety. He was the master, and he fully enjoyed his rights without feeling the least constraint. He continued to see Madame d'Etiolles regularly. On April 22 and 23, he invited her to dine for the first time with Monsieur de Luxembourg and Madame de Bellefonds, former friends of Madame de Châteauroux who had shared the King's grief just a short time ago. The invitation was a way of making his liaison official to his intimate friends. He now spent most of his evenings and nights with his new mistress. So great was his infatuation that he failed to go to the official reception given by the Spanish ambassador in honor of the Infanta's marriage! He merely sent Monsieur de Lugeac and Monsieur de Tressan as his representatives. He had just moved Madame d'Etiolles into the apartment that had been Madame de Châteauroux's and, before that, Madame de Mailly's. It was in the right wing of the château, on the second floor, above the gallery decorated by Mignard, and it included a bedroom, a study and a drawing room. Now everyone wondered whether the King would present the young woman at Court and "declare" her, as he had Madame de Châteauroux. He could very well just summon her whenever he wished.

Madame d'Etiolles's fate was played out at the end of April, shortly before her betrayed husband returned from his trip. When he walked into his home, he had the unpleasant surprise of finding that it had been thoroughly emptied. His uncle, *Fermier général* Le Normant de Tournehem, was waiting to tell him of his misfortune: unable to overcome her passion for the King, his wife had left him and taken all her belongings with her. Stunned by the news, Monsieur d'Etiolles fainted; however, his uncle soon alleviated his suffering by painting a very promising future for him, as he was handing him the extremely lucrative position of *Fermier général*.

By this time, word was out that the King was arranging the purchase of the marquisate of Pompadour for his new mistress. This settled the question: the Marquise de Pompadour would be succeeding the Duchesse de Châteauroux. The Court had no choice but to remain silent and turn its attention to the campaign of Flanders, for which the King set off on May 5. Would the lucky lady follow the sovereign? A rumor spread that she would be taking the waters at Saint-Amand,[16] a spa between Tournai and Valenciennes. Too astute to put herself in a situation that might be embarrassing, she preferred to resettle at the Château d'Etiolles, but only after she had asked her husband for a separation, in body and property.

Three

A STEADY RISE TO THE TOP

Jeanne-Antoinette Poisson, who later became Madame d'Etiolles, was
not born into high society, and her mother was not exactly a pillar of
virtue. Had Madame Poisson been of noble birth, her loose behavior
would have been of no great consequence, but because of her modest
origins, Madame Poisson's free-and-easy morals were damaging to her
daughter. Unlike the previous royal mistresses, Jeanne-Antoinette
could not pride herself on an aristocratic lineage dating back to the
eleventh century. It would have been more acceptable if her parents,
Monsieur and Madame Poisson, had at least belonged to the old bourgeoisie that was related to the nobility. Such was not the case. They
belonged to the world of finance, a milieu that was rapidly changing;
the nobility could not help but mix with this milieu, even though they
looked down with contempt on these proletarians who "without knowing a word of Latin, had found the secret of getting ahead."[1] The body
politic could not function without them. The investments they advised
were profitable and they willingly lent money to aristocrats in debt.
Hence, most gentlemen had no choice but to associate with them, in
spite of their feelings of contempt. Some even had to come to terms
with the idea of marrying their daughters off to them. In a society as
hierarchical as that of the Ancien Régime, where each person's place
was determined by birth, these flattering matches enhanced the prestige of the financiers. However, their milieu was far from homogeneous.

Long-standing fortunes and prestigious alliances in certain families had contributed to the creation of a new and invisible hierarchy within the microcosm, and in this world Monsieur and Madame Poisson were at the bottom of the ladder. They were viewed as recent parvenus of doubtful reputation.

If we can trust Police Lieutenant Feydeau de Marville, François Poisson, Madame d'Etiolles's father, began his career as a flunky in the service of Monsieur de Bernage, Intendant of Amiens.[2] The latter helped him get employment in supplies, and Poisson then became steward to the powerful Pâris brothers, who had been supplying the army since 1690. Police lieutenants are usually the best-informed men in the kingdom. Yet it is possible that this police lieutenant may have blackened Poisson's background in the hope of pleasing his supervisory minister, Comte Maurepas, Secretary of State in the King's Household, who had immediately announced that he was hostile to the new favorite. It is likely that Feydeau de Marville took pleasure in lowering Monsieur Poisson's origins, for it was commonly said that all financiers were sons of flunkies.

François Poisson's early years remain shrouded in mystery. We know only that in 1715, at the age of thirty-one, he commanded a nice fortune of 100,000 livres and purchased the office of Secretary to the King. This position was called "the knave's bar of soap" because it "cleaned off" commoners by conferring the first degree of nobility. For the ninth child of a weaver from Provenchères, a small town near Langres, this was no mean accomplishment! How had François Poisson amassed so much money, without an inheritance or marrying into money? In business, for he had indeed entered into service with the Pâris brothers, but probably thanks to one of his brothers-in-law who was a Superintendent of Supplies. That same year, 1715, he married Anne-Geneviève-Gabrielle Le Carlier, a young woman from the respectable bourgeoisie of Laon, whose father, a former Superintendent at the Mint, had moved to Paris. Prematurely widowed in 1718, Poisson immediately married Louise-Madeleine de La Motte, whom Feydeau de Marville describes as "as beautiful as a Venus." She was the youngest daughter of the meat supplier to the Hôtel des Invalides. Did

Poisson fall madly in love with this tender nineteen-year-old with insolent good looks, or had he accepted a deal offered by the Pâris brothers, in return for certain advantages? The second hypothesis seems most plausible. Several important men coveted Mademoiselle de La Motte. Marrying her was out of the question because her station was too inferior to theirs, but they couldn't treat her like an opera girl either and set her up in a "little house." Poisson had only to behave like an obliging husband and his career could take a new turn.

The marriage contract, dated October 6, 1718, carries the signatures of the family members, as well as those of the Pâris brothers, of Claude Le Blanc, Minister of War, and of the Duc d'Orléans, Regent of France, and his sister, Princesse Charlotte de Lorraine. It is not surprising to find Claude Le Blanc's signature on this kind of deed. He had overseen the army supplies for many years and knew the father of the bride very well, as he had lived in the Hôtel des Invalides for a long period of time. The signatures of the princes, on the other hand, are surprising. They are proof of the Pâris brothers' intercession. Philippe d'Orléans could not deny them anything, as they were the State creditors. Eager to humor Poisson, they had also obtained for him the grand title of "Quartermaster to the Duc d'Orléans," thanks to which he could call himself "Equerry to His Royal Highness the Duc d'Orléans."

Once the wedding celebrations were over, Poisson became the Pâris brothers' trusted assistant and they sent him on assignments in France and abroad while his charming wife began a career as a kind of paramour. First she was the mistress of Claude Le Blanc and then of his brother, César Le Blanc, Bishop of Avranches. They were succeeded by Monsieur du Laurens, Steward to the War Office, before Pâris de Montmartel took her as his lover, which did not prevent the *Fermier général*, Le Normant de Tournehem, from also enjoying her favors. Others for whom she had a conspicuous weakness included: Monsieur Fournier, Director of the Stores in Charleville; Monsieur Wedderkop, the King of Denmark's envoy; Prince of Grimberghen; Monsieur Graevenbrock, the Palatine Elector's Chargé d'Affaires; and Le Bel, Louis XV's valet. It can certainly be assumed that she gathered information for the Pâris brothers from her lovers. The brothers would be her lifelong protectors and her daughter's protectors as well, as she would be very generous in repaying her debt of gratitude to them when she became Marquise de Pompadour. In 1724, Pâris de Montmartel acceded to the most prestigious and lucrative positions in the world of finance; he was appointed Chancellor of the Royal Treasury and Court Banker. The first of these two functions gave him voting rights in the Council of State and the rank of Councillor of State. As for his brother, Pâris-Duverney, who became a Councillor of State in 1725, he had complete control over the supplies to the army and became Director General of Provisions in 1733. The two brothers, who managed a substantial fortune, belonged to the uppermost crust of their milieu.

When little Jeanne-Antoinette was born, on December 30, 1721, everyone wondered who her father was. Malicious gossip had it that Madame Poisson herself did not know. Her husband, who had always turned a blind eye to her love affairs, seemed an unlikely candidate. His compulsory, extended stay in Marseilles at the beginning of the year,[3] where a dreadful epidemic of the plague had detained him, did not exactly plead in favor of his daughter's legitimacy. Two putative fathers could be counted—Pâris de Montmartel and Le Normant de Tournehem. Madame Poisson's protracted love affair with Le Normant de Tournehem and his tenderness and concern for Jeanne-Antoinette would lead one to believe that she was his daughter.

Several days after her birth, her godfather, Pâris de Montmartel, and his niece, Antoinette Justine Pâris, carried the infant to the baptismal font of the church of Saint-Eustache. Two years later, Madame Poisson gave birth to a second daughter, who would not live long, and, in 1725, to a son, Abel François, who would play a role of some consequence in his older sister's life. In spite of their mother's dissipated life, no one wondered who had fathered the two youngest children. Poisson continued to travel for his employers and earned a lot of money. The family's successive moves testify to his growing financial prosperity. After living on the rue de Cléry where Jeanne-Antoinette was born, and later on the rue Thévenot (today the rue Réaumur), the Poissons first moved to a rented mansion in the Marais. Soon, however, they bought an elegant town house at the corner of the rue de Richelieu and the rue Saint-Marc, a neighborhood where the wealthiest financiers lived. With several servants in their pay, they began to live in grand style.

François Poisson's career still seemed full of promise when royal disgrace fell momentarily upon the Pâris brothers and their employees. In 1725, the fiscal measures imposed by Comptroller General of Finances Dodun and Pâris-Duverney led to disturbances that were further aggravated by the bad crops and consequent threats of famine. Poisson, at the time, was responsible for supplying the capital with wheat. He handled this assignment extremely well and was enjoying a peaceful existence when the young Louis XV (or more accurately Cardinal Fleury) decided, in 1726, that the ministerial term of the Duc de Bourbon, the Regent's successor, should be cut short. The King reshuffled the cabinet and dismissed the Comptroller General of Finances, who had worked very closely with the Pâris brothers. They had taken an active part in all the financial operations of the Regency. The Pâris brothers saw their positions abolished. And since it was difficult to prosecute men who had been in control of the State's finances and who might still be needed, a scapegoat had to be found. This is where Poisson came in. A Council commission investigated his accounts and found irregularities. He was accused of having speculated on wheat the year before and was sentenced to death by hanging; his worldly goods were also confiscated, for he had a debt of 232,430 livres. There is one odd detail: no trace of this death sentence was ever found. It is possible that the written verdict was subsequently deliberately destroyed. However, Poisson did not wait until April 27, 1727—the day the conclusions of the investigation were announced—to leave France, with a substantial sum of money given to him by his employers. He took refuge in Germany, settling in Hamburg, where he secretly stayed in touch with his superiors.

Left alone with her two children, the beautiful Madame Poisson had to face difficulties for which she was completely unprepared. She began by requesting a separation from her husband, which she obtained on August 12, 1727; this allowed her to recover her worldly possessions, which were in fact rather modest. The joint assets she had with her husband had been seized, so she quickly had to dismiss her large staff of servants and give up her house on the rue de Richelieu for a much more modest abode on the rue Neuve-des-Bons-Enfants. *Fermier général* Le Normant de Tournehem attended to her welfare, and that of Jeanne-Antoinette and her brother.

Reinette, as her family called her, was growing up. We do not know if it was Poisson or his wife who decided to send her to the convent of the Ursulines in Poissy, but we do know that Poisson, from his exile, kept a watchful eye on her. Though the letters the couple exchanged, in spite of their separation, have not been found, some bits and pieces of correspondence between Poisson and the convent have come down to us. They allow us to reconstruct several months in Jeanne-Antoinette's childhood.

In early 1729, Madame Poisson took her to the venerable convent, where one of her sisters and one of her cousins were nuns. This was not a disciplinary measure. Little girls from good families were usually placed in religious establishments until their marriage. The education they received there prepared them to be submissive and dutiful Christian wives. According to the letters the mother superior wrote to Monsieur Poisson, who received news of his daughter regularly, it seems that Reinette was happy in her convent. The nun praised the lovely personality of this seven-year-old child, who already knew how to charm her small entourage, her classmates as well as the schoolmistresses who were in charge of her. When she contracted "measles with pox" in February, she was looked after with great care.[4] She was kept in a nice warm bed and purged several times. By the end of the month, she had recovered her appetite, and the good nun recorded that she had "lost none of her plumpness." When Poisson worries about the diet his daughter would have to observe during Lent, the mother superior immediately reassures him: "As soon as the little children feel some discomfort, we treat them with due consideration. Whenever they are deprived of meat, they have fish or some fresh catch [*sic*] for lunch: carp, skate, whiting, cod or gudgeon; at night, they have boiled rice and eggs. You can be assured that we are like mothers to them when we have them in our care."[5]

Restored to health, Jeanne-Antoinette learned to read and write, but prayers and spiritual exercises took up a large part of the day. Yet the little girl was not bored (at least that's what the mother superior says). She thought about her father, prayed for him and said she was eager to learn how to write so she could tell him of her affection for him (this is still the nun speaking). However, the charm of convent life for Jeanne-Antoinette was probably entirely due to the presence of her cousin, Mademoiselle Deblois, with whom she struck up a deep friendship. The two little girls played and sang together. Monsieur and Madame Deblois[6] occasionally took them out for a ride; indeed, they looked after their daughter and niece more than Madame Poisson did. She hardly ever came to see Jeanne-Antoinette. It was Easter by the time she took her home for four weeks. She made her make a corset stay and several printed calico sheaths. As soon as she returned to the convent, Jeanne-Antoinette resumed her games with her cousin. "They never go around without each other," the mother superior wrote to Monsieur Poisson.

We have every reason to believe that Poisson paid for his daughter's expenses and that his wife pleaded poverty with him. "Because she thinks you provide extremely well for the girl, she only provides for her bare essentials," wrote Reverend Mother Perpétue—Madame Poisson's own sister—to her faraway brother-in-law. Poisson saw to it that his daughter, who was described to him as "very delicate," was lacking in nothing. She had permission to go to the Poissy fair with her cousin on Saint-Louis day, and to take part in the grape harvest in the beginning of autumn. When the cold weather returned, she contracted whooping cough and was again confined to her room. Attention and care were lavished on her. A pleasant fire was kept permanently blazing in her fireplace, and she was given warm soup, broth with fresh eggs, jam and compote. She was also allowed to play and amuse herself as she wished. Since she had not completely recovered by January 1730, her mother decided to bring her back home. "We have been told that she no longer has a fever," the mother superior wrote to Monsieur Poisson, "that she is well, and very happy to be with Madame her mother. It looks like she will remain there. Hence, Monsieur, we will no longer have such reliable news; though we will continue to ask after her often, since we are very interested in her and love her tenderly. She is still lovely and has an attractiveness that charmed all those who saw her."[7] Jeanne-Antoinette never returned to the convent.

Madame Poisson had used her daughter's frail health as an excuse for withdrawing her from the Ursulines. No doubt she had wanted to remove her from her father's influence at a time when the Pâris brothers were coming back into favor and Le Normant de Tournehem, her official lover, had just lost his mother. An opulent *Fermier général,* widowed several decades earlier, Le Normant had never considered remarrying. An inveterate workaholic, he was primarily interested in business and only incidentally in Madame Poisson. All this changed when Jeanne-Antoinette came out of the convent. He suddenly developed a great passion for her and wanted her to become a perfectly accomplished young woman. Lanoue and Crébillon[8] gave her lessons in declamation. Her singing teacher was Jélyotte, whom Paris audiences raved over whenever he stepped out on the stage of the Opera. The best ballet masters instructed her in dance. And Jeanne-Antoinette turned out to be a superb student. If Le Normant had not planned a great future for her, she might have become one of the best actresses of her day. Not only did she have an unmistakable talent for the stage, magnified by her beauty and grace, she was also pleasantly cultured, and that made her shine in conversation at an early age. Innately tactful, she always found the appropriate thing to say and already had insight into people's hearts and souls.

Marveling at her talents, Le Normant decided to introduce his ward into society, and some of the salons in the capital opened their doors to her. It was thanks to her daughter that Madame Poisson was able to infiltrate a society that had earlier preferred to ignore her. Jeanne-Antoinette was first noticed at Madame d'Angervillers's,[9] when she sang the great aria in Lulli's *Armide.* She so moved the audience that Madame de Mailly, who was then in great favor with Louis XV, went up to her and kissed her effusively. Jeanne-Antoinette demonstrated her gifts as an actress and opera singer in the theater that Tournehem had had built at the Château d'Etiolles. At sixteen she played in Voltaire's *Zaïre,* in the author's presence. "The actors at the Etiolles theater would not leave me in peace . . . ," he wrote. "One does not expect people

whose station is so remote from the theater to be such good actors. . . .
As for the women's parts, they are filled by Madame de Blagny and
Mademoiselle Le Normant, the *Fermier général's* daughter, who only
started acting this year but who displays all the natural abilities needed
to become a very good actress."[10] As we see, Jeanne-Antoinette was
indeed believed to be Le Normant's daughter.

Madame and Mademoiselle Poisson were often seen in the salon of
the scheming Madame de Tencin, whose brother, still Archbishop of
Embrun at the time, would soon become Cardinal and Minister thanks
to his sister's intrigues. Her salon was a meeting place for secretaries
of State, financiers, philosophers, writers and artists of all kinds. Montesquieu, the elderly Fontenelle, the Abbé Prévost, Helvétius and
Réaumur were among those who enjoyed her company. Marivaux,
Piron and Duclos brought life to her soirées with their witticisms, epigrams and philosophical discussions. Jeanne-Antoinette took in their
words, while closely watching the attitudes and reactions of those present. She absorbed reminiscences of the Grand Siècle and the Regency,
and longed to know even more. However, the renowned Madame
Geoffrin, who hosted the most sought-after salon in Paris, was loath to
receive the Poisson ladies. Though a bourgeoise herself, she had her
principles. She was horrified when mother and daughter turned up at
her house one day. She gave the much "reviled" Madame Poisson an
icy welcome on the grounds that she was a notorious "kept woman
from the streets of Paris," but was not as curt with Jeanne-Antoinette
who, she thought, "deserved courteous words."[11]

While Jeanne-Antoinette was enjoying her first social successes,
François Poisson returned from Germany. The Pâris brothers, for whom
he had never stopped working, had not gone to a lot of trouble to obtain
his pardon. Fortunately he had met the Commandeur de Thianges, who
had come to Germany on a diplomatic mission in 1733. Thanks to his
excellent knowledge of German, Poisson had helped him in his initiatives and accompanied him as far as Brussels. Not daring to get any
nearer to France, Poisson had asked him to intercede on his behalf.
Monsieur de Thianges pleaded his case to the Marquis de Breteuil, who
was then Minister of War, and Breteuil spoke to Cardinal Fleury. In

1736, Poisson was allowed to return to France on payment of 400,000 livres. In 1741, his case was re-examined and he obtained satisfaction. The commission's 1726 sentence was overturned and Poisson's rights were restored. Two persons had exerted themselves on his behalf—Madame de Saissac,[12] a friend of his wife, and Monsieur de Graeven-brock, the Palatine Elector's representative, who it might be recalled had been the latest person to enjoy Madame Poisson's favors.[13]

We have no idea how Madame Poisson welcomed this long-lost husband, whom she had not seen for ten years and from whom she was officially separated. Perhaps making the best of things, and in return for a few arrangements that we know nothing about, she moved into new lodgings with him and her children, on the rue Neuve-des-Petits-Champs. It was she who paid Flamand, the fashionable interior decorator, 10,000 livres for the remodeling of her apartment. Madame Poisson's financial situation had improved again, thanks to a series of family inheritances, the inheritance from her parents being the most significant. Consequently, on January 8, 1738, she was able to buy a house on the rue de Richelieu,[14] looking out on the gardens of the Palais-Royal. A short time later, she would have it torn down and another one built, more luxurious and better suited to her style of life.

In spite of her many charms and gifts, Jeanne-Antoinette was not a presentable match. Only a parvenu with no reputation would ever aspire to her hand. But Le Normant de Tournehem had plans for her future. He had probably long intended to marry her off to his nephew, Charles-Guillaume Le Normant, the son of his brother Hervé-Guillaume, Treasurer General of the Mint. Tournehem, who had no legitimate children, had brought up this boy in the hope that he would succeed him in his position of *Fermier général*. In 1738, when he had just turned twenty-one, the young man was indeed accepted as *sous-fermier*. Intelligent, cultured and talented for business, he could quite reasonably aspire to a good match in that his uncle had just designated him as his sole heir.[15] When Tournehem informed his brother of his marriage plan, he met with a haughty refusal. Proud of his newly acquired nobility, the Treasurer General of the Mint wanted to be recognized as a true gentleman. His daughter had just married François de Baschi, Comte de Saint-

Estève, and added to the family's prestige. His darling son could aim higher than Mademoiselle Poisson.

But Tournehem stood fast, and the marriage took place as he had planned. Pecuniary arguments prevailed over offended pride when the father realized that his brother's fortune might well pass into the hands of someone other than his son if he persisted in his opposition. As for the future spouses, they had certainly not been consulted. In those days, marriage was primarily an arrangement between two families. The tastes and feelings of the two persons concerned were irrelevant. Jeanne-Antoinette and Charles-Guillaume, like most young people their age, were presented with a fait accompli. They had known each other since childhood and had never had any particular affection for each other, but Tournehem's arrangement suited them. The beauty and exceptional charm of the woman Charles-Guillaume was being given made up for her mediocre origins. As for Jeanne-Antoinette, she had good reason to be satisfied. This marriage buried in oblivion everything that tainted her parents' reputation and gave her a social status that was far superior to her mother's—the status of a woman married to a future *Fermier général.* She was nineteen and he twenty-four.

The contract was concluded on March 4, 1741.[16] Mademoiselle Poisson brought a rather handsome dowry that included jewelry and a sumptuous trousseau valued at 30,000 livres. Added to this was the house on the rue Saint-Marc, which had just been returned to her father and which was valued at 90,000 livres.[17] Charles-Guillaume Le Normant, for his part, was rich in future prospects: he was to inherit from his parents, and his uncle Tournehem was cancelling the loan of 85,000 livres he had given him so he could become *sous-fermier.* Moreover, Tournehem pledged to maintain the young couple in style for as long as he lived, providing them with five servants, horses and carriages. The notarized deed was signed at the Poissons' residence, on the rue de Richelieu. It includes no distinguished signatures. The contract dinner was held in strict intimacy, since the young man's parents were less than thrilled about the union. On March 9, Jeanne-Antoinette and Charles-Guillaume's wedding was celebrated in the church of Saint-Eustache. The newlyweds chose to be called Monsieur and Madame Le Normant d'Etiolles, although Tournehem was the squire of

Etiolles. But since they planned to spend part of the year in this little château, it was a way of setting themselves apart from the other members of the family. The young couple, as prearranged, moved in with their uncle, who had just recently rented a mansion on the rue Saint-Honoré. Indeed, Tournehem had just separated from his brother, with whom he had shared a residence until then. The Treasurer General of the Mint refused to live under the same roof as his son and daughter-in-law and would nurse his grudge to the end of his life.

A brilliant life began for Madame d'Etiolles, whose personality quickly eclipsed her husband's; he was reduced to playing a minor part in her new world. Though he was not plain-looking, as legend had it, he was a serious bourgeois, very absorbed in his business affairs, and lacked the charm and panache that might have made Jeanne-Antoinette's heart beat faster. But this hardly mattered to her. She was carried away by her social successes and these were enough to fulfil all her desires. Her marriage had given her access to the Paris elite of the day, where the oldest nobility, the libertine clergy, the established magistracy, high finance, artists and men of letters rubbed shoulders. Though she continued to attend Madame de Tencin's salon, she was seen more and more often at the home of the Comtesse d'Estrades, a cousin of her husband.[18] This lady belonged to another milieu than his. Since she was about to be presented at Court, she frequently went to Versailles and received the pride of the aristocracy in her salon. This was where Madame d'Etiolles met the witty Abbé de Bernis, who found her charming but turned down her invitations because "the company" she kept "was not acceptable to him." Madame Geoffrin had finally welcomed her into her famed "kingdom of the rue Saint-Honoré," where all the celebrities of Europe met. And Jeanne-Antoinette did not hide "her happiness at being admitted into her Areopagus."[19] People invited Madame d'Etiolles with pleasure; her beauty, wit and talents were praised to the skies; but it was felt that visiting her would be demeaning. She had an air that fit into Paris, but not Versailles. She was aware of this and longed to acquire that tone of high society that she still lacked. "How fortunate you are!" she said repeatedly to Madame de Geoffrin's daughter, the Marquise de La Ferté-Imbault. "You live with that charming Duc de Nivernais,[20] that amiable Abbé de Bernis[21] and that Gentil-Bernard,[22] and can have them as much as you want! While I have all the difficulty in the world getting one of them to dine at my uncle de Tournehem's because his company bores them." She also begged the Marquise to allow her to visit her as often as possible so she could acquire "some wit and good manners" from her. "My uncle's company is made up of very decent people, but they have an unrefined manner," she added.[23]

Modest, discreet and kind to everyone who could contribute to her advancement, Madame d'Etiolles knew how to exercise a gentle authority in her household. She reigned over her uncle's house and especially over Etiolles, where she was the real chatelaine. Bought by Charles Le Normant du Fort, father of Le Normant de Tournehem, this property was located at the edge of the Sénart forest, north of Corbeil. It included a patchwork of woods, vineyards and meadows in the midst of which were a manor and a small, recently renovated château facing a garden designed in the style of the day. This was where Jeanne-Antoinette made her debut as a hostess. She received Crébillon and Jélyotte, her old friends, as well as Fontenelle, Montesquieu and Voltaire, who was already praising the "divine d'Etiolles." Moved by her gentleness and beauty, Président de Rocheret took her to visit his cousin Monsieur Bertin de Blagny[24] and read to him Richardson's novel *Pamela*.

At the time, amateur theatricals were all the rage. All the great ladies wanted to have a theater and perform onstage for an audience of friends. But they were not all as gifted as Madame d'Etiolles. By now she was sufficiently integrated into good society to be asked to play opposite the greatest names in France. Hence she was asked to perform at Chantemerle, at Madame de Villemur's, opposite the Duc de Duras and the Duc de Nivernais—a performance that was attended by the Duc de Richelieu. This brought her one step closer to the Court that she secretly dreamed about.

By an odd coincidence, the year that Jeanne-Antoinette got married, Louis XV bought the Château de Choisy, which he planned to use as an escape from the burdens of government. It became his habit to go there with agreeable company to amuse himself and surrender to his passion for hunting. Many noblemen began to spend time in the environs of Choisy.

Etiolles was always full and the hostess did not go unnoticed. The King's favorite equerry, Monsieur de Briges, paid assiduous court to her. She accepted his tributes merrily, but never agreed to let this elegant badinage go any further—though the gentleman was certainly not lacking in charm. Instead, she chose to stage appearances in the monarch's path.

Was it this theatrical game that gave ideas to her protectors? Or were they the inspired behind-the-scene directors? Though it is impossible to say with certainty, it should be recalled that the Pâris brothers lived not very far away, in grand style, in their Brunoy residence, where they had received the King and the most notable figures of the Court, including Louis XV's mistresses. Madame de Tencin, who spent several days there in 1743, wrote to Richelieu that they "were swimming in wealth. They have a lot of friends, dispose of all possible channels, and money to hand out. Given these things, as you can see, they can do either good or bad,"[25] she added. At that time, the Pâris brothers enjoyed the trust of Madame de Châteauroux, but they knew that royal favor was fickle and were intent on keeping the sovereign's trust through his mistresses. Changes had to be foreseen and they knew how to make use of women. They had formerly used Madame Poisson for obscure but lucrative assignments. They could ask more of her daughter. For many years, they had invested a great deal in both mother and daughter; it was time for the daughter to take over. Madame de Châteauroux's sudden death provided her with a golden opportunity. As for Tournehem, he was ready to assist the Pâris brothers. This became clear when his niece went to Versailles for the first time. It was he who sent Charles-Guillaume on a well-timed trip and who informed him of his fall from grace. His behavior during this period suggests that he had foreseen and planned everything. And he had no compunctions about siding with Jeanne-Antoinette rather than the scorned husband, even though he was his nephew. Moreover, he chose to follow the new favorite to Versailles, while insisting that the betrayed husband leave on assignment for Grenoble and Provence to fulfill his obligations as *Fermier général*, a position from which he resigned in his nephew's favor. Coerced and pressured, Le Normant d'Etiolles complied, to the great relief of his wife, who never wanted to hear of him again.

Four

THE SUMMER OF FONTENOY

Madame d'Etiolles's dazzling success stunned the Court; her advancement to the rank of royal favorite was seen as a masterpiece of intrigue,
surely not a miracle of love. Unworthy of the King because of her birth,
she was considered a loose woman, an expert in voluptuous pleasure, in
whose company Louis XV found "a mistress well trained to rule over
him." Thus thought the Marquis d'Argenson, who saw her as the "gracious instrument of the most unfortunate designs."[1] His vitriolic portrait of her (which remained unpublished until 1857) closely resembles
those found in most of the correspondence and memoirs of the time.
Nearly all these writings trot out the same aggressive and contemptuous words with regard to the future Marquise. People passed judgment
before knowing her. This did not prevent her detractors from subsequently putting on a show of adulation in the hope of using her to
obtain the monarch's favor. At Versailles, for nearly twenty years,
people would never stop talking about her, would watch her every
move, and keep a vigilant eye for the faux pas that might herald her
fall. No one would show the slightest concern for her feelings or moods;
it was taken for granted that she was driven solely by ambition. Prudent, possibly even distrustful, Jeanne-Antoinette rarely confided in
anyone and retained an aura of mystery.

No extant letters between the two lovers have come down to us,
though they kept up a prolific correspondence during their first separa-

tion. Voltaire, who went to Etiolles several times in the summer of 1745, left an eyewitness account that was said to be rather accurate. "She was well brought up, well-behaved, amiable, full of charm and talent, born with common sense and a kind heart. I knew her well; I was even the confidant of her love for the King. She admitted to me that she had always had a secret presentiment that she would be loved by him and that she had violent passionate feelings for him that she didn't really unravel. This idea which might have seemed fanciful for someone in her situation came from her having often been taken on hunts in the forest of Sénart where the King went. . . . When she finally held the King in her arms, she told me she firmly believed in destiny and she was right."[2] Louis XV was regarded as the epitome of the seductive male: "He had a ravishingly handsome head. . . . No painter, even very skillful, could sketch the movement of this monarch's head when he turned to look at someone. One felt compelled to love him instantly. . . . I was certain that Madame de Pompadour had fallen in love with that face,"[3] said Casanova.

It seems more than likely that Jeanne-Antoinette was enjoying a period of perfect happiness when Louis XV set off for the campaign in Flanders, at dawn on May 6, 1745. Her lifelong dream had just come true and a bit of solitude did not frighten her. She needed the calm to recover from such enormous joy and to prepare for the glorious destiny that awaited her. She was confident of the King's love, for he wrote to her almost every day. He had promised that as soon as he returned to Versailles, she would be presented at Court so she could live in close proximity to him.

The monarch's decisions concerning his mistress had been kept secret. Even Police Lieutenant Feydeau de Marville did not know of them. "Rumor has it that Madame d'Etiolles will not be around for long, and they say she is quite a beautiful creature," he confides to Maurepas, convinced that the favorite had left for Normandy.[4] On learning that she is actually in Brunoy, at Pâris de Montmartel's, the "usual sojourn for the mistresses of our rulers," Marville claims she is six weeks pregnant.[5] This was false. Since Jeanne-Antoinette finally settled in Etiolles with her mother, Feydeau de Marville thinks she "has been the

King's perfect dupe, he amused himself with her for a few days and then left her there. She is neither baroness, nor countess, nor marquise; all she brought back from Court were regrets for all the mad steps she had taken."[6] Three days later, on May 13, he states that she "will not last long and it is absolutely false that she has been named a marquise."[7] On May 18, a new rumor is going around Paris that he passes on: Madame d'Etiolles has retired to a convent, "where she will spend the rest of her life if the King does not summon her back to Court. If this resolution is true," adds the police lieutenant, "it is said that Madame d'Etiolles may never leave the convent."[8]

Jeanne-Antoinette was enjoying a peaceful stay in Etiolles with her mother, Le Normant de Tournehem and her young brother, Abel Poisson, a chubby twenty-year-old boy who lacked neither cleverness nor ambition. But the summer, that year, would not just be devoted to rest and the usual distractions of château life. The King's new mistress had to be initiated into the subtleties of a world that was unfamiliar to her, the world of the Court. She had to master every last nuance of the sacrosanct Court etiquette, first codified by Henri III and established as inviolable by Louis XIV. Louis XV endured it reluctantly, but demanded that it be scrupulously observed. And nothing was more difficult to understand than this dogmatic ritual, which was almost as complex as the Vatican's. Madame d'Etiolles also had to know all the histories of those families who were close to the throne and who had distinguished themselves for centuries, or for even just decades. It was essential to remember births, marriages and distant family relationships; to be aware of liaisons, friendships, enmities and the networks of protégés within the microcosm; to have a clear idea of the clans and their power; to know how cabals were formed; and be aware of the issues that were hotly debated and that had to be avoided at all cost. Above all, she had to try to acquire that inimitable tone of the old aristocracy, that Court manner that seemed a privilege of birth.

The King had assigned the task of educating Madame d'Etiolles to two noblemen, the Marquis de Gontaut and the Abbé de Bernis. The first was an intimate friend of Louis XV, who liked him for his lively character and discretion. Since he had no personal fortune, he had married the granddaughter of one of the richest financiers of the Regency and was therefore in a better position than most to appreciate the difficulties that Madame d'Etiolles might encounter. But the man who really had the role of mentor was the Abbé de Bernis. The youngest child of an old, illustrious family, François-Joachim de Pierre de Bernis had sought a career in the Church, though he completely lacked any religious vocation. Having lost all hope of obtaining a benefice, he had received only minor orders and was leading a life of leisure, which might have been the life of a perfect sybarite had he had a larger income. Baby-faced, with sensual lips and an alert gaze, he loved women and they were rarely indifferent to his charm. He wrote pretty verses to the muses, "doting on love." Having become, as he himself put it, "the darling" of the salons, and admitted into the French Academy at twenty-nine, he waited for fortune to smile on him, though pride forbade him from requesting anything. He was most surprised when Madame d'Estrades informed him that Madame d'Etiolles, Louis XV's new mistress, "wished to consider him a friend and the King approved." Fully understanding the meaning of the mission he was being given, Bernis began by protesting. "I was very loath to sanction this arrangement, in which I had actually played no part, and that seemed inappropriate to my profession. They were insistent and I requested time to think about it. I consulted the most respectable people. They all agreed that since I had done nothing to encourage the King's passion, I should not turn my back on the friendship of an old acquaintance, or suppress the good that could result from my advice."[9] He thus decided to respond to Madame d'Etiolles's pledge of "eternal friendship" when he dined at her house for the first time. They agreed to see each other often.

Jeanne-Antoinette liked the company of the young abbot, whom she took to calling "my clumsy pigeon," because of his pleasant portliness. Completely won over by this lovely and witty woman, the "pigeon" took no offense at this familiarity and fulfilled his duties of adviser very conscientiously and gallantly. "I had no need to give her advice about cherishing and seeking out people of quality," he said. "I found this principle established in her mind. At the time the only fault

I noticed in Madame de Pompadour was a pride too easily flattered and wounded, and an overall distrust that was just as easy to excite as to calm."[10] Nevertheless, Bernis resolved always to tell her the truth, at the risk of displeasing her. "I must say in praise of her that for over twelve years she preferred my truths, though sometimes harsh, to other people's flatteries."[11]

At that time, the mood in France was one of jubilation. *Te Deums* were being celebrated everywhere in honor of the decisive victory at Fontenoy, which the French forces had won against the English, who had received support from the Dutch and the Austrians.[12] Louis XV was at the peak of his popularity. For the first time since the battle of Poitiers in 1356 (a defeat remembered with horror, in which King Jean le Bon was killed), a monarch had faced enemy fire with his son by his side. Louis XV and the young Prince immediately announced the marvelous news to the Queen. The Dauphin's prose exuded barely contained emotion, whereas the King's letter was chilly and representative of the tone that had been characterizing his relationship to Marie Leczinska for some time. Unfortunately, Louis XV's letter to his mistress and her reply were destroyed. Some courtiers claimed that Bernis and Voltaire wrote Madame d'Etiolles's letters for her. They probably did give her some well-turned sentences, and some verses perhaps. But there is no reason to underrate the favorite's epistolary skills to the point of assuming that the two poets had to be holding her hand.

Recently appointed Royal Historiographer and Ordinary Gentleman of the King's Chamber,[13] Voltaire had turned into an attentive and somewhat obsequious courtier. The day after Fontenoy, he wrote to the fortunate chatelaine of Etiolles: "I am more interested in your happiness than you think, perhaps there is no one in Paris that takes a livelier interest in it. I am talking to you not as an old, gallant flatterer of beautiful ladies, but as one good citizen to another, and I request permission to have a small word with you in Etiolles or Brunoy, in May. . . ." These lines were preceded by some rather convoluted, but gallantly turned, verses:

> *When César, that charming hero*
> *Whom Rome idolized,*

Defeated the Belgians or the Germans,
Compliments were paid
To the divine Cleopatra.
This hero of lovers as well as warriors
United myrrh with laurels;
But the yew is now the tree I revere,
And for some time I attach greater importance to it
Than to the blood-soaked laurels of the proud god of battle,
And the myrrh of Cythera.[14]

The reply was quick to follow. Voltaire was graciously received at Etiolles. From then on, he shared his time between the Château de Champs, where he was the guest of the Duc de La Vallière, and the Château d'Etiolles. He courted the chatelaine assiduously. He saw her as the rising star that might light up his career. He consulted her, heaped praise on her and extolled her lover. Indeed, he had just written a lyric ode to Louis XV's glory, *La Bataille de Fontenoy*, which came off the press on May 16, and immediately received the approval of the censor (who was none other than Crébillon). It was a dazzling success and in its fourth printing by May 26. Voltaire added about ten verses to each new printing, glorifying the King's and the Dauphin's great feats of arms, and those of the entire nobility from whom he sought recognition and gratitude. "How do these gentle, lively, amiable courtiers/ Become invincible lions in combat," he wrote. "In trying to please everyone, he produced a great many malcontents," grumbled the Duc de Luynes, though he acknowledged that the ode contained "some very beautiful verses."[15] The historiographer was specifically criticized for his exaggerated praise of the Duc de Richelieu's merits, Richelieu being one of his protectors and the sovereign's intimate friend. Outside the Court, Voltaire was berated for his indifference to the "subordinate heroes" who had paid for their loyalty to the sovereign with their lives.

Flattered by Voltaire's attentiveness, Madame d'Etiolles championed him with the King. In this, she was following Bernis's advice, for he had encouraged her to "protect men of letters. It was thanks to them that Louis XIV was called Louis the Great,"[16] he had said to her. What greater writer could she dream of having by her side than Voltaire, whose works were already held in the highest esteem throughout Europe? Jeanne-Antoinette stood by him and bubbled with indignation over the criticism his poem aroused. "I don't know why people clamor about your poem. It seems to me the most unjust thing in the world. You must not let this distress you. Being envied is the fate of great men."[17] She lavished the warmest encouragement on him at suppers where generous quantities of Tokay wine flowed. Voltaire sang her praises. "She is better read at her age than any elderly lady in the country where she will reign and where it is most desirable that she reign," he wrote Président Hénault. To Richelieu he admitted that the favorite's kind gestures "fill him with gratitude. . . . I am tenderly attached to her and think I can count on her kindness as much as anyone."[18] Madame d'Etiolles, with Richelieu's agreement, had just commissioned an opera from him to the glory of Louis XV, for which Rameau was to compose the music.[19]

Never before had Jeanne-Antoinette known such happiness. While Madame de Châteauroux's former apartment was being renovated for her at Versailles, she received the official ruling of her legal separation from her husband. And then, on July 11, the day Ghent was captured by the Maréchal Lowendal, Louis XV sent her the certificate of her title, Marquise de Pompadour. The King, who could confer titles of nobility whenever he pleased on whomever he pleased, had arranged for the estate of Pompadour, in the Limousin, to be purchased for his mistress.[20] Pâris de Montmartel had loaned the Royal Treasury 200,000 livres for this purpose. Now Marquise de Pompadour, Jeanne-Antoinette was the owner of a château and surrounding buildings where she would actually never set foot. She immediately assumed the coat of arms— three castles on an azure ground—of the Pompadour family, the last member of which had recently died without leaving an heir.

The news spread like wildfire. This time, the police lieutenant had no choice but to tell Maurepas that the new Marquise's letters of nobility would very shortly be registered in parliament and at the *Chambre des comptes*.[21] The Duc de Luynes noted in his *Journal* that the King had already written over eighty letters to his mistress since the beginning of the campaign. Delivered at Pâris de Montmartel's in

Brunoy, and carefully sealed, they bore the motto "discreet and faithful." "More in love" with the young woman "than ever," the monarch wrote to her constantly.[22]

In principle, the new title of nobility elevated Jeanne-Antoinette to the same rank as many women at Court and allowed her to be "presented." However, for the courtiers, this undeserved favor could not wipe out the new Marquise de Pompadour's origins as a commoner. More rigid than their master, they persisted in seeing her as the daughter of the contemptible Poisson couple. Nevertheless, they knew that they would have to put on an act and treat her like a woman of noble birth. This made them simmer with anger, while Voltaire, at Etiolles, composed some verses to celebrate the happy event. They are far from sublime:

> He knows how to love, he knows how to fight;
> He sent to this beautiful abode
> A certificate worthy of Henry the Fourth
> Signed Louis, Mars and Cupid. . . .

But it is still preferable to be exalted unimaginatively by a great man than by some rhymester of unrecognized genius.

The summer continued as it had started. Just one tragic incident occurred. On July 9, the inhabitants of Etiolles were roused by a dreadful din and the drawing-room door was shattered by a mysterious, violent impact. One league away, the Essonne gunpowder mill had just blown up, causing the death of about thirty people.

The rest of the stay was idyllically peaceful. Madame de Pompadour listened to her instructors or chatted with Madame d'Estrades and Madame de Tencin. The latter believed that the little Poisson girl's success was partly hers. She asked her insistently to get her brother, the Cardinal de Tencin, appointed Prime Minister. Madame de Pompadour listened but promised nothing. The charming group often went to visit Montmartel, who held glittering receptions in Brunoy. And Bernis composed verses near the "solitary woods where the young Pompadour went to daydream."

Meanwhile, the campaign of Flanders was going well. The royal army had taken Tournai, Ghent, Alost, Bruges, Audenarde and Ostend; Nieuport fell on September 5. Louis XV was getting ready to return to Versailles. Crowned with the laurels of victory, he was supposed to participate in the festivities prepared in his honor by the Paris councillors. The joyous city was getting ready to acclaim the conqueror of Fontenoy in lavish style. The lovers would soon be reunited.

On September 2, escorted by four footmen wearing plumed, three-cornered hats and suits with silver trimmings, the Marquise de Pompadour left Etiolles in a six-horse coach. On her arrival in Paris, she settled in a pied-à-terre in the Château de Tuileries, not far from the Duc de Richelieu's lodgings, which were connected to the monarch's apartment. Appearances had to be maintained.

On September 7, at four in the afternoon, Louis XV, the Dauphin and their retinue arrived at La Villette, where a light meal had been prepared for them. But in his rush to get to the Tuileries, the monarch shortened the ceremonies and merely changed coaches. At four-thirty, he reached the Porte Saint-Martin, where the Duc de Gesvres, Governor of Paris, the Provost of Merchants and the aldermen were kneeling and waiting for him. After receiving the city keys, he made his entrance into the capital, through streets decked with flags and tapestries. A huge crush of people acclaimed him as he passed. It was six o'clock by the time he finally arrived at the Tuileries, where the royal family and the courtiers were waiting for him at the palace windows. The enormous crowd that had been following him since the Porte Saint-Martin spilled out into the gardens, where they cheered even more loudly. Louis XV stepped out of his carriage, smiling and relaxed; he kissed the Queen, the Dauphine and his daughters, who had come downstairs to welcome him. Pale and thin, the Dauphin gamboled among his relatives like an overexcited dog. The King and his son stayed to chat for a while in the hall before retiring to their separate apartments to change clothes. The King let it be known that he had no intention of attending any ceremonies that evening. He said he wanted to rest and spent only a half hour at his wife's card table. He then supped with her, *en grand couvert*, in other words, in public and with musical accompaniment. Once he had fulfilled that obligation, he put an end to the conversation after a quarter of an hour. Then, as the Duc de Luynes puts it, "everyone went to bed."[23]

The following day was devoted to ceremonies and fetes, and it started with the celebration of a solemn mass at Notre-Dame that lasted until one-thirty. Then the monarch had to receive the city representatives and the ladies from the market, who recited their customary congratulations. In the evening, the entire royal family was driven by coach to the Hôtel de Ville, where several apartments had been prepared for their use so they could rest whenever they wanted. The papal nuncio, ambassadors, foreign ministers, courtiers and the representatives of the main bodies of the State were already assembled in the large reception room, where platforms had been built under the windows to allow those present to admire the fireworks on the square of the Hôtel de Ville. Afterward, the guests were invited to a concert, where the small violins played a divertimento composed for the occasion, entitled *Le Retour du Roi*. A supper followed. The King and the Queen presided over a table that included their children, the princes and princesses of royal blood and several guests whom Their Majesties especially wanted to honor. Meanwhile, the Marquise de Pompadour was dining incognito, in a small apartment above the large room. Madame d'Estrades, Madame de Sassenage, Le Normant de Tournehem and the young Abel Poisson were keeping her company. Before her arrival at the Hôtel de Ville, the Duc de Gesvres, the Provost of Merchants and the police lieutenant, Feydeau de Marville, had come to see her to "inform her of everything."[24] The Duc de Richelieu and the Duc de Gesvres went up to see her during the banquet. She left the Hôtel de Ville at eleven-thirty, though the King still had to ride through Paris by coach to admire the lighted streets extending all the way to the Place Vendôme. It was two in the morning by the time he returned to the Tuileries. On September 9, the monarch accepted congratulations from the sovereign courts and spent the remainder of the day resting. The following day, after dining at the Louvre, Louis XV and his retinue headed back to Versailles.

Throughout those days of celebration, the Marquise de Pompadour had been the main subject of conversation. Though her presence was very discreet, it was known that she had seen the King again, in spite of his many obligations. The whole Court looked forward, with a barely concealed impatience, to her official presentation, which was to take place several days later.

Five

THE COURT

It had been ages since Versailles had known such excitement. The end of the war, a princely marriage, the reception of a foreign sovereign— none of these created as much excitement as the Marquise de Pompadour's presentation at Court. Tuesday, September 14, 1745, would remain a memorable date in the royal annals: the Poisson girl, estranged spouse of *Fermier général* Le Normant d'Etiolles, was officially admitted into the monarchy's inner sanctum, where the only aristocrats accepted were those who could show supporting documents tracing their lineage back to the year 1400! However, not all the noblemen could pride themselves on an ancestry dating that far back. Many had received their titles of nobility recently, benefiting from a presentation "by order or grace of the King."[1] But they were separated from their plebeian origins by at least two generations. On that day, the newest aristocrats were not necessarily the most lenient in their attitude toward the new Marquise.

At the end of the afternoon, hundreds of courtiers were milling around in the King's and the Queen's antechambers. Mocking, malevolent, in a word pitiless, they had flocked to the strange spectacle of a love-struck sovereign whom they regarded as heedless of his duties. They strongly hoped the "flighty chatterbox" would make an irreparable faux pas that would spell her ruin. Since every new applicant had to be sponsored by two ladies of the Court, the courtiers wondered "which harlot would dare" lend herself to this charade. They fully expected to see Madame d'Estrades chaperon the favorite, but certainly not the Princesse de Conti.[2] The illustrious dowager, forgetting the scandals of her bygone youth, had needed a bit of coaxing when the King imposed this patronage on her. But the promise of seeing her debts repaid had overpowered her hesitations. Yet, fearing that she would be demeaned in the eyes of the royal family and the rest of the Court, she repeated to all and sundry that she had never met Madame d'Etiolles. She had also been scrupulous about informing the Queen that she bore no responsibility for this disgraceful show.

Before appearing in front of this audience whose cold hostility she had foreseen, Madame de Pompadour rehearsed her movements and gestures and the lines she had to deliver as though it were a stage performance. She took several "curtseying lessons" from the master of ceremonies. The day before, she made the customary visits to the Queen's Lady-in-Waiting and wardrobe lady.[3] No doubt her heart beat very fast on this solemn occasion. Though she was confident of the King's love, for he had again supped alone with her, the tiniest blunder could call her new status into question. Not for anything in the world did Jeanne-Antoinette want to disappoint her lover. This added to her anxiety, for "in this country"[4] the slightest mistake in etiquette could be fatal.

At six o'clock, Madame de Pompadour appeared, majestic and gracious, wearing a formal court dress well fitted at the waist and with a long train. She was accompanied by the Princesse de Conti and Madame d'Estrades, followed by Madame de Lachau-Montauban. After crossing the threshold of the King's council chamber, the Marquise made a deep curtsey, took several steps and bowed down again, then walked right up to the monarch and bowed deeply for the third time. "The conversation was very brief and the embarrassment great on both sides,"[5] remarked the Duc de Luynes. With confident movements, the Marquise walked backward, curtseying again three times as required by protocol. The same test awaited her at the Queen's. Everyone wondered what the scorned wife would say to the triumphant mistress. They thought she would pay her some compliments on her dress, "a very common topic among ladies when they have nothing to say to one another."[6] When, after the three curtseys, the Marquise lifted the hem of the Queen's dress with her ungloved hand and respectfully kissed it, Marie Leczinska spoke not about her clothes but about Madame de Saissac. She said she was happy to have made the acquaintance of that lady, a friend of Madame de Pompadour. We do not know if the newly presented Marquise heard all the words uttered by the Queen, who spoke in a rather low voice, but she was heard assuring the sovereign "of her respect and her desire to please her."[7] Not one single word of this exchange eluded the public. It was exceptionally long for this kind of ceremony and consisted of twelve sentences! Nothing escaped the courtiers. Flustered, Jeanne-Antoinette dropped a glove and it was hastily picked up by the Princesse de Conti.[8] Then Madame de Pompadour took leave of the Queen in the same manner as she had taken leave of the King, by walking backward and bowing three times. The same ritual had to be repeated for the Dauphin, who gave her an icy reception; the Dauphine, who was very distant; and Mesdames Henriette and Adélaide, Louis XV's daughters, who had no intention of being in the least gracious with their father's mistress.

Like any other presented woman, Madame de Pompadour could now pay court to the King, the Queen and the other members of the royal family in the morning after mass and in the evening at the card tables. She could ride in the King's and Queen's coaches, be invited to suppers in the private apartments and go to all the Queen's balls. But the status of official mistress was very different from that of "presented lady." Since no rules defined it, in a world codified down to the last detail, the Marquise had to impose her sovereignty very fast in order to make it impregnable. She had to stamp her reign with a style immediately, a reign which she sensed was fraught with fearsome pitfalls. Now was the time to recall the advice given to her by Bernis, who had tried to unravel for her Versailles's complicated tangle of rites and intrigues.

"Everyone hates the Court and everyone makes it their paradise," the Marquis d'Argenson remarked. Since 1682, Versailles had become a mythical place. It was the royal residence and the center of both government and entertainment, where Louis XIV had assembled the pride of his aristocracy and reduced them—after their decades-long rebellion against the monarchy—to a gentle captivity. Whether from fear or from hope, they had decided to serve this monarch, who was the sole dispenser of every honor and every favor, as it pleased his mood. By imposing a rigorous etiquette on the aristocracy, the princes, the royal family and himself, Louis XIV had defined a way of life from which none was allowed to deviate; anyone who did was in danger of being excluded from this microcosm, which exhibited itself to the world as a spectacle in which he, the Sun King, was the central shining star. Each person in his entourage played his or her part according to rank. Louis XIV was on perpetual show. He submitted to the same stringent rules of protocol no matter what his state of health; he never changed his daily ritual and demanded the same discipline from his entire family. "We are not like ordinary people, we owe ourselves entirely to the public," he said to his daughter-in-law, Maria Anna of Bavaria, on a day when she felt too ill to appear at a ball. "You could be three hundred leagues away, and with an almanac and a watch, you would know what he was doing," asserted Saint-Simon. For the Sun King, this Court clockwork was not just a ceremonial affair, it was an instrument of domination.

The rituals were maintained, but the times and the people had changed. Louis XV admired Louis XIV. He liked his impressive château, which all the European sovereigns had taken as a model. Like his ancestor, he used etiquette to show the distance that separated him from the princes and, all the more so, from the nobility, even though bellicose initiatives were no longer to be feared from them. But Louis XV refused to live like the Sun King. He could not bear the dogmatic theatricality and the rhetoric of appearances his ancestor had cleverly worked out. Being respectful of tradition, he endured the royal ceremonial unhappily and performed it conscientiously but wearily. As a way of escaping from the burden of his royal obligations, he arranged a double life for himself, which contributed to altering the interior of the palace and to changing the spirit of the Court.

His official existence took place in the formal apartments, punctuated by the public ceremonies of the *lever* (the rising) and the *coucher* (the going to bed), the daily mass and the days with formal suppers, called "*jours de grand couvert.*" A large crowd flocked around the monarch at those times, for the château was not restricted to courtiers. It was open to any visitor, provided he was properly dressed. Men were required to wear a sword on the hip and these could be rented at one of the stalls set up at the entrance to the château. Thus courtiers and country people rubbed shoulders amidst a throng of administrators and servants of all ranks, proud holders of positions, who bustled about in the halls. But only the three or four thousand persons who had been "presented" participated in the life of the court. The others were merely chance spectators. They never attended the concerts, balls, games or fetes over which the King and the Queen presided several times a week. The common people were only invited to festivities on exceptional occasions, such as the wedding of a Dauphin.

As a way of protecting his private life, Louis XV created his own personal domain where no one could enter without his permission. Very ill at ease in the Sun King's sumptuous bedchamber, which he left unchanged and where he complied with the public *lever* and *coucher*, as of 1738 he decided to spend his nights in a more modest but more intimate room. This was where he slept and woke up, before the official *lever*. Louis XIV had kept a private apartment as an alternate to his formal apartment. Louis XV had it modernized so it would be more inviting and comfortable. However, in spite of the alterations that had been made, the private apartment lacked intimacy. The King was never alone in it. He sometimes had to seclude himself in his dressing room to find peace and quiet. He felt truly at home only in a string of small rooms, reached by interior stairways on the third and fourth floors and the mezzanine in between, called the "*petits cabinets.*" These were decorated and furnished with a refined taste and had undergone many alterations over several decades, with the dining rooms, kitchens and bathrooms changing places several times.

A stairway giving out on an interior courtyard, called the King's "small ladder," led to this retreat. It allowed him to grant personal audiences without anyone knowing. Ministers as well as a few pretty women slipped in through "the back." Though nothing leaked out about these repeated meetings, the Court was intrigued by them. Few people knew that Louis XV worked in this private retreat and indulged in his hobbies—geography and physics—undisturbed. He spent hours consulting his map collection or using the precision instruments assembled in his laboratories. This secret apartment also served when he entertained for pleasure. The King enjoyed spending part of his evenings here, far from the rest of the Court, among the hand-picked few, particularly after he instituted the "suppers in the private apartments" to which he invited people whose company he valued. His previous mistresses always hosted these meals, where he behaved like a nobleman receiving his friends in his castle.

This signal privilege extended to a few intimate friends aroused many jealous feelings. "If you want attention to be paid to you, you must be attached to a minister or dine in the private apartments. If you have that good fortune you will find the Court pleasant,"[9] the Comte de Sade wrote to his son. Many noblemen felt that the King was neglecting them, or worse, that he was ignoring them. In Louis XIV's time, it had been sufficient to be seen regularly by the monarch to obtain his favor. Now the courtiers lived in a state of permanent rivalry, eyes riveted on the King, from whom they expected positions, distinctions and pensions. They preferred the Paris social life to the monotonous pleasures of Versailles, and they went to Court out of obligation, sometimes with regret, and always out of self-interest. Most of the aristocrats kept up with the King's ministers, mistresses and friends assiduously in order to retain the rights they had acquired and acquire new ones. Bernis was indignant at the greed of his table companions: "They love money and request it without blushing and sometimes just take it. . . . They are conceited but lack genuine nobility. Nothing is rarer today than finding *characters* at Court: no one appears above anyone else; everyone there seems to be of the same height."[10] The courtiers were jealous and spied on one another. "Nowadays friends are as fickle and unfaithful as in the past and enemies are not irreconcilable; relationships at Court change from day to day."[11] The King's appetite for a private life, his intermittent presence at Versailles and his apparent lack of interest in some of his nobility prompted the emergence of cabals and intrigues that had to be disentangled by the ministers. "The chain of protection and influence extends from the Crown's highest officers down to the footmen," asserted d'Argenson.

Though Louis XV seemed elusive, even the most modest among those "presented" tried to attract his attention. For they knew that the King's whim could change a person's destiny. And the King, a creature of habit, had his occasional caprices. An elaborate strategy was required in order to succeed in arousing his interest. You had to respect every detail of his rigid etiquette scrupulously, show deference when he crossed your path, pay court to him, hunt with him, join his card table and, most important of all, make yourself liked. A courtier seeking favor spent his time on visits where conversation invariably centered on what the King and the royal family had done the day before and what they planned to do tomorrow. "The life of an assiduous courtier resembles that of a valet, or of anyone living in servitude," said Dufort de Cheverny. "I have seen the Duc de Luynes, the Duc de Saint-Aignan, Président Hénault, Moncrif and so many others narrow their mind with such unvaried conversation that I could neither get used to it nor concentrate on it. . . . The boredom a stay at Court necessarily entails had to be diversified, for it is only bearable for a thinking man if he is engaged in active or continual service or engaged in intrigue."[12] If he had the unusual good fortune of succeeding in his aims, the courtier had to be attentive to his master's every desire; or better yet, he had to anticipate them. Though he could not speak sincerely with the monarch, he had to know instinctively how to please, reassure and entertain him, for the life of princes was always weighed down by boredom. The person who obtained this invaluable honor, which so many people envied, became obsessed with keeping it. Then "flattery would be disguised as wisdom and love."[13] The courtier who had the signal favor of being admitted into the King's intimate circle had to be lively, find ways of saying amusing things without shocking propriety, never question the sovereign about anything and always let him choose the subjects of conversation. Hence the King always talked about science, art or hunting. If he commented on any burning issues, his every word would be interpreted in thousands of different ways.

A woman coming from a different background had to have exceptional qualities to become Louis XV's chosen female companion. The sovereign's passion would not have sufficed in maintaining a mistress in such a position. Though she incurred the danger of succumbing to even greater blows from those who wanted her dismissal, the Marquise had to adapt at once to the customs of "this country." The masterful way in which she had handled her presentation and the Queen's mass the following day had disarmed several of her detractors. Offended at having to associate with a marquise of such low extraction, the women suppressed their frustration, whereas the men were impressed by her charm and inclined to be more lenient.

Louis XV, who had had very little time to rest since his return from the campaign, decided to leave for Choisy, with a select group, on September 16. The only ladies invited were Mesdames de Lauraguais, de Sassenage, de Bellefonds, de Saint-Germain and, of course, Madame de Pompadour. A select group of gentlemen accompanied them—the Ducs de Richelieu, d'Ayen, de Duras and Monsieur de Meuse. The Princesse de Conti had declined the monarch's invitation so she could pay conspicuous court to the Queen. Thanks to this trip, the King avoided seeing his father-in-law, the King of Poland, who was expected at Versailles for a visit. Having no desire to meet his son-in-law's new favorite, Stanislas had stopped for a short stay at Dampierre, the Duc and Duchesse de Luynes's château. By the time he arrived at his daughter's home, the sovereign and his retinue were in Choisy.

The stay at Choisy, which the two lovers had greatly looked forward to, turned out not to be the hoped-for honeymoon. The King fell ill (with what was probably a tooth abscess), and the physicians thought it wise to bleed him twice. Fortunately, the fever soon subsided and so did everyone's fear. But the Queen, who had been notified of her husband's condition, requested his permission to come to his bedside. To her amazement, the King suggested she come to Choisy where she "would find," said he, "a good dinner, vespers and salvation."[14] Louis XV was courteous in receiving his wife, and had her dine with all the ladies in his company, including the charming Madame de Pompadour, who had pride of place. The sovereign wanted the Queen to visit the château, where he had just undertaken important renovations.[15] The royal apartment had been enlarged, the terrace overlooking the Seine extended, and a new main building was being built by the architect Gabriel. To decorate the hall, Louis XV had just commissioned Parocel for a series of frescoes commemorating his victories in Flanders. Marie left in the evening, after spending a long time on her religious duties.

Stanislas Leczinski then felt obliged to visit his son-in-law, though the latter had no desire to see him. However, Louis XV could not shut the door in his face, so he received him in his bedchamber, where Madame de Pompadour, in a hunting outfit, was playing *quadrille* with three other people. It was a very cold welcome and the King of Poland stayed only a half an hour. The Dauphin, the Dauphine and the King's daughters soon followed suit and came to wish their father a prompt recovery. The joys of love therefore had to be postponed to the stay in Fontainebleau, where they would be going after Choisy.

Louis XV always held Court in Fontainebleau during the first weeks of autumn. He arrived on October 1 with Madame de Pompadour, whom he lodged in Madame de Châteauroux's apartment. That very evening he dined in his private apartment with her, Madame de Lauraguais and Madame de Sassenage. The Marquise showed great discretion. She made herself available to her lover at all times, rarely left her own quarters and paid conscientious court to the Queen, who was relatively lenient toward her. Marie Leczinska was completely resigned to her fate. Since her intimate relations with her husband had ceased long ago, she knew she would have to tolerate his mistresses. She thought that a woman of low birth would be more considerate of her than the arrogant Nesle sisters, who had taken pleasure in haughtily crushing her. And she was right. Madame de Pompadour went out of her way to show her a deep respect.

Louis XV fell into new habits with his mistress. Once he was up and dressed, he went down to see her and stayed with her until the hour of mass. After the service, he returned to eat a soup and a cutlet with Jeanne-Antoinette and only left her apartment at around five or six o'clock to go to work. Whenever he had a formal supper obligation *en grand couvert*, the Marquise, whose chef was excellent, held small suppers to which she invited a few close friends and relatives. On evenings when theater performances were held at the château, the King and his favorite were seen together behind the wire netting of the same box. Louis XV was more attentive to her than to anyone else. This became clear when Jeanne-Antoinette caught a cold and had to take to her bed and be bled. On that day, the King interrupted his supper, leaving his friends in the middle of the meal, and went to keep her company. When he returned to the dining room, he asked Monsieur de Meuse and Monsieur de Soubise to take turns at her bedside to relieve her boredom. When they understood that this liaison might last much longer than they had thought, the courtiers started to have much kinder words for Madame de Pompadour. "Everyone finds Madame de Pompadour extremely polite; not only is she not nasty and never unkind about anyone, she does not tolerate unkind words in her quarters. She is cheerful and talkative,"[16] wrote the Duc de Luynes. Feydeau de Marville was the only person to predict that she would soon fall out of favor.[17]

The Marquise was not so intoxicated by her advancement as to forget her origins. To everyone's surprise, even in the King's presence, she spoke of her family readily and did not repudiate her relatives. She visited Monsieur Poisson, who had rented a house in town, but asked him not to appear at the château. However, Jeanne-Antoinette, who was still adapting to her new position, had a Parisian turn of speech and used expressions that were "extraordinary in this country." Luynes feared that this might annoy or shock the King. It never occurred to this great nobleman that the sovereign was charmed by his mistress and that her speech added a harmless piquancy to his rigidly regulated existence.

When the Court was about to leave Fontainebleau for Versailles, it became known that the sovereign had made the thoughtful gesture of inviting his wife to Choisy, something he never did in such circumstances. It was clear to everyone that Madame de Pompadour had inspired this sensitive gesture. She had recently confided to the Duchesse de Luynes, the Queen's Lady-in-Waiting and intimate friend, that if the Queen had "treated her badly, she would have been truly distressed, though she would never have complained about it; that therefore, there was nothing extraordinary . . . in her seeking to please her in every possible way."[18] But the Dauphin and Dauphine did not show Jeanne-Antoinette the same kindness as their mother did. Taciturn, somber and steeped in religion, the young Prince saw her as the devil posing as a lovely woman. His sour-tempered wife bestowed a few contemptuous smiles upon the sinner whom she hoped to see disgraced. People said that when Madame de Pompadour had accidentally fallen in a basin in Fontainebleau, the Dauphine had graciously mumbled that she was a "fish [*poisson*] returning to her element."[19] The King's daughters shared her feelings. Among the young princes, the influence of the Church party, called the "*clan des dévots*," was unrelenting.

Six

DEBUT IN "THIS COUNTRY"

There was no escaping the obvious: never before had Louis XV seemed so in love with a mistress. She seemed to have qualities that meant more to him than any of her predecessors. More subtle and astute than the Nesle sisters, Jeanne-Antoinette instinctively understood the melancholic monarch's temperament; she understood that he needed constant reassurance and had to be pulled out of the depressive state that always threatened to engulf him. She was always natural and unaffected with him, whereas a woman of the Court would not have been. She had frequented milieus with which he was completely unfamiliar; she had met writers, scholars, scientists and artists, and had had experiences that were banal but could appear extraordinary to a sovereign confined to his palaces. She was like a huge breath of fresh air for him, for his knowledge of real life was very limited, restricted to what a swarm of obsequious courtiers were willing to tell him.

She enveloped her lover with a warm tenderness and "had the art of bantering" with him in a tone that was completely novel in "this country." She described the small events of the Court and the city with unparalleled charm, and these narratives enchanted Louis XV. She always found the opportune moment to tell him what she wanted him to hear and did so so skillfully that she always attained her objective. Jeanne-Antoinette anticipated the King's every desire and he marveled at the surprises she expertly contrived for him. "She was, as required, magnificent, imperious, calm, cheeky, mischievous, sensible, curious, attentive,"[1] and she also had the gift of tears, an extremely rare quality at Court, where impassivity was the norm. She completely changed the sovereign's life; she could behave both as a mistress and a wife, on one occasion candidly pointing out, quasi-publicly, that the lace of his jabot did not match the lace of his cuffs.[2] Louis XV, who was no longer bored, was convinced that he "would never find a person with whom he could spend such quiet and happy days."[3]

At Versailles, where they moved at the end of November, the King maintained the habits he had adopted in Fontainebleau. He spent several hours in his mistress's apartment, adjoining his private apartment. With its nine windows looking out on the northern flowerbeds and with a view of the Neptune basin, the favorite's residence was elegant and comfortable. Hanging over the fireplace in the antechamber to her apartment and giving depth to the room was a mirror dating back to the time of Louis XIV. The door to the left opened onto a vast drawing room with a large alcove used as a dining room. This was where the Marquise held her exquisite suppers. To the right of the entry, a double door led to the bedroom, wainscoted with large scalloped panels in the style of Verberckt. The sleeping alcove, under an arch crowned by an escutcheon and flower motif, was located between two small rooms with wood paneling concealing wardrobes. The apartment also included a kitchen and bathroom. The height of luxury was a flying chair that allowed Jeanne-Antoinette to go up to her apartment without tiring herself. In spite of the claims of an oriental-style lampoon dated 1745, this lift had not been built for her but for Madame de Châteauroux, who died before being able to use it.

Madame de Pompadour still needed Bernis's guidance in avoiding the innumerable pitfalls of "this country." Hence she had arranged to meet with him for one or two hours a week. But these private conversations provoked such alarm among the courtiers that she decided to discontinue them. She then received her mentor in a circle of select guests, and he transmitted to her in writing "everything that could concern the King's greater glory and the happiness of decent people."[4] This elegant turn of phrase in describing his advice to the Marquise is worthy of admiration.

She was eager to shed her role of novice and dreamed of leaving a glorious name in the history of royal favorites. She was dazzled by the favorites of Louis XIV's reign. In order to know more about them, she asked to be given the unpublished manuscripts of Dangeau's *Journal* and Saint-Simon's *Mémoires*. She wanted to be the organizer of the King's and the Court's pleasures as Madame de Montespan had been. Though she lacked that illustrious predecessor's good health and sensuality, she had the advantage of a creative imagination and a keen intelligence. Madame de Montespan's misfortunes were a warning to her against the follies of jealousy. A magnificent woman, she had fallen into disfavor after becoming involved in sordid activities because of her desperate desire to keep the King's love.

Madame de Maintenon's fate exerted an even greater fascination on Madame de Pompadour. She wanted to probe the secrets of a woman who had been born in the Niort prisons and whom the most powerful European sovereign had ended up secretly marrying! Queen without a crown, Madame de Maintenon's amazing success was deeply troubling to Jeanne-Antoinette. She admired her for having known how to keep the King's love and fidelity, in spite of the odds, and for having been the only person of her sex to exert a undeniable influence over an absolute monarch, who called her "Your Solidity." With supreme skill, this austere, religious woman had claimed a special place for herself in history. Madame de Pompadour wanted nothing less.

As soon as they returned to Versailles, it became clear that the pretty Marquise's role was not going to be restricted to satisfying the King's desires. On December 4, 1745, when Louis XV dismissed Philibert Orry, his Comptroller General of Finances, it was rumored, correctly, that Madame de Pompadour had been involved in the decision. The love she felt for the monarch did not prevent her from remaining the devoted friend of the Pâris brothers. As creditors of the State and suppliers of the army, it was very much in their interest for the war to continue so they could make deals and command their own prices. This brought them into conflict with Orry on several occasions, for he did not want to squander the funds of the kingdom, which he had been managing since 1730. Most recently, Orry had warned the King of the exorbitant expenses brought about by an inordinately long conflict whose out-come was still unclear in spite of the French army's victories. Moreover, the minister had been thinking of resigning since the previous spring.[5] When informed of his intentions, the King had asked him to stay on. But in the early fall, the relationship between the minister and the Pâris brothers had grown more acrimonious. An argument broke out over the price of bread supplies, with Duverney wanting to sell at thirty-two deniers a pound and Orry maintaining he could buy through other middlemen at twenty-eight. "The conversation became extremely curt and Monsieur Duverney added that he would never work with him again in his life."[6] Assured of Madame de Pompadour's support, the Pâris broth-ers put pressure on her to get what they wanted from the King.[7] Louis XV, it seems, hesitated a long time before parting from his upright aide and used greater tact with him than he had ever used with a minister in requesting a resignation. He also listened to Orry's suggestions for choos-ing a successor. The Pâris brothers were sorely disappointed when Louis XV appointed the *Intendant* de Hainaut, Machault d'Arnouville, instead of Monsieur de Boullongne, whom they knew they could count on.

For the first time, Madame de Pompadour had made use of her influ-ence to assist those who had helped her rise to her present position. Le Normant de Tournehem and Abel Poisson would be the next benefici-aries of her ability to influence the monarch's decisions. She wanted them to be assigned the important position of Director of the King's Buildings that became vacant with Orry's resignation. As a cost-saving measure, not only was Orry Comptroller General, he had concurrently been in charge of what could be called the Ministry of Fine Arts. Over-burdened by his many responsibilities, he had neglected the Buildings, an area in which he had shown himself to be extremely parsimonious. The person holding this office was responsible for the management of the royal châteaux, parks and gardens. When he felt it was called for, he could suggest the construction of new buildings and negotiate with contractors and artists. He was also responsible for directing the Royal Academies of painting, sculpture and architecture, and for supervising all scientific assignments. The officeholder had the privilege of working directly with the monarch, who informed him of his wishes.

Louis XV hesitated for some time before yielding to his mistress's request. The King was very interested in architecture and buildings; he did not know Tournehem and was not really open to new people. Jeanne-Antoinette had to apply all her persuasive gifts to sway his will. The sovereign met secretly with Tournehem, who succeeded in convincing him that he had the qualifications for the position. This unexpected nomination provoked much agitation at Court. And when word was out that the Marquise's brother, Abel Poisson, who had recently become the Marquis de Vandières, had been given the position as a legacy,[8] no one had any more doubts concerning the new mistress's power.

Madame de Pompadour was loved and her prayers had been answered. The year would have been idyllic except for the death of her mother on December 24, 1745. It was claimed by vicious gossips that she had died from indigestion, whereas in fact she had been wasting away with cancer for several months. Jeanne-Antoinette was devastated by this loss and she had to take to her bed. Moved by her grief, the King offered to put off their trip to Marly, though it had been planned for a long time. The Marquise mastered her sorrow and replied that her mother had been too modest a person for the Court to endure any inconvenience on her account. Only about ten people attended Madame Poisson's modest burial in the crypt of Saint-Eustache.[9] The Marquise remained at Versailles, where the King never left her side. On the evening of December 31, he even kept the Queen waiting at a presentation of automatons that he had promised to attend. He preferred to keep the Marquise company. On the following day, however, Marie Leczinska had the pleasant surprise of receiving a magnificent gold snuffbox with a watch, though it had been years since her husband had given her a gift. It would certainly have tarnished her joy to find out that this fine object had originally been intended for the late Madame Poisson!

On January 8, 1746, two weeks after her mother's death, Madame de Pompadour reappeared at Court. To distract her from her grief, the King took her to Choisy for several days, where he invited only a few intimate friends. Never before had Louis XV showed such kindness and consideration for someone. When she returned to Versailles, Jeanne-

Antoinette shed the relative reserve she had maintained till then. She began to share the monarch's public as well as private life. To celebrate Mardi-Gras, they left for Paris together, in the company of a few friends. They danced all night at the Opera ball and returned to Versailles only at seven in the morning. The next day they rose at five-thirty in the afternoon. Though she disliked hunting, a pastime Louis XV engaged in three or four times a week, she accompanied him on horseback and usually rode with the princesses. On hunting evenings, they supped in a small group in the private apartment.

In early 1746, Madame de Pompadour initiated the custom of inviting the monarch for supper in her own apartment with friends whose company he liked: Madame d'Estrades, the Duchesse de Brancas, the Comtesse d'Egmont, Madame du Roure[10]; the Duc d'Ayen, the Duc de La Vallière,[11] the Marquis de Gontaut, men who had been very close to Madame de Châteauroux and were now respectfully attentive to her; and the Prince de Soubise,[12] who praised the new favorite to the skies. Monsieur de Croissy[13] and Monsieur de Coigny[14] sometimes joined this small group of friends. However, some of the King's close friends, whom the Marquise was obliged to invite, hardly concealed their contempt for her. This was the case of the Prince de Conti.[15] Furious that his mother had lowered herself by presenting the favorite at Court, he still felt anger for this woman whom he regarded as a schemer. As for the Duc de Richelieu, long-standing confidant of the King's love affairs, regarding Jeanne-Antoinette, he maintained all the prejudices of a great nobleman toward an upstart "grisette," a young French working-class woman of easy virtue. She feared this libertine, whose respect for women was very limited, particularly when they were not well born. For the time being, she was spared his presence. Richelieu was preparing a landing on the coast of England that, as it turned out, would never take place. To please his mistress, Louis XV told her she could include her brother, the Marquis de Vandières, who was wickedly nicknamed the Marquis "d'avant-hier" (of the day before yesterday).

The Marquise also hosted the suppers in the King's private apartments. All the courtiers dreamed of being invited to one of these evenings. The young Prince de Croÿ, though he went hunting with the monarch regularly, was very unhappy at not being invited. "Having learned that practically the only way to be admitted was through the Marquise, and since I was on good terms with the Pâris brothers, I begged them and Monsieur de Tournehem, to talk to her about it."[16] The happy effects of this conversation were not long in coming. Several days later, "the King put him on the list which the usher read off at the door. Guests went in one by one, up the small stairway, to the private apartments. . . . Once upstairs, you waited for supper in the small drawing room. The King only came in time to sit down at the table with the ladies. The dining room was charming and the supper extremely pleasant and unconstrained," though there were eighteen guests "tightly packed around the table" for almost two hours. "We were served by only two or three footmen of the wardrobe who retired after giving each of us what we were supposed to have," the Prince continued. "The King was cheerful, free and easy, but always maintained a grandeur that didn't let us forget who he was. He didn't seem at all shy, talked well and a great deal, enjoying himself and knowing how to enjoy himself. He seemed very much in love with Madame de Pompadour, and didn't conceal the fact at all. He had shed all shame, and appeared to have made up his mind, either because he was infatuated or for some other reason, and had accepted the ideas of society on this subject, without accepting others, in other words, he had adjusted his principles, as so many people do, to his tastes and passions.

"I noticed that he talked to the Marquise. . . . It seemed to me that he spoke very freely with her, as with a mistress whom he loved, but whom he liked to tease. And she behaved extremely well, had a lot of influence, but the King always wanted to be the master, and was adamant about that." After supper, Louis XV walked over to the small drawing room, helped himself to coffee on his own, asked his guests to sit down, and they started playing cards. Madame de Pompadour was not very fond of card games, but she forced herself to play games of *comète* with her lover. On the evening when the Prince de Croÿ attended the supper, he saw the Marquise fight against increasing sleepiness. The King noticed it and said to her cheerfully in an undertone, "Come! Let's go to bed!"[17] The ladies then bent down before the sovereign and curtseyed respectfully, and he responded in kind. It was one in the morning. And the guests made their way through the private apartment's maze of hallways and stairways to reach the State bedchamber so they could be present for the monarch's public *coucher*. Once he had finished the ceremony and observed the ritual in minute detail, the King slipped into his dressing gown, and went back to his private apartments and up the stairs to be with Madame de Pompadour, who was waiting for him. His nights were spent with her and in the morning he would return to his bedchamber for his *lever*.

The courtiers were quick to grasp that they had better not cold-shoulder a mistress with whom the sovereign seemed so in love and who had just demonstrated her power in a striking manner by getting a minister dismissed. The representatives of the oldest nobility now solicited the honor of being presented to her. "She received the whole Court in her quarters, she acted almost like a hostess and everyone went there."[18] At eleven o'clock, as she was finishing her toilette, princes, noblemen, writers and artists clustered around her, spoke about everything with her and presented her with petitions and requests. "She handled all this extremely well, in a grand manner, with a very light touch, and infinite gaiety and grace."[19] To everyone's surprise, her visitors remained standing while she was seated in an armchair. She stood up only for princes of royal blood, cardinals and several exceptional personalities. One day, the Marquis de Souvré casually perched on the arm of her chair. Madame de Pompadour said nothing, but complained to the King of the breach in her unspoken rules. Louis XV scolded the insolent Marquis for thinking he could take such a liberty. Without the slightest embarrassment, Souvré replied that feeling "fiendishly tired, and not knowing where to sit, he had helped himself as best he could."[20] The matter went no further, the King having laughed heartily at this rather casual answer. However, Madame de Pompadour was vigilant about people observing protocol with her, dictated solely by her intuition concerning the obligations a royal mistress was entitled to expect. She regarded these obligations as an indirect homage being paid to the monarch through her. In other words, she regarded herself as something of a queen. And, of course, her court eclipsed that of the real Queen.

A strange *modus vivendi* developed between the Queen and the favorite. It seemed as if Jeanne-Antoinette sought forgiveness and legitimacy from Marie. She worried about her health, her tastes, and paid court to her regularly. On the *"jours d'appartements"*[21] she attended the Queen's dinner and game. At the end of the evening, when she knew the King was waiting for her, she stood up graciously, made a formal curtsey and asked the Queen for permission to retire. "Go,"[22] said Marie, with a smile. The Queen showed no hostility toward the favorite, whom she did not regard as a rival. Madame de Pompadour treated her as a sovereign and not as a humiliated wife. Furthermore, since his liaison with the Marquise, the King had a different attitude toward her. He had become much more thoughtful and would soon give her 40,000 écus to pay back the debts she had contracted from her innumerable charitable gifts. Poor Marie knew she owed this unexpected generosity to the Marquise's good offices. She was sometimes annoyed by so much solicitude, but was careful not to show it. She would never have wanted to antagonize an all-powerful favorite of that splendid and fearsome husband whom she had never succeeded in contenting.

Jeanne-Antoinette wished that the Queen would regard her as one of the ladies of her Household. With this in mind, she asked the Duchesse de Luynes if she could attend the Queen's *coucher*, as did some princesses and a few privileged persons who were entitled to this great honor. Marie let her know that she was willing to accept her presence. When the night arrived, she kept Madame de Pompadour around a bit longer than the other ladies. Extremely flattered by this sign of favor, the Marquise thought that she now had entry into the Queen's bedchamber, in other words, the right to attend the *coucher* every night. This was not at all the case. She was given to understand that the welcome had been completely exceptional.

Madame de Pompadour beat a prudent retreat, but showed her zeal again during Lent. Again through Madame de Luynes, she offered to help the Queen during the Supper ceremony, on Holy Thursday. On that occasion, the Queen designated fifteen ladies to help her pass the dishes of food to the indigent little girls whose feet she had previously washed. Marie Leczinska declined the offer, giving as an excuse that the ladies assisting her for this ceremonial had already been chosen. In truth, she would have been incensed at assigning a duty of this kind to a woman who was openly living in sin and moreover was known to have an independent mind and be nonbelieving. However, Madame de Pompadour did not consider herself beaten. She wanted permission to take the collection in the royal chapel at the Easter mass. Once again the Queen refused to grant a request that she considered offensive to the holy service. Though she trembled before her husband, Marie Leczinska would have readily stood up to him if her religious convictions had been at stake and had to be defended.

The favorite met with another refusal when she expressed a desire to ride in the Queen's coaches without being invited to do so. Annoyed by this clumsy insistence, Marie finally relented. As soon as there was a vacant place in her carriages she arranged to have it given to the Marquise and even invited her to dine with the ladies of her household.

Only once did the Queen show resentment for her husband's mistress—and it backfired. Madame de Pompadour was in the habit of sending the Queen huge bouquets of flowers. One day, it is not known why, she decided to bring them to her personally. When she arrived at the Queen's apartment carrying an armful of fragrant branches, the sovereign asked her, with a pinched air, to choose an aria and sing it since she had such a lovely voice. Disconcerted by this welcome, Jeanne-Antoinette quickly pulled herself together and, to the astonishment of those present, self-confidently sang the aria of the sorceress Armide[23]:

> *Finally, he is in my power,*
> *That deadly enemy, that magnificent conqueror . . .*
> *Everything on earth yields to this young hero.*
> *Who would believe that he was born only for war?*
> *He seems made for love.*

Eyes were lowered; no one dared look at the Queen or the favorite, yet she sang her aria to the end without a single mistake. After bowing to the sovereign, she laid the flowers down and left the drawing room.

She had just won a victory, not so much over poor Marie as over the Court before which she had dared to assert her power.

The King's children, however, still had their prejudices against the Marquise. Very attached to their mother, they could not understand how she could be lenient toward the upstart who was usurping her place. Fearing that Madame de Pompadour might harm them with the King, they affected a purely superficial amiability with her. The Dauphin, with his narrow-minded piety, was her fiercest enemy, and his aversion to her was reinforced by the fact that his relationship with his father had never been one of mutual trust. Louis XV regarded him as a hypocrite who wanted to succeed him on the throne as soon as possible. The King and his son were deeply suspicious of each other. The Dauphine, who was always sullen, followed her husband's instructions to the letter. She refused to encourage a close relationship with the sovereign even though he viewed her with paternal affection. Indeed, for several weeks he had been openly showing his joy: the young woman was expecting an heir at the beginning of the summer. But in spite of all the attentiveness lavished upon her, Marie-Thérèse Raphaëlle isolated herself in a hostile silence.

Louis XV's daughters sided with their brother and sister-in-law. Only two lived at Versailles. The eldest Princess, Madame Elisabeth,[24] was married. She had left Versailles in August 1739, at the tender age of twelve, to marry the Infante of Parma. Since then she had been living in Italy, where she had not found happiness. Madame Henriette,[25] her twin, had remained at Court. Vivacious and lively, she had been madly in love with her cousin the Duc de Chartres, and he returned her feelings. But the elderly Fleury had felt that this union was not in the dynasty's interests: Henriette, the King's favorite daughter, had had to give up the love of her life. She remained disconsolate. Nattier, who painted her as Flora, left the portrait of a gracious young woman, stretched out on the grass at the edge of a stream. In contrast to the melancholic Henriette, Adélaide, called Madame Troisième,[26] stood out for her impetuous, almost virile character. Athletic, indefatigable at the hunt, she would have gladly commanded an army. The Marquis d'Argenson thought that one could "expect violent extremes" from such a determined person who was the only Princess not to be intimidated by her father. She was only thirteen at this time. Three other little princesses were boarders at the Abbaye de Fontevrault, where they had been taken shortly after their births, and their parents never went to see them.

At Versailles the young royal family was guided by Monseigneur Boyer, Bishop of Mirepoix, leader of the Church party and very hostile to Madame de Pompadour. The prelate condemned the favorite for her lack of religious feeling. It was known that she had received guests such as Voltaire, Fontenelle, Cahusac, Montesquieu, Maupertuis and the Abbé de Bernis whom the Jesuits disliked and who had caused a scandal by escaping from a seminary of *Sulpiciens*. "This kind of social set, governed by laughter, follies, philosophical reasoning and a consistent gaiety, threatened the Jesuit spirit that Fleury had introduced at Court. Boyer, who wanted to keep this spirit alive in the King . . . feared that because of the favorite's ideas, he would lose his religious opinions and his respect for worship, and embrace principles that were contrary to the interests of the French clergy."[27]

Seven

"THE ORACLE OF THE COURT"

Madame de Pompadour was beginning to exercise a power that was cause for alarm among the King's ministers. They feared her and treated her with great consideration. Machault, who had just succeeded Orry as Comptroller General, tried to please her. The Cardinal de Tencin was mindful to flatter her in the hope that she would intervene on his behalf and encourage Louis XV to make him Prime Minister. But Maurepas, Secretary of State in the King's Household, and the d'Argenson brothers—who were, respectively, Secretary of State in the War Office and Secretary of State in Foreign Affairs—couldn't bear her.

A cold and calculating courtier, familiar with all the mysteries of the Court, the Comte d'Argenson[1] had acquired the King's trust since the victory at Fontenoy. He was much too clever to denigrate Madame de Pompadour, as he was aware of her ties to the Pâris brothers with whom he had regular dealings.[2] However, it was quite obvious that he hoped the favorite would be dismissed. His brother, the Marquis,[3] was a tireless worker; he had directed Foreign Affairs since 1744 and had nothing but contempt for fashionable circles and social life. No one cared for the company of this ugly, sad man, nicknamed "d'Argenson the beast," and no one knew about his scathing writing talent. The passages devoted to Madame de Pompadour in his *Mémoires*[4] are among the cruelest ever recorded about her. He blames her for her low origins, her thoughtless spending and above all her power over the monarch.

However, the Marquise's most treacherous enemy was the Comte de Maurepas. Born and bred at Court, so to speak, he had become Secretary of State at fourteen, after the resignation of his father, the Comte de Pontchartrain.[5] He controlled the Navy, the King's Household and the city of Paris. It will be recalled that it was Maurepas whom the police lieutenant, Feydeau de Marville, plied with information about Madame de Pompadour. Maurepas was a past master in the art of satire; he composed nasty epigrams that hit their mark. Madame de Châteauroux, whom his evil tongue had not spared, had almost succeeded in getting him dismissed. He had avoided disfavor by a hairsbreadth, thanks to her sudden death, for Louis XV had made up his mind. But since he was amused by his witticisms, the King decided to keep him in office. Confident of impunity, Maurepas no longer put any check on his malicious gossip. His house "was the meeting place for the most brilliant people. The King was told what was said there and what wasn't; the people who thought they were most well-connected, the King's lady friends, were not treated gently."[6] Maurepas had never been able to bear the sovereign's mistresses, for he was terribly jealous of their favor. There was no reason for him to spare Madame de Pompadour. He began by making fun of her appearance. "He caricatured her manners; he knew how to mimic her bourgeois way of speaking and heaped ridicule on her, a ridicule he mastered with much facility and grace."[7]

When the favorite moved to Versailles, two factions had formed—her faction, which drew inspiration from the philosophical spirit, and the Dauphin's. The first included numerous opportunists whose primary concern was to secure as many advantages as possible and who saw Madame de Pompadour as a woman who could make the King adopt progressive ideas and reforms. The second faction was of Jesuit inspiration and included a heterogeneous coalition of *dévots* (believers) and freethinkers (like Maurepas). They claimed to be fierce defenders of absolute monarchy and were outraged by the intrusion at Court and in the King's bed (the ultimate desecration) of a woman from a shameful background who might make the sovereign—who was a slave to sexual pleasure—commit the worst political and religious errors.

With tact and diplomacy, Madame de Pompadour went about reinforcing her position. She increased the number of devoted servants in her midst. Given the title of *Intendant*, Collin, who was prosecutor at the Châtelet (the Court of Justice), now managed her affairs. This attractive, pleasant man who was in his forties had been useful to the Poissons in earlier times and had helped arrange Jeanne-Antoinette's separation from her husband. He grew rich in the Marquise's service while never neglecting her interests. The Chevalier d'Hénin, though he descended from an ancient family, was willing to serve as her equerry. Nicole du Hausset, the widow of a Norman country squire, became her First Lady of the Bedchamber and confidante; the other women in her service were very devoted to her. The Marquise was eager to make friends in every way possible and make people obliged to her. She had just negotiated the marriage of Pâris de Montmartel, who had become a widower, and Mademoiselle de Béthune,[8] from the illustrious Sully family. The world of finance thereby allied itself with the oldest nobility. Madame de Pompadour would soon find a new ally in the Maréchal de Saxe—the man who had just led a surprise attack on Brussels and taken it from the Austrians. "I do not know Monsieur le Maréchal-Comte de Saxe; I very much want to meet him for it must be said he is the only general we have,"[9] she had exclaimed when the hero of Fontenoy arrived in Versailles and the King embraced him.

This unexpected victory, in the middle of the winter, was received with enthusiasm by the Paris population. Welcomed triumphantly in the capital, the great warrior was crowned with laurels at the Opera, where he was well known to young women seeking lovers. The Marquise praised him ceaselessly and always called him "My Maréchal." Responsive to women's charms, the likable roughneck, born of an affair between the King of Poland, August II,[10] and the Countess von Koenigsmark, paid discreet court—with only the most honorable intentions—to the favorite of the King of France, his master.

This new success encouraged Louis XV to take command of the troops again for the next campaign. A separation of several months was not a pleasant prospect for Madame de Pompadour, who "pointed out to the King that her health was too delicate for her to accompany him."[11] She was subject to persistent headaches and occasionally coughed up blood, which alarmed the monarch's entourage. Though "chest ailments" had not yet been diagnosed as such, it was known that such symptoms were a sign of serious and contagious illness. The Marquise was exhausted from the life of perpetual show she had been leading for several months; the obligation she had of always being beautifully dressed and seductive for her demanding lover; and the late hours she had had to keep at suppers during which large quantities of champagne and liqueurs were consumed. A period of rest could only do her good. But Jeanne-Antoinette feared being separated from the King and the intrigues of her enemies. However, she cared too much for the monarch's glory to try to keep him by her side. Fortunately, the Dauphine's confinement, due at the end of June, gave hope of a more rapid return than the previous year, for Louis XV had promised to be by his daughter-in-law's side for this great event.

The King enjoyed a last escapade with Jeanne-Antoinette at Choisy and left for the army in the night of May 1 to May 2, 1746. That evening he held a formal State dinner with the Queen, who was unable to hide her tears. After the meal he chatted with his children and his wife, and she kissed his hands repeatedly. They all wanted to wish him a last farewell just before his departure. After promising them that he would give them the opportunity to do so, he retired to Madame de Pompadour's, where he stayed until one in the morning. Then he changed his clothes and boarded his coach. According to Luynes, the family embraces were brief and cool.[12]

The two lovers had agreed that Madame de Pompadour would live at Choisy during the sovereign's absence, though she would make occasional visits to Versailles to pay court to the Queen. Before leaving on the campaign, Louis XV had given his mistress a magnificent gift—the château of Crécy, located two and a half leagues from Dreux.[13] She went there as soon as the sovereign had left, in the company of Tournehem and Montmartel. She found a handsome but rather badly maintained building that had been built some twenty years earlier. A succession of drawing rooms ended in some rooms that could easily be converted into two apartments, one for herself and one for the King. The building lacked an elegant, wide stairway leading to the first floor, but several small staircases led to a corridor from which other well-distributed and well-furnished apartments fanned out. There were also outbuildings with less elegant but comfortable lodgings that could be used by guests. The flowerbeds in front of the château led to a terrace jutting out over a large valley with a river. Beyond were forests abounding in game. It was hard to imagine a more rural setting for a royal romance. Before going back to Choisy, the Marquise commissioned the most pressing renovations from the architect Lassurance whom the King had put at her disposal.[14]

During the sovereign's absence, Jeanne-Antoinette rested and received only her intimate friends and family in the royal residence that Louis XV had so amorously assigned to her. She lived on the second floor and was served by her own staff. By the time the King returned she had regained her health and felt able to meet the obligations of her position. Everyone was waiting for the Dauphine to go into labor. The King grew impatient and appeared to miss camp life. It seemed as if he might even return to Flanders before the Prince's birth. But it was respectfully pointed out to him that after returning for this event it would have been very odd for him not to wait for it to happen. Then, as time dragged on, news came of the sudden death of Philippe V of Spain, Louis XV's uncle and the Dauphine's father. The question was, should the Dauphine be told of her father's death? After much reflection, it was decided that the sad news would be concealed from her. As a result, the Court did not go into mourning for this sovereign though he had been born a French prince.[15]

Finally, on July 18, the Princess started to have labor pains. After an exhausting delivery, she gave birth to a girl. Her husband was the only person to seem happy. Life was beginning to return to normal when suddenly, on the twenty-second, Marie-Thérèse Raphaëlle died of complications from childbirth. Though she had not been very loved, her death deeply upset the royal family. The King was possessed again by his morbid demons; the Queen and her daughters wept with the Dauphin. A few hours after this sudden death, Louis XV decided that the Court would go to Choisy, while preparations for the funeral ceremonies were being made at Versailles. The Dauphin found it difficult to leave the château. While travelling in his father's coach with his mother and sisters, he suffered a nosebleed; this alarmed the sovereign, who had no idea that his son was prone to this kind of affliction. They arrived in Choisy at eight in the evening. "First there was a long silence, followed by many tears and a sad conversation that included all the most heartbreaking details."[16] The King left his family to assign apartments to everyone present.

Louis XV had wanted Madame de Pompadour to accompany him. Her task was to find the words and gestures that would lift his somber mood. In fact, the monarch's health was alarming. "A movement of bile"[17] was feared, similar to the one that had caused the dramatic accident in Metz two years earlier. Fortunately he quickly recovered.

An oppressive sadness weighed on Choisy. Everyone was bored. The sovereign got up at eleven, but no one was allowed into his bedroom before noon. The Dauphin attended his *lever*. The Queen and the princesses would come down to see him only after he had dressed. Then the royal family went to mass. After the service, Marie would go back upstairs to her quarters and dine with her daughters, while Louis XV worked with his ministers and then spent time alone with his mistress. He would reappear again at seven for a walk. Sometimes he would stroll briefly with his wife and daughters, but usually Marie went her separate way. At nine o'clock the royal family ate supper in the Queen's antechamber. An hour and a half later, supper was served for the rest of the Court in the presence of Madame de Pompadour. Afterward, the King had long conversations alone with his son, while the Queen and the princesses went to bed. At around midnight, the King joined his guests in the drawing rooms. Seated by his mistress's side, he spoke tenderly to her and also took part in the general conversation. Everyone retired to his or her own quarters at around one in the morning.

At Versailles, where they soon returned, the atmosphere was even gloomier than at Choisy. The Dauphine's remains, saluted by representatives from the main branches of the State and sprinkled with holy water by the princes and princesses, had just been driven to the Cathedral of Saint-Denis in great pomp. She had been buried, as required by tradition, without the royal family being present. When the King and his family returned to the château, they had to go into mourning for both the King of Spain and the Dauphine, which certainly helped complicate the tedious questions of etiquette. The King was obliged to wear a purple suit for six weeks. The Queen and the princesses were required to wear black dresses and mantles for the same period of time. And theatrical entertainments and concerts were out of the question for at least three weeks.

These funereal arrangements depressed the King, who toyed with the idea of rejoining the army—a prospect that alarmed the Marquise. Though it has generally been thought that she was not involved in politics at this early stage, she was already corresponding with the principal military commanders, the Prince de Soubise, the Maréchal de Luxembourg and especially the Maréchal de Saxe—whom, it will be recalled, she greatly admired. Since she knew that the Maréchal de Saxe had no desire for the sovereign to be on the front, for obvious security reasons, she urged him to dissuade Louis XV from his plans to rejoin the front. And she herself sought to distract the King by every possible means. They went on a few escapades to Choisy, and soon she convinced him to come to Crécy. He agreed, with very little coaxing, and during a brief, bucolic stay in this château, with which he had been unfamiliar, he completely gave up his plan of leaving for the army. The Maréchal de Saxe had informed him that no large-scale action was foreseeable at that time. "You know I'm very fond of you," the Marquise wrote to the Maréchal. "I believe whatever you say like the Gospel. So I believe you, and hope there will be no battle and that our adorable master will not be missing an opportunity to gain more glory. It seems to me that he follows out your wishes to a sufficient extent. I put all my trust in you, my dear Maréchal. Your way of making war gives me hope for a good and lasting peace."[18]

Madame de Pompadour was beginning to gauge the extent of her influence. She now spoke with a certain authority and engaged in subtle maneuverings. While she was doing everything she could to get the Maréchal de Saxe to share her views, she also actively supported the ambitions of his rival, the Prince de Conti. Though he had never distinguished himself on the battlefield, Conti dreamed of recognition for his merits. Knowing that Louis XV had a great deal of affection for this distant cousin, whose gifts lay in diplomacy rather than war, she urged the King to give him the title of Generalissimo. She thought this would bring her into Conti's good graces, for he did not like her, and would be a way of thanking his mother, the Princess, for having presented her at Court.

The Marquise could well imagine the Maréchal de Saxe's resentment, since he was infinitely more qualified than Conti for a distinction of this kind. She tried to minimize the matter with him: "You know the King gave the Prince de Conti a title," she wrote him. "Between us, this title satisfied him and restored his reputation, which he thought was lost. This is what he thinks, while I think it is an embarrassing thing for the King and will prevent Conti's being called to serve as much as he thinks. In any case, this doesn't apply to you, we will always make you safe from the effects of the title. Don't tell a soul about this. Farewell, my dear Maréchal, I like you as much as I admire you. Which is saying a lot."[19]

The favorite knew that "her Maréchal" would not turn against her. He was too much in need of her in carrying out a plan that was very dear to him—the marriage of the Princesse Marie-Josèphe de Saxe, daughter of his half-brother King August III of Poland, to the Dauphin. Indeed, the young Prince was required to remarry as soon as possible in order to ensure the posterity of the dynasty. The day after the Infanta's death, Louis XV had examined all the possible candidates to replace her. Madame de Pompadour, who had suffered from Marie-Thérèse Raphaëlle's hostility, dreamed of a dauphine who would be her ally and wanted to be involved in the selection.

There were not that many possible matches. Only a Catholic princess from a house that was not at war with France could aspire to this great destiny. Ferdinand VI, the new King of Spain, had offered to send his young sister Antonia to replace the deceased. But Louis XV had politely sidestepped this proposal by claiming that in France you were not allowed to marry the sister of a woman with whom you have had children. The truth of the matter was that the King of France did not trust Philippe V's successor. This left the princesses of Sardinia and Saxony. As the son of the lovely Adélaïde of Savoy, the King fervently wished for a Piedmontese alliance. In her constant eagerness to please him, Madame de Pompadour had encouraged his inclinations, and the Pâris brothers had sent emissaries to Turin to gather information concerning the three marriageable young women.[20] But the King of Piedmont's evasiveness, and his decision to side with Austria despite an accord signed with France, quickly dashed the sovereign's hopes.

Thereupon the Marquise began supporting the plans of Maurice de Saxe, who wanted to see a princess from his family mount the throne of France. "I hope that what you want will happen," she said to him in the letter where she broached the delicate subject of the Prince de Conti's title. She pleaded the cause of Marie-Josèphe de Saxe eloquently to the King. Though not much of a beauty, the fifteen-year-old girl enjoyed excellent health; and the women in the royal family of Saxony were regarded as exceptionally fertile.[21] But neither the Queen nor the Dauphin were prepared to accept her as Dauphine. Marie Leczinska harbored a rather legitimate grudge against the King of Saxony for having dethroned her father. As for Prince Louis-Ferdinand, though he tried hard to distract himself, he still mourned the blue-eyed redheaded Infanta, whom everyone else at Court had already forgotten. The brilliant victory of Rocoux, won thanks to the Maréchal de Saxe, removed the last obstacles to this marriage. The Marquis de Valfons,[22] in boots and covered with dust, arrived in Fontainebleau for the King's *lever* on October 16, 1746, and gave Louis XV the first detailed account of the battle. After relating everything to the sovereign, the young man went to see the Queen and then Madame de Pompadour.

She received him alone in her quarters, with great gaiety. "We have time to chat, the King will be here only in an hour,"[23] she said, inviting him to sit down in an armchair by her side. "So, tell me everything, don't hide anything," she continued, showing him letters from the Prince de Soubise and the Maréchal de Luxembourg to prove that she was kept abreast of events on the front. Since she knew the young Valfons was a protégé of the Maréchal de Saxe, she inquired about everything he had done. "My Maréchal must be very pleased!" she exclaimed. "How handsome he must be at the head of an army, on a battlefield! . . . You can write him that I share his successes and am very fond of him."[24]

At the point when she expected the King, the Marquise dismissed Valfons, but not without promising him that she would intervene on his behalf so that he would get a promotion.

Several days later, on October 21, Louis XV decided that his son would marry the Princesse Marie-Josèphe. "I received a letter from the Very Christian King," Maurice de Saxe wrote to his brother, the King of Poland. "He informs me of all the objections he endured on the part of his wife the Queen and that had to be dealt with; *that's where Madame de Pompadour helped us enormously.*[25] . . . The master and the favorite were on our side. . . . Finally I did so many things that the King wrote me that he had made up his mind and since I had defeated his enemies, everything should give in to me (this is a gallant remark on his part)."[26] However, in spite of this success, Maurice de Saxe was still deeply hurt that the King had appointed Conti Generalissimo rather than himself.

On the day of his arrival at Fontainebleau, Maurice de Saxe dined at Madame de Pompadour's with Louis XV. When he left the dinner, late at night, he went to meet Valfons, who was waiting for him. Unable to contain himself, he gave free rein to his bitterness: "This is the country of falsehood," he said to him, "and gratitude for services rendered does not always exist here. I get fine words, and Monsieur le Prince de Conti gets to be Generalissimo. . . . They had better not humiliate me or haggle with me; I was not born their subject and they would be sweating ink [*sic*] if I followed the plan prompted in me by their injustices and my discontent,"[27] he continued, and he railed against d'Argenson, the Minister of War, whom he saw as responsible for Conti's promotion. Though he was envied for the special treatment he received from the sovereign, he shrugged his shoulders. "The King talks to me, that's true," he said, "but not any more than he talks to Lansmatte [a nobleman of the venery]."[28] While he was licking his wounds, he had the pleasant surprise of being promoted to the rank of Maréchal de France, a title that had been given to Turenne, one of the greatest military leaders in the seventeenth century. This repaired the injustice, and, having recovered his serenity, the Maréchal could pay court without any reluctance to the Marquise de Pompadour, whose power was growing with each passing day.

Count Loss, the Saxon ambassador, warned the future Dauphine that she would have to reckon with the favorite. "Madame de Pompadour plays a big part," he said to her, ". . . the friendship with which the King honors her, the interest she showed in the Dauphin's alliance with a Saxon princess, the insinuations she made to the King to help him decide, all of these things will oblige the Dauphine to thoughtfulness and good behavior. The Marquise has an excellent character; she will be eager to please the Dauphine, and the Dauphine will be paying court to the King by showing friendship toward a lady that the Queen showers with polite gestures."[29]

Jeanne-Antoinette reigned over the King's heart and over his Court. People crowded to her toilette in the morning in greater and greater numbers. "She knew about everything."[30] A large number of petitions were submitted to her and "many transactions were done through her."[31] The Duc de Gesvres[32] came to take orders from her for the princely marriage festivities planned for February 9. The Provost of Merchants brought her the plans and the drawings of the triumphant cortege that was to cross the capital during the city celebrations. She gave her opinion about everything and even settled tricky problems of protocol. Nothing was done without her. "The King had so many reasons for believing that she was essential to his life's happiness that his heart no longer inclined toward the pleasures of fickleness."[33] According to the Marquis d'Argenson, Madame de Pompadour had become "the oracle of the Court."

Eight

THEATER IN THE
PRIVATE APARTMENTS

The year 1747 began most auspiciously for Madame de Pompadour. On the morning of January 1, Louis XV gave her diamond-studded tablets on which the royal arms and the towers of Pompadour were side by side. This was the King's way of symbolizing the narrow ties uniting him with his mistress. Jeanne-Antoinette had the pleasant surprise of finding a promissory note for 50,000 livres inside the tablets. She was thrilled and no grumbling was heard from the Court. The Marquise was far too important a personage by now for anyone to make malevolent remarks. Only some small intimate groups could indulge in nasty gossip.

Jeanne-Antoinette was actively preparing the Dauphin's wedding, in which she felt personally involved. The young Princess was expected in the first days of February. Escorted by the Duc de Richelieu, Ambassador Extraordinary in Dresden, Marie-Josèphe de Saxe was crossing the German States and making many stops on her way to Paris. The King decided that she would be met at Choisy. Only the princes and princesses, the great officers of the Crown and their wives, and those holding the highest positions were invited to join the royal family. The favorite was among those invited. She then requested that Madame de Baschi be invited as well. This whim was bound to seem astonishing, as Madame de Baschi, the wife of a penniless Provençal nobleman who had just been presented at Court, was none other than Le Normant d'Etiolles's younger sister.[1] Instead of treating this woman with contempt, for her presence might have reminded her of a scorned husband, the Marquise was eager to promote her at Versailles. She probably wanted to create more beholden protégés, show off her power and take revenge on the Le Normants. But she also wished to please Tournehem, Madame de Baschi's uncle.

Very proud of the nobility she had acquired through marriage, and swallowing her shame, Madame de Baschi had no hesitation about soliciting the kindness of a sister-in-law whom she might have considered unworthy of her attentions in other circumstances. But she was ready to stoop to anything if Jeanne-Antoinette could help her husband's career—a career with the outstanding characteristic of being nonexistent. After serving in the King's musketeers in his youth, the Comte François de Baschi, who was twenty years older than his wife, had lived modestly on his estate. In order to escape from this lackluster existence, Madame de Baschi had decided to move to Paris. She now kept house for her uncle Tournehem and hoped soon to lead a more exciting life. Madame de Pompadour turned out to be just the good fairy that they expected. It was she who found the subterfuge that made it possible to include the ambitious newcomer in the privileged Choisy group. She said laughingly to the Duc de Gesvres that "she saw herself as entitled to being admitted among the highest office holders and that consequently Madame de Baschi, her sister-in-law, could be put on the list."[2] Amused by his mistress's playfulness, the King added the name of Madame de Baschi in his own hand to the list of the elect.

Louis XV trusted his favorite completely. He allowed her to give out the invitations for the formal ball. When the Duc de Gesvres, master of ceremonies, told him of his hesitations about whom to invite, the King said to him: "You have forgotten the Paris ladies; give me your list; Madame de Pompadour knows them and will make the arrangements."[3] Louis XV and Jeanne-Antoinette looked over the list together, and the sovereign followed his mistress's advice in making his choices.

Shortly before leaving for Choisy, Madame de Pompadour was undoubtedly pleased to learn from her lover that he had dismissed the Marquis d'Argenson, Minister of Foreign Affairs, who did not like her. She had played no part in his disgrace, but was delighted to learn that a very close friend of Pâris de Montmartel, the Marquis de Puisieulx, was his successor. This was one more person whom she could consider an ally.

Louis XV and his retinue settled in Choisy on February 6. On the following day, the King and the Dauphin went to meet Marie-Josèphe de Saxe on the Corbeil road. The King was much more gladdened by the arrival of this German princess than was his son. The Dauphin still mourned the Infanta and regarded his wedding as a horrendous ordeal. He was ice-cold with his new wife, just barely granting her the kiss on the cheek required by protocol. The sovereign had to go to great lengths with his young, bright-eyed daughter-in-law in order to counterbalance any negative impression. Though she was not beautiful, Marie-Josèphe was not lacking in elegance and "this pretty ugly duckling could, it seemed, turn many heads."[4] Her wholesomeness and simplicity seemed to presage a pleasant personality and good health. Marie-Josèphe made a favorable impression on Madame de Pompadour, whom she addressed with a well-turned compliment. This was a great relief to Jeanne-Antoinette, who had not forgotten the Infanta's contemptuous chilliness. Alas, she would soon be disillusioned.

After a two-year interval, the festivities for the Prince's wedding were repeated with almost no changes. On February 9, the same entertainments took place after the religious ceremony. In the evening, at the costumed ball, Madame de Pompadour was admired for the gracefulness with which she danced the minuet just after the princesses. Afterward, the Court attended the ceremony of the newlyweds' *coucher*. The new spouses got into bed, in their nightdresses and nightcaps, and were blessed by the Court's grand chaplain. Once the two young people were in bed, the curtains of the canopy were quickly drawn and reopened. The point was to show the world that the princely union was about to be consummated. The newlyweds were then left to enjoy their privacy after the nuptial bed curtains were drawn shut again. Marie-Josèphe de Saxe impressed everyone present by her kind dignity, while her husband buried his face under the sheets trying to conceal the sobs he was choking back. "Everyone walked out feeling somewhat pained, for it looked like a sacrifice,"[5] Maurice de Saxe wrote to his brother, King August III.

On the following days, celebrations and amusements followed one upon the other, according to the immutable ritual adopted in such circumstances. Madame de Pompadour attracted everyone's attention.

On the night of the costumed ball, she followed her handsome masked lover, the King, with her gaze. He was hardly recognizable, but the Duc de Croÿ, who was watching Jeanne-Antoinette, knew who he was from "the worried look that escaped her" as the King contemplated the ravishing Comtesse de Forcalquier.[6] But it was a false alarm. Louis XV sat at his mistress's feet and "seemed madly in love" with her.[7]

The young members of the royal family were finding the flaunting in broad daylight of this liaison more and more intolerable. At the end of February, the Dauphin and his sisters drew the innocent Marie-Josèphe into a little conspiracy. Act One was performed during a hunting expedition that the princesses followed, as always, with the favorite. In the barouche going back to Versailles, Louis XV's daughters had agreed not to address a word to Madame de Pompadour and not to reply if she talked to them. "She was furious, fuming,"[8] said the Marquis d'Argenson, who was all too happy to spread the story of this nasty episode. The young princesses did not stop there. Madame Henriette indoctrinated her sister-in-law. She wanted her to share the disgust the children felt for their father's mistress. The unhappy Dauphine did not know what to do. Whereas the Saxon ambassador and the Maréchal had advised her to treat Madame de Pompadour with respect, Mesdames were asking her to join their conspiracy against her. Spurned by her husband, who did not show her the least tenderness and who loathed the favorite, she had no choice but to side with her sisters-in-law. It was the only way she could get closer to the Dauphin.

With the Queen's support, the Prince and Mesdames elaborated a plan that they naïvely hoped to impose on their father. Convinced that there were surely "many things that repulsed him about his mistress and the company she kept," they wanted to "make him ashamed of having placed his tenderness in such a low place."[9] Their aim was to get him to dismiss Madame de Pompadour and live in the intimacy of his family. They could accept, regretfully, that this thirty-seven-year-old man was attracted to the beautiful sex, and were prepared to tolerate some discreet passing affairs, provided they were with women from the Court.

The young people had decided to make life difficult for the favorite. Louis-Ferdinand was rude to her and d'Argenson claims that the

Queen did not discourage her son's attitude. Neither Louis XV nor Madame de Pompadour was taken in by this little game. Too clever to complain, Jeanne-Antoinette nevertheless succeeded in getting her lover to clear up a situation that was becoming unbearable and that was reported on explicitly in the Saxon ambassador's correspondence. Fearing the Dauphin's churlish personality, Louis XV said nothing to him. He preferred to speak to his daughter Henriette, "to whom he gave a dressing down,"[10] bidding her to stop exercising a negative influence on Marie-Josèphe. The King insisted that Madame de Pompadour receive the Dauphine. The Marquise was supposed to convince her to go directly to the sovereign when she wanted something. A short while later, Louis XV received the young couple personally and asked his daughter-in-law to have another confidential talk with his mistress.[11] To her great humiliation, Marie-Josèphe had to admit that certain people (whom she could not name) sought to harm her relationship with her. The schemes of the Children of France were thus quashed. Madame Henriette wept; the Dauphine moped; the Dauphin remained gloomy; and Adélaide nurtured wild plans of revenge against the woman they now called "*maman-putain*" (whore mommy).

The Marquise triumphed. The King still loved her. He even flirted with her in public.[12] "Too actively," according to the Prince de Croÿ, who was slightly shocked by these conspicuous liberties. However, Madame de Pompadour did not rest on her laurels. She knew she would have to devise new amusements constantly to keep the monarch's passion alive and outdo her rivals in remaining the perpetual object of his desires. This was when she came up with the idea of performing onstage, in front of him, as she had formerly done in the theater at Etiolles and in Chantemerle at Madame de Villemur's. Trained by the best teachers, she was a genuinely talented actress, singer and dancer. By appearing before her lover in the most flattering costumes and showing her body and voice to advantage, she was sure to fan the ardor of this man who could so easily become apathetic. Furthermore, Madame de Pompadour knew that she would take great pleasure in resuming her involvement in pastimes that were all the rage in good society and to which she had dedicated herself with passion several years earlier.

Now that she lived in Versailles, the Marquise went to Paris rarely and she could no longer follow the theatrical scene as she used to. She had to be content with the performances given every Wednesday in the hall of the Cour des Princes by the actors of the Comédie Française and the Comédie Italienne, and the opera singers of the Royal Academy of Music. But the actors performed with greater restraint before the Versailles audience than they did in the city. And while performances were plentiful and dazzling, premieres were no longer given at Versailles as they had been during the reign of Louis XIV. Only rather conventional spectacles were given there. The Marquise missed the warm ambience of the Paris theaters and the endless discussions generated by new plays. As soon as she moved to Versailles, she tried to give the King a taste for theater.[13] It was said that she had even suggested to Louis XV that they stage comedies at Choisy in which the royal family and the courtiers would perform.[14]

Prior to Madame de Pompadour's arrival at Court, the sovereign showed very little interest in theatrical productions. He acquiesced in the suggestions made by the persons in charge of organizing them, the Ordinary Gentlemen of the Bedchamber.[15] But soon his mistress's tastes prevailed over theirs. Under her influence, the repertoire had already changed. There was no increase in the number of tragedies performed, for they had gone out of fashion, but the comedies of Molière were often replaced by the comedies of popular contemporary playwrights, such as Dancourt, Regnard, Dufresny, Destouches. . . . Oddly enough, Marivaux was performed only five times![16] On the other hand, Voltaire's works were performed often. The Marquise's interest in him had contributed to strengthening his position as historiographer of the King and favorite playwright. Yet the two big entertainments that he had recently written for the Court had been semifailures. *La Princesse de Navarre* had received a cool reception at the Dauphin's first wedding celebration. And the *Temple de la Gloire*, commissioned by Madame de Pompadour after the Fontenoy victory and performed on November 27, 1745, did not please the sovereign. Voltaire apparently wanted to give Louis XV a lesson in enlightened despotism by using Trajan as an allegory. Though Voltaire praised his hero to the skies, the King had been

annoyed by his audacity and not in the least amused. He had kept a gla-
cial silence when the writer had dared to whisper to him, too familiarly,
as he came out of his box, "Is Trajan pleased?"[17]

This did not make it any easier to convert the monarch to the pleasures of the theater. Madame de Pompadour beat a temporary retreat
and no longer mentioned performing. During Lent of 1746, her lover
allowed her to give spiritual concerts in her quarters, and she sang religious music. Hence she showed Louis XV and the Court that her artistic
talents could contribute to the meditative mood of the moment. Captivated once again by his mistress's incomparable charms, the King finally
yielded to her requests. He gave her permission to stage performances for
a limited public that he reserved the right to choose with her.

The Marquise organized her troupe in the greatest secrecy. She
made the Duc de La Vallière its director. An eminent nobleman, a protector of Voltaire and the *philosophes*, a friend of Pâris de Montmartel
and a close friend of the King, this well-read, refined and enlightened
bibliophile was a passionate theater lover who haunted the wings of the
Paris theaters. His well-known liaison with Mademoiselle Le Maure, a
singer at the Opera, and his intimacy with the theatrical Favart couple
were subjects of gossip, but this flaunted libertinism shocked neither
the King nor his mistress. Moncrif, a member of the French Academy,
reader to the Queen and La Vallière's protégé, was appointed under-
secretary of the amicable company, which included several members.
Foremost among the women was the favorite, of course. After her was
the Dowager Duchesse de Brancas, who had just turned thirty-eight;
followed by the ravishing Madame Trusson, the Dauphine's Lady of the
Bedchamber; Mesdames de Pons, de Sassenage and de Livry; and a
young woman full of charm, Madame de Marchais,[18] daughter of *Fermier général* Laborde. She was married to the son of Binet de Marchais,
the Dauphin's valet, who had played a not unimportant role at the
beginning of the King's affair with Madame de Pompadour. Among
the men were Louis-Philippe, the Duc de Chartres, the future Duc
d'Orléans,[19] the Duc de Nivernais and the Duc de Duras—who had
formerly played opposite Madame de Pompadour at Madame de Villemur's—the Comte de Maillebois, the Marquis de Courtenvaux, the

Duc de Coigny, the Marquis d'Entraigues, Monsieur de La Salle and several others.

Jeanne-Antoinette drafted the statutes of her theater in a professional manner and the King approved them. The statutes were modeled on those of the Comédie Française. No beginner was accepted into the troupe. Role assignments were definitive, and no one had the right to refuse to perform a part on the grounds that it did not suit him. The female members of the troupe had considerable privileges. They decided which works to perform and how many rehearsals there would be, set up the schedules and determined how much to fine late actors. They also set the date for the public performance.

The Marquise did not want to restrict herself to comedies; she also wanted to mount musical entertainments, ballets and even operas. An orchestra was assembled, mixing amateurs and professionals. Among the professionals was Mondonville, Superintendent of the Music in the King's chapel, and the most famous tenor of the period, Jélyotte, who was not asked to sing but to play the cello! Nearly all the chorus members were professionals, as were the members of the corps de ballet. But the star dancers were recruited among the Marquise's close friends: the Marquis de Courtenvaux stood out as the most talented; the Comte de Langeron, Monsieur de Beuvron and the Comte de Melfort were rather gifted and held first and secondary roles. The workshops of the Menus-Plaisirs,[20] which made the sets and costumes, also provided the countless props[21] whose lists have come down to us. Finally the Abbé de La Garde, the Marquise's librarian, acted as secretary and prompter.

Rehearsals began in Choisy in December 1746 and the first performance took place at Versailles, on January 16, in the hall giving out on the stairway of the Ambassadeurs. At intermission, the actors retired and changed costumes in the Cabinet des Medailles. The Marquise had chosen *Tartuffe* for the inauguration of her theater group, and it is believed (without certainty) that she performed the part of Dorine for the select audience of invited guests. The entrance tickets, with fine artwork by Cochin, were distributed parsimoniously. The King, who had personally selected the fourteen guests, sat enthroned in an ordinary chair. Only the Marquise's friends, Mesdames d'Estrades and du

Roure, the Abbé de Bernis, Vandières, Tournehem and several chosen few, had the opportunity of applauding the star performer. This was an exceptional privilege, for clapping was never allowed in the King's presence, and Louis XV had waived the rule in this instance. This *numerus clausus* infuriated many people. The Prince de Conti, though the King was fond of him, was refused an entrance ticket, as well as the Maréchal de Noailles, his son the Comte de Noailles and several other eminent noblemen. In principle, even the Dauphin had no knowledge of the event.

On the following Monday, the Marquise and her troupe performed two pleasing comedies, *Le Préjugé à la mode* (the fashionable prejudice) by La Chaussée and *L'Esprit de contradiction* (argumentativeness) by Dufresny. After the performance, supper was served in the King's apartment, followed by a ball where the King joined in dancing the quadrilles. The Marquise danced a minuet with Monsieur Clermont d'Amboise. This new institution, of a private nature and presided over by the favorite, puzzled the Court. The Queen was annoyed that her reader, Moncrif, had agreed to be a member of the troupe without asking her permission. The Dauphin and his sisters felt scorned, once again, by their father and his favorite. As for the courtiers, they adopted a wait-and-see attitude in the hope that, miraculously, they would one day be admitted to this new inner circle. The Duc de Luynes noted prudently in his *Journal* that according to hearsay Madame de Pompadour "performed marvellously."[22]

Performances were interrupted for the Dauphin's wedding celebrations and resumed on February 27 in the presence of the newlyweds. That evening, a comedy by Dancourt, *Les Trois Cousines* (the three female cousins), was performed, in which Madame de Pompadour surpassed herself in the role of Colette. Nor did she stop there. She sang opposite the Duc d'Ayen in *Les Amours déguisés* (disguised loves), an opera-ballet by Bourgeois, which was only moderately successful in spite of her lovely voice and the choreographed performances of Monsieur de Courtenvaux and Monsieur de Luxembourg. *Les Trois Cousines* was performed again on March 13, followed by the premiere of *Erigone*, an opera in one act. It so enchanted Louis XV that he requested a second performance for the Queen. Given her husband's insistence that she agree to honor the theater in the private apartments with her presence, Marie could not refuse. On Saturday, March 18, accompanied by the Dauphin and the princesses (but not the Dauphine, who pleaded that she felt unwell), she settled in a chair next to her husband and sat through the triumph of Jeanne-Antoinette, who gave an excellent performance in *Le Préjugé à la mode*. The subject of the play was risqué, given the circumstances: it was about a love-struck husband who feared showing his feelings, since conjugal love was considered the height of ridicule. The Queen applauded the King's mistress—an excellent actress in her own right, she pretended to be pleased. According to the information he gleaned, the Duc de Luynes wrote that "Madame de Pompadour sang extremely well. She does not have a very full-bodied voice, but a lovely tone and her voice has range; she has a good knowledge of music and sang very tastefully."[23]

Nine

PLEASURES AND DAYS

Le Préjugé à la mode had concluded the theater season. With the return of spring, Louis XV was preparing to rejoin the army as he had done in previous years. The war was dragging on, but the King hoped that after the invasion of Holland that was being planned by the Maréchal de Saxe this campaign would be decisive. In the interim, before his departure scheduled for the beginning of May, the monarch treated himself to several pleasure trips with his mistress. They went to Choisy three times and, to Madame de Pompadour's great joy, they spent several days in Crécy, with a small group of people. When Louis XV lived in his favorite's château, it took on the status of royal residence and the courtiers who accompanied him wore green outfits that differed from those worn in Choisy by "a simple trimming and gold buttonholes."[1]

Madame de Pompadour feared the King's long absences, but they were also an unexpected opportunity for her to rest, and this was something she greatly needed. In spite of her youth, her health was fragile. Subject to frequent colds that degenerated into bronchitis and the coughing of blood, she also had persistent migraines during which she had to keep a bright smile. She exhausted herself in the service of this man whom she adored but who loved her selfishly, without ever giving a moment's thought to the reserves of energy that she had to summon to be up to what was expected of her. The King was always by her side and never did anything without asking her advice. In the most sophisticated

Court in Europe, they formed a very close-knit couple. And though very little is known of their quasi-conjugal intimacy, it seems very probable that this was a love affair in which tenderness soon came to play a greater part than sensuality. Several episodes in the private life of the two lovers are known from the secrets confided by Madame du Hausset, the Marquise's Lady of the Bedchamber, whose discretion in the service of her mistress was always exemplary.[2]

After his *coucher*, Louis XV was in the habit of joining Jeanne-Antoinette in her quarters, where she waited for him in bed. One night she burst into Nicole du Hausset's bedroom like a madwoman. "Come quickly, the King is dying!" she cried. And the two women, in their nightgowns, ran to the bedside of the wheezing monarch. Madame du Hausset immediately recovered her sangfroid, threw some water on the King's face and made him take a few Hoffman drops. When he came round, Louis XV asked that she summon Quesnay,[3] the Marquise's physician who lived very close by. "Tell him that your mistress has passed out," he whispered, "and tell his people not to talk." Madame du Hausset executed his orders at once. Imagine the good doctor's surprise on discovering the monarch in such a bad state. He took his pulse. "The crisis is over," he muttered, "but if the King had been sixty years old, it might have been serious." After sprinkling scented water on the patient, he gave him some "drops of General de La Motte," which had a salutary effect. In the meanwhile, Madame du Hausset told a wardrobe girl to fix some tea and the King drank three large cups full. He rose a short while later, slipped on his bathrobe and made his way back to his apartment leaning on Doctor Quesnay's arm. "What a sight to see all three of us half naked!" writes Nicole du Hausset. "Madame put on a dress as quickly as possible, and so did I, and the King changed behind his curtains, which were very decently drawn. He talked about his brief illness and showed much appreciation for the care that he had been given. An hour later I still felt great fear at the thought that the King might have died in our midst." On the following day, Jeanne-Antoinette received a little note from him: "My dear friend must have had a great fright," he wrote, "but she can stop worrying. I am fine and the physician will bear me out."[4] After this episode, which was never talked about, Quesnay received a pension of 1,000 écus and Madame du Hausset, a promissory note for 4,000 francs. And Louis XV gave the Marquise a clock and a snuffbox decorated with his portrait.

The pleasurable habits of the monarch and his mistress were interrupted once again by Louis XV's departure. The Marquise left immediately for Crécy. The residence was being altered under the expert guidance of Lassurance, and the Marquise supervised the expansion and other improvements. She could often be seen, pen in hand, annotating the architect's plans and the decorators' sketches. She cared most about the interior renovation. She wanted her house to be a haven of peace and refinement. Verberckt and Rousseau had just made new paneling for the large "assembly room," and Jeanne-Antoinette put in countless orders with the art dealer Lazare Duvaux[5] for furniture and precious objects. She was very involved in the final installation of her library and the octagonal cabinet she had designed. She commissioned Boucher to paint eight allegorical canvases with children representing the Arts and Sciences. Her daughter Alexandrine was portrayed in the group representing Sculpture. These paintings can be seen today at the Frick Collection in New York.

The Court offered few attractions at the time. Many noblemen had followed their master, and the restrictions of another period of mourning had been imposed by the death of Queen Catherine Opalinska, mother of Marie Leczinska. Until the month of September, the sovereign's apartment had to be draped in violet and the Queen's and her children's had to be draped in black. All distractions were banned. The young princes delighted in talking about death and catafalques, and engaged in macabre pastimes. The Dauphin asked his wife and sisters to play cards in the light of yellow candles under a black canopy, with drawn curtains. They sang *Tenebrae* (Holy Week hymns) in the Dauphine's bedroom, where the body of the Infanta Marie-Thérèse Raphaëlle had been exhibited the previous year. Sometimes they even imitated recumbent statues and exclaimed, "We are dead."[6] "Childhood prevails over thought,"[7] noted the Duc de Luynes.

The King's absence allowed the Marquise to escape from the

burdens of the Court. She could savor a relative solitude whose every detail recalled to her the power she had, a power she owed to the monarch's love. Better informed than the Queen, she was kept apprised of everything, particularly military matters, for the Maréchal de Belle-Isle sent her detailed reports every day. While she waited for her lover to return, she paid regular court to Marie Leczinska, spent several happy moments with her intimates and looked after Alexandrine.

It was during this period that she obtained letters patent of nobility for her father as a reward for his services rendered in food supplies. The act stipulated that this ennoblement was in reparation for Monsieur Poisson's unjust disgrace, whereas he had exerted himself in the service of the State with considerable "zeal" and "selflessness"! An écu with two fish in the shape of gold cornflowers—these became the Poisson arms as designed by Monsieur d'Hozier, the King's genealogist. This was meant permanently to erase the disgrace of his sentence and now, presumably, Madame de Pompadour could no longer be looked down on as the daughter of a lowly commoner. But no one was fooled by this charade.

The Marquise went one step further for her father, even though he had never showed her that much affection. She paid his debts, which totaled 400,000 livres, and arranged to have land given to him. By a sleight of hand that stunned the Court, the King personally gave the erstwhile felon the land of Marigny. Louis XV agreed to pretend that he owed Poisson the sum of 200,000 livres, for the "supplies and advances he had made," and to give him the land of Marigny, in Brie, in payment.[8] The Marquise remembered her brother as well. The young Abel Poisson, Marquis de Vandières and future Marquis de Marigny, was given the stewardship of Grenelle by the King, who paid the 100,000 livres needed for the royal warrant. Vandières lost no time reselling it to the Prince de Soubise for 180,000 livres.[9] The Marquise had great expectations for her brother, who was handsome, intelligent and gifted in the arts. Luckily, also, the King happened to like him. To the Court's annoyance, he was often invited for supper in the private apartments, and the monarch showed no contempt for his conversation. Madame de Pompadour wished that her brother would live up to her great plans for him: a brilliant career and a prestigious marriage. She tried to tempt him with the most splendid alliances—marriage to the daughter of the Maréchal de Lowendal, or of the Duc de La Vallière or of the Princesse de Chimay. But he stubbornly chose to remain a bachelor during his sister's lifetime. After her death, he married Marie-Constance Filleul, who was rumored to be Louis XV's illegitimate daughter, and the marriage turned out to be a very unhappy one.

In late September 1747, accompanied by Mesdames de Brancas, d'Estrades, de Livry and du Roure, Madame de Pompadour went to join the King in Compiègne, his last stop before Fontainebleau. It was a passionate reunion. The King basked in the glory of the Lawfeld victory and the capture of Berg-op-Zoom.[10] Everything pointed to an advantageous peace for France.

During the stay in Fontainebleau, which followed this hopeful return, the gloomiest courtiers (except for the Marquis d'Argenson) could note that the monarch's passion for his mistress had not cooled. This became obvious during a memorable hunt where the kill occurred under the Marquise's windows. The hunted deer had jumped into the large ornamental pond in the Cour des Fontaines, which was right outside the Marquise's apartment. The city residents had rushed to the château and the courtiers mingled with them waiting for the kill; the Dauphin and Dauphine watched the scene from a terrace just above Madame de Pompadour's windows. As the animal struggled in the water, Louis XV appeared on horseback. Though he was a passionately devoted hunter, he postponed the final act to speak to Jeanne-Antoinette. The kill that followed was like a public homage to the favorite's charms.

Never had the Marquise been lovelier; the slight plumpness she had acquired over the summer suited her wonderfully. "She had many flirtatious wiles for the King and employed the art of the most refined amorous intrigue to retain him."[11] The Prince de Croÿ, who had the honor of dining in the private apartments, found the monarch "more and more charming, gentle, gay, amiable, talkative, and speaking very well, with constant pertinence and wit."[12] He credited Madame de Pompadour for the happy changes he noticed in his behavior. She had, he said, "the talent of her position. . . . She meddled in many things without seeming to, or even seeming interested. On the contrary, whether genuinely or tactically, she looked like she was busier with her theatrical endeavors, and other trifles, than all the rest."[13] But it was known that no favor was granted without her mediation. And she attracted in her wake "the court of a Prime Minister."[14]

At Fontainebleau the Marquise prepared the theatrical season that was to open on December 20, 1747, at Versailles. Once again the performances took place in the small hall, which had recently been renovated. The space reserved for the audience had been enlarged and the orchestra was now placed between the stage and the public, handicapping those performers whose voices did not project all that well. Finally, dressing rooms had been built in back of the stage allowing the actors to change in greater comfort. Madame de Pompadour was not in the cast of *Le Mariage fait et rompu* (marriage made and broken) by Dufresny,[15] the play that inaugurated the new season. She watched the performance and then slipped away to appear in a pastoral, the true apotheosis of the evening. Written by Moncrif in honor of the King, with music by Rebel and Francoeur, this divertimento was a hymn to the favorite whose praises were sung by the poet:

> *In the games which we take care to create for you,*
> *Your enchanting talents bring you a thousand conquests;*
> *It was to crown your art of charming everything*
> *That Cupid invented our festivities.*[16]

The King complimented the authors and the performers with unusual enthusiasm. As he returned to his quarters, he kept repeating, "That was a charming spectacle."[17] The piece was bold enough to rekindle the religious party's combative mood, further unleashed by a few verses by Voltaire.

The Marquise had scheduled her troupe to perform Voltaire's *L'Enfant prodigue*[18] on December 30. This maudlin comedy, which would inspire one of Greuze's most famous paintings, had absolutely nothing subversive about it. Voltaire had aimed for "a mixture of seriousness and humor, comedy and soul-stirring."[19] Jeanne-Antoinette played the part of Lise, the abandoned fiancée; the Duc de Chartres played the father and the Duc de Nivernais, the prodigal son. Madame de Pompadour, who still protected Voltaire in spite of the King's reticence, had prevailed on her royal lover to invite the authors of the plays to the performances in the private apartments. Though this favor filled his patroness with joy, it aroused the great writer's irony: "Rising by degrees to the highest of honors, I have been admitted to the theater in the private apartments in between Moncrif and d'Arboulin. But my dear Cideville," he wrote to his friend, "Moncrif's dazzling splendor has not seduced me."[20] Yet he composed some gallant verses for the Marquise:

> Hence you bring together
> All the arts, all tastes, all the talents that please:
> Pompadour, you embellish
> The Court, Parnassus and Cythera.
> Charm of all hearts, and one mortal's treasure,
> May a fate so beautiful be eternal!
> May festivities mark your precious days!
> May peace return to our fields with Louis!
> May you both be without enemies,
> And both keep your conquests.[21]

Flattered at seeing herself immortalized as the equal of a goddess and as the monarch's one and only glorious love, the favorite did nothing to keep this little poem secret. It soon became known in the city and the Court, and provoked great indignation in the entourage of the Queen and the princes. Marie Leczinska, as always, took refuge in prayer; the Dauphin cursed the "maman-putain," whom he hated; "Mesdames saw this parity of glory as detrimental to their father's honor."[22] In Paris Voltaire's enemies allied themselves with the Marquise's enemies—first among them Maurepas—and replied sharply to the brazen Voltaire through the voice of a versifier using the name of Roy:

> Tell me, rash stoic,
> Why your bold verses

Dare unveil before our eyes
What ought to remain a mystery?
The loves of kings and gods
Are not for the common people:
When one wishes to intrude in their sanctuary
With inquisitive glances,
Respect for their taste and silence
Are the best approaches.[23]

This little scandal took on such proportions that the angry Voltaire decided it was wiser to leave for Cirey, in Lorraine, with his mistress, Madame du Châtelet, a learned woman who translated Newton into French.

The whole incident, which is not even mentioned by the Duc de Luynes, hardly troubled Madame de Pompadour. It was just one more episode in the small war waged against her by the religious party. During the stay in Marly, she "looked very beautiful" and the King seemed "more in love than ever."[24] When they returned to Versailles, the troupe, of which she was the magician, gave performances with a regularity worthy of professionals. *Tartuffe* was performed again. In *Les Dehors trompeurs* (misleading appearances), a comedy by Boissy, she played the part of Lucile, an innocent girl who learns about life. "Are you naïve?" she was asked by her seducer. "Oh very much so!" she replied with a blush. . . . That same evening, she also sang the title role in *Eglé*, a pastoral written by Laujon with music by Lagarde.

The performance of Gresset's *Le Méchant* (the villain) was the great event of the season. The play, which had its first performance on April 15, 1747, at the Comédie Française, was having considerable success in Paris. It was quite a challenge for amateurs, but Madame de Pompadour had promised the author that she would stage it in her theater. She kept her word and the troupe rehearsed feverishly for two months. "The more I see this play, the more I find studies made from nature," wrote d'Argenson sarcastically. "Cléon or the Villain is a composite of three people I have known well: Monsieur de Maurepas for his tirades and his hasty judgments—of both men and intellectual works—the

Duc d'Ayen for his malicious gossip, and my brother for his heart of hearts, his pleasures and in his bearing."[25] From all accounts, the Marquise and her friends had a well-deserved success. "I fear that the clever depiction of contemporary vices caused more delight than conversion to virtue,"[26] noted d'Argenson, caustic as ever. The Duc de Nivernais played the part of the wise Valère with so much natural simplicity that the Marquise asked the King for permission to invite the actor Roseli, from the Comédie Française, to see Monsieur de Nivernais so he could draw inspiration from his performance. (It is not known whether Roseli appreciated the gesture.)

The troupe revived a few old plays and gave the first performances of two operas, *Almasis*,[27] and *Les Amours de Ragonde*.[28] The second opera's performance was completely improvised. One Saturday, Madame de Pompadour decided at supper that it would be performed on Tuesday to celebrate the end of Carnival. She wrote to the Duc de La Vallière that night and he received her letter at four in the morning. By Sunday they set to work: the text had to be learned, the costumes and set prepared. The bustle amused the King; he then admired his mistress in a male role on the day of Mardi-Gras! She played the young shepherd Colin, loved by a buxom woman farmer performed by Monsieur de Sourches, who was making his first stage appearance in the private apartments. "Madame de Pompadour was dressed as a man but it was a woman's riding outfit; it was a very decent costume,"[29] the Duc de Luynes makes a point of saying.

On March 4, a tragic event prevented the revival of *L'Enfant prodigue*. The actors, in costumes and powdered wigs, were waiting for the curtain to rise when the King cancelled the performance. News had just come of the Comte de Coigny's[30] death, a person for whom Louis XV had great affection. Deeply distressed, the sovereign took to his apartment immediately. "We were in despair over the tragedy of the unfortunate Coigny," wrote the Marquise. "The King's reaction was such that it frightened me. . . . Fortunately, reason won out."[31] At first, it was thought that Coigny had had a fatal accident between Versailles and Paris, not far from Auteuil, caused by a violent snowstorm, but soon the truth was learned. On the evening before that fatal morning, he had lost a considerable sum of money to the Prince de Dombes at the King's game. "Only a bastard could have so much luck,"[32] he had exclaimed. The Prince de Dombes, grandson of Louis XIV and Madame de Montespan, demanded reparations for the insult, and the two men agreed to a meeting at "daybreak" by the banks of the Seine, between the village of Auteuil and the farm of Billancourt. They fought by torchlight and Coigny's throat was slit with one whip of the sword. The details of the duel were soon known and on everybody's lips. The scene of the fight became a place of pilgrimage, soon baptized *Point-du-Jour* (daybreak). "Even if no one had liked Coigny, his accident would have moved everyone, and you know when I love, I love well,"[33] Louis XV wrote to Richelieu six weeks later.

A week later, the Marquise gave another performance of *Almasis* and *Ismène*. The Prince de Dombes was at his usual music stand in the orchestra and quietly played the bassoon. There were performances of *Zénéide* and *Erigone* before the season ended on March 30 with *Cléopâtre*, an act excerpted from *Fêtes grecques et romaines*.[34] This was a grand operatic spectacle for which the Menus-Plaisirs had surpassed themselves: the Queen of Egypt's boat, it seems, was much more elaborate than the one at the Paris Opera,[35] and the props included impressive serpents with springs to end the heroine's life. For the dress rehearsal, on March 29, Madame de Pompadour invited friends from Paris, including Madame de Châtelet. After the last performance, the Marquise distributed gifts on the King's behalf to the performers and authors.

In spite of a bad cold, which prevented her from singing for several days, Jeanne-Antoinette organized the kind of leisure activities that could reasonably be allowed during Holy Week. As in the previous year, she gave concerts of religious music in her apartment. The works performed were Lalande's *Miserere* and Mondonville's motets. The soloists and choristers were among the best performers from the private apartments. The Marquise, Madame de Brancas, Madame Trusson, Madame de Marchais and the Duc d'Ayen's son, Monsieur de La Salle, were universally liked. Jélyotte, a Paris favorite, took part in almost all the concerts. Yet Holy Week did give the Marquise cause for concern.

The King, who had last received the sacraments during the Metz scandal in 1744, seemed overcome with remorse at this time of the year. He was deep in thought as he listened to the sermons of the preachers denouncing adultery and lust. If he chose the road to repentance, he would have to renounce his love affairs. . . . But he did nothing of the sort. Jeanne-Antoinette could breathe again.

Ten

"A WELL-TRAINED ODALISQUE"

The success of the French army did not prevent the war from dragging on in the Netherlands and Holland. In the Court as in the city, there were some people who accused Maurice de Saxe of behaving like a roughneck and needlessly prolonging operations. The Maréchal's recent victories led to a widespread hope that a peace would be rapidly concluded. If d'Argenson is to be believed, the Marquise, still under the influence of the Pâris brothers, wanted the conflict to continue, though she stood to benefit in other ways than her friends. "During the winter, she exhausted herself in amusements"[1] for a sovereign who constantly had to be rescued from boredom. D'Argenson claimed that she needed "this campaign time to stimulate the King's liking for her." Choiseul in his *Mémoires* asserts, on the contrary, that the Marquise feared separations.[2] Whatever the case, Louis XV had decided to end the war.

The French, English and Austrian ambassadors plenipotentiary began peace talks at the end of March at Aix-la-Chapelle. The conquest of the Netherlands and the invasion of Holland had placed France in an advantageous negotiating position. The capture of Berg-op-Zoom and the capitulation of Maastricht on May 7, 1748, further strengthened Louis XV's position. The diplomats easily agreed on the preliminary articles proposed by the French that became the basis of the negotiations. Everyone was surprised that Louis XV "did not want to make peace like a merchant but like a king," which meant a return to the *status quo ante*. He returned the Netherlands to Maria Theresa, Maastricht to the Dutch, Nice and Savoy to the King of Sardinia. Frederick II kept Silesia, and Maria Theresa, whose sovereign rights were recognized by confirmation of the Pragmatic Sanction, had to yield Parma, Modena, Piacenza and Guastalla to Don Philippe, Louis XV's son-in law.[3] The English and the French were to return the conquests made in their respective colonies, and Louis XV recognized the legitimacy of the Hanovers on the British throne. He also promised to drive away the Stuart pretender, whom he had encouraged in his ambitions. On June 5, the Comte de Saint-Séverin, the King's principal representative at the Congress of Aix-la-Chapelle, came in secret to Versailles to receive his final instructions. People were looking forward impatiently to the end of this war, "which it would have been difficult to carry on much longer,"[4] since the French Navy could not compete with the British one. And it was hoped that the special taxes created to finance this conflict would be abolished.

The King seemed satisfied with the way negotiations were going and the Marquise appeared as content as her lover. To add variety to their lives, they came up with the idea (instigated, no doubt, by Jeanne-Antoinette)[5] to visit the Luynes in their château of Dampierre. Rambouillet, where Louis XV often went hunting, was in the vicinity of this residence where the Queen and her children were frequent visitors. But the King had only ridden through the grounds. Once he had entered the first courtyard, but had gone no farther. Yet the Duc had urged him to honor him with his presence. In June 1748, the sovereign "was pleased to recall what he had made him hope for"[6]: he wished to spend the evening and night of Whittuesday at Dampierre. The monarch was traveling with Madame de Pompadour, whom he treated publicly as his chosen lady companion. Madame d'Estrades and Messieurs d'Ayen, de Bouillon, de Fleury, de Soubise and de Luxembourg accompanied them. Escorting the King and his friends were twelve bodyguards, four of their officers, two brigade chiefs and two noncommissioned cavalry officers, a head equerry, a barracks equerry, a barracks surgeon, a first valet, two assistant valets, a coat carrier, four pages, four footmen, five coachmen, five postilions, five harness boys and some kitchen and pantry officers. Exclusive of the bodyguards' mounts, sixty horses for the use of the King and his suite were put up in the stables.

They arrived at six-thirty in the evening and after making a thorough tour of the château, Louis XV and Jeanne-Antoinette strolled along the edge of the artificial pond and into the small woods. They crossed through the English-style flowerbeds on their way back to the residence. When the King sat down to eat at nine, he placed the Marquise at his right and the Duchesse at his left. The Duc served him for half an hour, and then the sovereign ordered him to take a seat near him. "He was in very good spirits during the supper and seemed to find it good."[7] At eleven-fifteen, Louis XV rose and had coffee, which he himself had prepared. He admired the illumination of the grounds before going on to the card games. The sovereign and his mistress played games of *comète* until two in the morning. The following morning, they appeared only after eleven to hear mass celebrated in the chapel of the château by the Dampierre parish priest. "He could not have appeared more at ease, more cheerful and more even-tempered,"[8] noted the Duc de Luynes after his master's departure.

Madame de Pompadour had every reason to be perfectly satisfied. At the time, d'Argenson compared her to "a well-trained odalisque who skillfully managed the superintendence of His Majesty's pleasures."[9] The King did not just treat her as his official mistress at Court, he now exhibited himself with her in the residences of his most illustrious subjects. And he continued to shower her with sumptuous gifts. At the beginning of the winter, he had given her a house in Montretout,[10] which the same d'Argenson described as a *"guingette"* (an open-air dance hall), adding that its evocative name ("show all") gave rise to many humorous remarks.[11] Since this residence revealed itself to be too cramped, the monarch soon bought[12] the château of La Celle-Saint-Cloud for the Marquise as a place where she could stay when he was absent from Versailles. La Celle was just a country house, a place to go to for supper or to spend several days during the fair season. The two lovers therefore agreed that once peace was restored, Louis XV would arrange to have a new residence built near Meudon. The sovereign, who had just acquired the Pontchartrain mansion as a place for lodging ambassadors extraordinary, gave his mistress a large apartment on the second floor so she would have a place to rest during her trips to Paris.

The King often joined Jeanne-Antoinette in La Celle. On one evening in July, he organized a lavish entertainment for her, in the presence of Messieurs de Soubise, de Luxembourg and de La Vallière. Just as dessert was being served, about ten young people, dressed as shepherds and shepherdesses, unexpectedly surprised the guests in the dining room, offered the Marquise flowers and performed a divertimento with singing and dancing. Afterward, the King led his favorite to the window and they watched a fireworks display. Louis XV did not return to Versailles, but spent the night with his "odalisque." After the traditional trip to Compiègne, during which Madame de Pompadour was the true Queen, the King stopped in Crécy before returning to La Celle, where his mistress held an impromptu entertainment for him on September 1.

At the end of the meal, while they were still sitting at the table, several costumed musicians burst into the dining room and played a little tune. The Marquise rose and sang the praises of the sovereign. "Come, everyone, follow me," she hummed at the end of the last couplet. Louis XV stood up immediately. Led by the musicians and followed by the guests, he went down into a grove that had been set up like a theater. There, waiting for them, were the Duc d'Ayen as the god Pan, Madame de Marchais as Flora and Madame Trusson as Victory. They performed a ballet. Soon the convivial party was led to the illuminated canal, where Monsieur de La Salle, dressed like a shepherd, recited an encomium to the monarch. Like all the other guests, Louis XV put on a domino and a mask at the entrance to the ballroom that had been created in a small wooded area. He stayed until three-thirty. But he didn't dance. He looked sullen and no one knew why he was sulking.

The Marquise's enemies began hoping again that she would fall from grace. Everyone started talking about the attention the King was paying to the Princesse de Robecq. Had he not disappeared for a quarter of an hour with her during a walk in Bagatelle and requested the

Queen appoint her Lady-in-Waiting at the nearest opportunity? In Choisy he showed an unusual harshness toward the Marquise, who had not come down to the assembly hall because she had felt unwell. Annoyed, he had ordered his surgeon, La Martinière, to go see what was wrong with her. When the physician confirmed that she was truly ill, the monarch asked if she had a fever. When La Martinière replied that she didn't, Louis XV demanded that Jeanne-Antoinette come down. Some courtiers thought that the King had finally recognized "the shame of his fetters." They prayed that "he would put an end to this shameful life with a mistress who reflected so badly on him."[13] They were also convinced that the Duc de Richelieu, her longtime enemy whose return was expected, would bring about the disgrace of this woman who was "born among buffoons" and who "had got her claws into governmental affairs, the choice of ministers and important positions."[14]

The stay in Fontainebleau was dreary, but on November 29, when Madame de Pompadour appeared at the review of troops in the Sablons plain, she was radiantly beautiful. The Court crowded into her toilette in the morning, and the theatrical season looked as if it would be even more dazzling than the previous ones. A new theater had been set up in the stairwell of the Ambassadeurs. It could accommodate an audience of fifty to sixty people, could be set up in twenty-four hours and fully dismantled in fourteen. Musicians and spectators had comfortable seats and the acoustics were far superior than in the small hall. Unfortunately, the first production, an opera by Rameau with a libretto by Moncrif and de Gentil-Bernard entitled *Les Surprises de l'Amour*, followed by ballets, was a fiasco, although Madame de Pompadour was superb in the role of Venus. The King yawned in the middle of the performance, and said rather loudly to someone in a neighboring seat, "I'd prefer a comedy." The opera *Tancrède*, given on December 10 in the presence of the sovereign, the Dauphin and the Dauphine, might have been a success if Maurepas had not handed Louis XV a letter during the performance informing him that the Stuart pretender had just been arrested, *manu militari*, in Paris.[15] This ruined the evening. Finally, the audience laughed heartily at a rather crude spectacle by Moncrif entitled *L'Opérateur chinois*, for which the Marquis de Courtenvaux had composed the music.

No one hesitated when it came to criticizing Madame de Pompadour's taste for expensive shows. And she knew it. "What are people saying? That the new theater the King just had built on the big stairwell cost him 2 million?" she said one morning at her toilette. "I'd like them to know that it cost only 20,000 écus. Please tell me whether the King isn't entitled to spend that amount on his pleasure, and the same goes for the houses he builds for me."[16] Once again Jeanne-Antoinette had disappointed the hopes of her detractors. D'Argenson himself had to recognize that the King was "more smitten with his favorite sultana than ever. She sang so well and performed so well in the last ballets at Versailles that H.M. praised her publicly and, caressing her in front of everyone, told her that she was the most charming woman in France."[17]

Ever since she had been elevated to the rank of official mistress, Jeanne-Antoinette made it her duty to protect men of letters. But how was she to exercise literary patronage with a king who was only mildly interested in books and distrusted writers? In addition, for several decades, the careers of writers had been made in the city and not at Court, as used to be the case. It was in the salons of the capital that trends and reputations were made and unmade. "With everyone back in Paris," wrote Grimm, "and all the judges flocking there, the authors hastened to appear before them to get their works judged."[18] The Court was too hostile to new ideas for writers to seek its approval. Madame de Pompadour could not possibly impose the *philosophes* on a world that was content to bask, for its enlightenment, in the glow of its own radiance. She was not even free to receive whomever she pleased in her own quarters. She had to go downstairs, to Quesnay's, to meet the most brilliant minds of her day. The good physician received them modestly in his quarters. Yet Louis XV was not completely indifferent to some forms of progress, though he preferred scientists to writers, whom he considered subversive and dangerous.

The Marquise supported Voltaire in spite of the King's prejudices, and this earned her the good graces of the enlightened public. She had succeeded in convincing Louis XV to allow him to be elected to the French Academy, even though the King saw him as nothing more than an impious *philosophe* and an ambitious flatterer. However, ever since he had written the verses that had caused a scandal, the Marquise could not defend him with the same warm enthusiasm. She was reduced to encouraging Gresset, the author of *Le Méchant*, and the Abbé Le Blanc, the regular critic of the salons in the *Mercure*—two perfectly innocuous writers.

Voltaire's enemies then made a point of telling the favorite that Crébillon, her former teacher, was living in poverty in the Marais neighborhood of Paris. Crébillon's name at the time was "the rallying cry for Voltaire's enemies."[19] They liked to think of him as the "Sophocles of the century," even though his tragedies were hardly ever performed anymore. They spoke in front of Madame de Pompadour about the great man being abandoned and growing old without any assistance just because he wasn't a schemer. This was bound to touch her weak spot. "'What are you saying?' she cried out; 'Crébillon poor and lonely?'"[20] She obtained a pension of one hundred louis for him at once. Crébillon rushed to thank his benefactress. As she was ill, she received him in bed. While he kissed her hand effusively, the King was announced. "'Oh, Madame!' said the poet, 'the King has caught us unawares; I am lost.' This witticism on the part of an elderly man of eighty amused the King. Crébillon's success was assured."[21] His work was praised to the skies, his selflessness was extolled and *Catilina*, the tragedy he had just completed, was spoken of as the "wonder of the century."[22] Madame de Pompadour wanted to hear it. It was read to her, in the King's presence, and they resolved that the play would be performed at the Comédie Française with even more sumptuous sets and costumes than Voltaire's *Sémiramis*, which was getting a lukewarm reception.

Voltaire had returned to Paris to attend the performances of his play, which had been previewed before the King and the Court at Fontainebleau. When he learned that Madame de Pompadour was taking an interest in Crébillon, he condemned her openly. How dare she pay heed to the most outmoded writer in the kingdom? How could she forget him—he who had written the glorious poem *Fontenoy*, the *Epître sur la victoire de Lawfeld* (epistle on the victory of Lawfeld) and, more recently, the *Panégyrique de Louis XV*, where he praised the peace of Aix-la-Chapelle without reservation? Blinded by rancor, he refused to see that the recent publication of *Zadig* had further aggravated his case with the King. The Court of Moabdar described in his philosophical tale was clearly Versailles with all its pettiness and turpitude. In it, he lambasted the religious faction, and this of course had been brought to the attention of the Queen's party, starting with Boyer, Bishop of Mirepoix, who was caricatured under the name of Yébor. Why had he taken sides? Madame de Pompadour could no longer praise such a dangerous protégé.

On the day when the royal mistress went to applaud *Catilina*, Voltaire became very angry. Louis XV, who had had supper that evening with some friends—among them the Prince de Croÿ—waited impatiently for the Marquise. "Well! Did we win our case? Did we succeed?" he asked her eagerly as soon as he saw her. The favorite's presence and Crébillon's supporters had helped arouse audience enthusiasm. It cooled thereafter and, in spite of praise by Montesquieu and Helvetius, *Catilina* had a run of only ten performances. Very embittered, Voltaire became violently resentful of the Marquise, though the thought of injuring him had never entered her mind. He was openly furious at her and boldly said to the Marquis d'Argenson: "The people who took the ministry away from you support *Catilina*."[23] He then wrote an epistle on life in Paris and Versailles (*La Vie à Paris et à Versailles*), where he vented his feelings against the Court. He quickly sent it to Frederick II, who had been urging him to come to Berlin for some time.

The following summer Voltaire, who had still not reconciled himself to the success of *Catilina*, decided to write his own tragedy on the same subject. This was *Rome sauvée* (Rome saved), with which he hoped "to avenge France for the infamy of *Catilina*."[24] He notified the favorite and sent her translations of *Panégyrique de Louis XV* in several languages.

"I received the translations you sent me, Monsieur, and was pleased to present them to the King," she replied. "H.M. put them in his library with kind attentions for the author. . . . I see that you are distressed by people's nasty comments and evil deeds. Shouldn't you be accustomed to this and realize that it is the fate of all great men to be slandered during their lifetime and admired after their death? Remember what happened to Corneille, Racine, etc., and you will see that you are no more mistreated than they were. I never thought that you did anything against Crébillon. It wouldn't be like you, a talent that I like and respect. I defended you against the people who accused you, since I have too high an opinion of you to believe you capable of such disgraceful behavior. You are right to point out that I myself am the target of shameful acts[25]; I react to all these horrors with complete contempt and my mind is at rest. . . . I find my reward in my heart, which is pure and will always be pure. Farewell, and stay in good health. Don't contemplate going to the King of Prussia's no matter how great a king he is or how sublime his mind. How can one want to leave our master when one is aware of his admirable qualities. Privately, I would never forgive you."[26]

The Marquise's letter was of no great solace to Voltaire, who also must have become disconsolate over the death of Madame de Châtelet, which occurred a short time later. The following year, when he learned that Louis XV had given Moncrif "entry into the bedchamber," he was furious. "And I don't have it in spite of my work," he fumed. He was hurt that the King never showed him any regard. So, in a fit of ill humor, he decided to leave for Prussia and resign from his position of *gentilhomme ordinaire*. He solicited an audience with His Majesty in Compiègne, and Louis XV did nothing to keep him. He simply told him he "could leave whenever he wanted."[27] Madame de Pompadour, aloof, asked him to convey her respects to the King of Prussia. She could no longer do anything for her favorite author, given the way the King had spoken to him. Voltaire would never return to Versailles. Actually all of this should have been anticipated. Voltaire was not made for the Court, and there was no way Madame de Pompadour could have sponsored a genius—even one who was a courtier—in the kingdom where convention ruled.[28]

Eleven

THE "POISSONADES"

At the end of December 1748, Richelieu's return created great excitement at Court. Would the great organizer of royal love affairs convince the King to give up this degrading bourgeois liaison? The circumstances seemed very favorable to Jeanne-Antoinette's detractors. The peace of Aix-la-Chapelle, whose provisions were finally known, displeased almost everyone; and inevitably the vagaries of French politics were attributed to the favorite who was luring the sovereign away from his duties. She was the target of a number of cruel songs. In one, she was called a "trollop's bastard daughter." Nor was her brother spared, "a small master, dazzled by a futile sparkle."[1] This was only the beginning. Soon the King himself was attacked: "this monarch beloved of the whole universe, . . . the slave of a council that has become too haughty," responsible for a "shameful" peace "that dishonored him."[2] Harping on his old hatred of Madame de Pompadour, d'Argenson noted that "she was attacked for the failings in the affairs of the kingdom, domestic and foreign, particularly domestic, for the Pâris brothers governed the household like the stewards of a ruined lord."[3]

Since her accession, Madame de Pompadour was regarded as Duverney and Montmartel's creature. The two brothers had financed the war, and the powerful influence they exercised over the Marquise and Puisieulx, Secretary of State of Foreign Affairs, had probably allowed them to prolong the war. The Pâris brothers shared their ideas with the minister, who transmitted them to the favorite and the monarch.[4] "The King has gone from the cardinal's stick [Fleury] to the Pâris's," d'Argenson exclaimed.[5] "Today all financial credit lies with the Pâris brothers; the King has great consideration for finance. Indeed what would become of the machinery of State without the illusory machinery of this credit as it is today?" he thundered several weeks later.[6] He believed that Madame de Pompadour's favor was entirely due to the money of the two financiers. "The great thing," he asserted, "would be to present the King with a way of getting money that would allow him to do without his dangerous auxiliaries."[7] Though extremely respectful of the monarchy, the disgraced minister minced no words in painting a distressing portrait of Louis XV: "He has adopted a jargon of feelings," he said, "a jargon of political arguments, composed of different comments that he has heard from different people, without the slightest inclusion of common sense and feeling, or even of comprehension. He is compared to nuns who speak Latin and pray to God in Latin without understanding a word. . . . From this it follows that he does contradictory things. . . . He jabbers with one person one way, with another in an opposite way, everything according to the theme he has constructed."[8]

Recently promoted to Maréchal of France, Richelieu returned to Versailles with an aura of glory he had acquired in Italy. On the day he arrived, the King conversed with him alone until two in the morning. The very next day there was a crush of courtiers at the Maréchal's *lever*, and he immediately adopted "the most imposing tone, making the Court fear him and the master respect him." Consumed with ambition, he saw himself as worthy of exercising the same functions with Louis XV as his grand-uncle, Cardinal de Richelieu, had exercised with Louis XIII. He began by openly criticizing Puisieulx's policies and the diplomacy of Saint-Severin, negotiator of the Aix-la-Chapelle peace agreement, who had just been admitted to the Council, with Madame de Pompadour's support. At the same time, he tried to win the favor of the other ministers. Maurepas, overcoming his aversion for him, promised him the support of the Queen and the young princes if he succeeded in extricating the King from the clutches of the favorite and the Pâris brothers.

But Richelieu lacked the breadth of intelligence needed to attain his grand objectives. His primary intention was to "pick fights with

Madame de Pompadour and treat her like an Opera girl."[9] He engaged in a real battle of nerves against her. Since his position of First Gentleman of the King's Bedchamber gave him authority over the organization of the Menus-Plaisirs, he thought he had found a way of frustrating Jeanne-Antoinette. The famed theater in the private apartments came under his jurisdiction, and he was determined not to be as easygoing as his predecessor, the Duc d'Aumont, who had let the Duc de La Vallière carry out the Marquise's wishes. In the beginning of January, while affecting an exquisite politeness toward Madame de Pompadour, Richelieu forbade the personnel of the Menus-Plaisirs to obey any orders other than his own. This led to a serious altercation between the two noblemen, during which the Maréchal behaved almost insultingly toward the Marquise's artistic adviser.

Apparently indifferent to these quarrels, Louis XV was very friendly with his old confidant; he enjoyed talking with him and this could not fail to alarm Jeanne-Antoinette. Her greatest fear was that this master in libertinism would place in the King's arms some dream creature who could replace her.

On January 10, 1749, the courtiers were burning with curiosity. The performances in the private apartments were starting up again after their break for the New Year ceremonies and the question was, would the Maréchal attend? To everyone's surprise, he did. As a courtier who respected customs (even if they were not bound by etiquette), he sat behind the King . . . next to the Duc de La Vallière. That evening, as in all the subsequent performances, Madame de Pompadour surpassed herself. She redid two acts of *Les Eléments*, an opera by Roy and Destouches in which she had the part of Pomone, and sang an act from *Philémon et Baucis*. On January 16, she scheduled revivals of *La Mère coquette* and *L'Opérateur chinois* in the Queen's presence. But never had anyone seen a more dazzling performance than on January 23: after Quinault and Lulli's opera *Phaéton*, the audience saw Campistron and Lulli's *Acis et Galatée*, in which Jeanne-Antoinette played Galatée. A gouache by Cochin immortalizes the scene. Galatée-Pompadour, in a fitted pink corset and white taffeta skirt with large panniers embroidered with motifs of reeds and shells, is being courted by Acis-Rohan, wearing a splendid garment, while a Cyclops is trying to aim a rock to drop on the bashful lover. In the first row in the balcony, to the left of the Queen in her black headdress, Louis XV, dressed all in gray, seems completely absorbed in contemplating his favorite, the unmistakable star of the opera.

The Marquise was fighting back with her own weapons and prevailing over the cabal concocted against her. The King treated the criticisms and veiled hostility of his Court with disdain. He could not do without this mistress, whom he liked better than any other woman, even if there were some pretty ladies whom he occasionally felt tempted by. When the feud between Richelieu and La Vallière reached its peak, Louis XV went to live at La Celle with Madame de Pompadour for two days. She had begged him not to invite her personal enemy: "You don't know Monsieur de Richelieu," he replied, laughing, "if you chase him from the door, he'll come in through the chimney."[10] The two lovers burst out laughing because the chimney affair was the subject of sarcasm in all the salons. In order to meet his mistress while eluding a jealous husband's suspicions, Richelieu had installed a revolving platform inside the chimney of his apartment, adjacent to the bedroom of his ladylove, who lived in the neighboring mansion. This gave him discreet admittance into her quarters. The betrayed husband, the wealthy *Fermier général* La Poplinière, eventually discovered the stratagem. He lost his temper and threw his wife out of the house. It had been ages since a scandal had caused such a great stir. The Maréchal's misadventure stimulated Madame de Pompadour's witty eloquence. She had no hesitation in making fun of her enemy with her lover, who at that time was in the habit of spending his nights at La Celle and returning to work at Versailles in the morning.

The sarcastic d'Argenson had to admit, with a heavy heart, that "everyone bowed before the Marquise and her dependents." (Indeed, La Vallière continued to exercise all his assigned functions.) The chimney affair had heaped ridicule on a man who thought himself destined to govern France and had not even succeeded in taking control of the theater in the private apartments. He had lost all influence at Versailles. But since he still seemed determined to hound Madame de Pompadour, the King asked him casually, as they returned from hunting, how many times he had been to the Bastille. "Three times," he answered.[11] Richelieu understood the hint full well. Madame de Pompadour was at the pinnacle of her power. "Woe betide a State governed this way by a coquette!"[12] exclaimed d'Argenson.

The Marquise was establishing herself at Court at a time when public opinion was raging against her and the King. Insulting lampoons, satires and songs were making the rounds. On February 12, the day of the official peace proclamation, the public kept away from the celebrations scheduled in the capital. The meager tax relief measures promised by the ministry failed to bring about any rejoicing—on the contrary. The Paris population was impervious to the cry of *Vive le Roi* (long live the King) proclaimed by the herald who had come to announce the end of the hostilities; not only did they not respond, hoots were even heard as the official cortege went by. To make matters worse, almost a hundred people were killed on the quays during the evening of the fireworks. The royal government's incompetence was considered responsible for the tragedy. "What does a peace like this, celebrated with such horrors, foreshadow?"[13] people grumbled. It was a harsh winter and the cost of living had increased considerably. It was known, from more or less reliable sources, that the kingdom was in financial difficulty. People blamed the money men in the King's entourage and his favorite on whom exorbitant sums were spent. Sacrifices had been made during the war and nothing had been gained in return. The monarch was accused of irresponsibility for selling off his conquests so cheaply after so many resounding victories. Why had France obtained nothing except the Italian duchies of Parma, Piacenza and Guastalla for the Infante Don Philippe, husband of Madame Elisabeth, daughter of Louis XV? In the Halles, the covered market, the new form of insult among fishwives was, "You're as stupid as the peace." There was a persistent feeling of bitterness in the capital and certain verses were repeated ad nauseam, verses that made the King and his mistress shudder with horror:

> *Cowardly squanderer of your subjects' property,*
> *You who count the days by the evil you do,*
> *Slave of a minister and of a miserly woman,*
> *Louis, know of the fate that heaven prepares for you.*

If for a time you were the object of our love,
It was because your vices were not fully visible yet.
You will see our zeal ebb every instant
And swell in our hearts a rebellious flame . . .
Amidst the ham actors who reign with you
Who could now recognize his King?
Your treasures are open to their mad expenses
They plunder your subjects, exhaust your finances
Not so much to renew your tedious pleasures,
As to better satisfy their shameful desires.
Your State is in dire straits, Louis,
And it is your own doing;
But beware the storm that will soon descend on you . . .
You will no longer find souls sufficiently vile
As to celebrate your so-called exploits
And it is to abhor you that there are still Frenchmen.[14]

In spite of Jeanne-Antoinette's prodigious efforts to distract him, the King lapsed into one of his abnormal, melancholic states. She never left him alone; she tried to liven him up, stir him and divert him from his gloomy thoughts; she reassured him and surrounded him with a giddy gaiety that she excelled at feigning. She invited more and more people to the suppers in the private apartments and increased the number of escapades to the smaller châteaux. "We are always on the road; Choisy, La Muette and a retreat near the gate of the Dragon, at Versailles, where I spend half my life. It is eight *toises* long and five *toises* wide, no more, so you can imagine how beautiful it is; but I go there alone or with the King and very few people, hence I'm happy there," she wrote to her friend Madame de Lutzelbourg,[15] as though she needed to persuade herself of the existence of a happiness that was gravely threatened. She knew that Maurepas and d'Argenson were insinuating to Louis XV that she should be sacrificed to calm an increasingly hostile public opinion. Would the *Bien-Aimé* let himself become an object of contempt for his people because of an "obscure woman"[16] to whom he was surrendering power? A print was making the rounds clandestinely: it showed the King chained to his mistress and to Puisieulx, and being whipped by foreign monarchs.

Early in March some insulting verses, sung to the melody of *Les Trembleurs*, brought the favorite's indignation to a climax:

> *The great noblemen are getting debased,*
> *The financiers are getting rich,*
> *All the Poissons [Fish] are getting big:*
> *It is the reign of the good-for-nothings.*
> *Finances are drying up*
> *In buildings and expenses;*
> *The State is falling into decadence,*
> *The King puts order into nothing, nothing, nothing.*

> *A small bourgeoise*
> *Brought up in a bawdy way,*
> *Measuring everything to the toise*
> *Is making the Court into a slum.*
> *The King, in spite of his scruples,*
> *Has a mad, burning passion for her;*
> *This ridiculous flame*
> *Arouses everywhere in Paris, laughter, laughter, laughter.*

> *This inferior harlot*
> *Governs with insolence*
> *And it is she who awards*
> *Honors for a small fortune.*
> *Before the idol everyone bows, the courtier humiliates himself;*
> *He endures this infamy*
> *And is all the more indigent, gent, gent, gent.*

The author then denounced the favorite's faded beauty, her "yellow, speckled skin," her "spotted" teeth, her foul breath, her "quavering voice" and her "gossip's" vulgarity:

She wants to be extolled
For her little talents
And thinks she is firmly
On the throne for a long time;
But her foot slips up.
The King recovers from his error,
And this sacrifice gives him back our heart.

Furious and humiliated, the Marquise made an immense effort to look serene before the pack of courtiers who wanted her downfall. Quite obviously, the author of these *"poissonades"*[17] belonged to the small, closed world of Versailles. "It is clear from their carelessness and malice that these verses were made by Court people; the hand of the artist is absent and besides, only people who live at Court would know some of the details contained in it," noted the playwright Collé, an expert in this area. It was suspected that the attack came from the three ministers who were enemies of the favorite. The name of Maurepas was whispered most often, for, much to his friends' amusement, he had always cultivated the art of the insolent epigram. Madame de Pompadour was convinced of his guilt. She remembered that Maurepas's sarcasm had formerly been aimed at the Duchesse de Châteauroux whose disgrace he had wanted. It was even rumored that he had poisoned her. Deeply distressed by the violence unleashed against her and the King, Jeanne-Antoinette was terrified that an attempt might be made on her life. She had someone taste all the dishes that were brought to her and requested that a surgeon sleep next to her room, which annoyed her lover.

Still in a state of depression, the King could not give her any comfort. She had to bring him cheer and entertainment. An abominable tract praising regicide, entitled *Réveillez-vous, mânes de Ravaillac* (Wake up, shades of Ravaillac; Ravaillac was the assassin of King Henri IV), further aggravated the sovereign's low spirits. He became convinced that he would be assassinated like Henri IV. This happened in the middle of Lent, a period of the year when he was always oppressed by remorse. Had he incurred God's wrath? Was he not doomed to a violent death in expiation of his sins? Though he had long conversations with Father

Pérusseau, he did not make confession. In spite of the fear of hell, inculcated in him since earliest childhood, he had no intention of giving up the life he had been leading for years.

Louis XV had of course given orders to find the authors of these lampoons, and the police had carried out arrests in the circles known for producing gutter writing. Most of the known pamphleteers had been incarcerated, but not the real culprits. When some courtiers hypocritically asked Berryer, the lieutenant of police, if he would be able to catch those dreadful lampoonists, his terse response was, "I know Paris like the back of my hand, but I don't know Versailles."

The Marquise demanded exemplary punishments and had sworn to herself that she would bring about Maurepas's downfall, since he was poisoning her existence. Exhausted by this perpetual struggle, she had a miscarriage at the end of March. (It was the third, apparently, since she had become Louis XV's mistress.[18]) As soon as she had recovered she went to the despised minister, accompanied by Madame d'Estrades. "It will not be said that I summon the ministers; I come to them," she said to him with hauteur. Then she added: "When will you know the authors of those songs?"

"When I know them, Madame, I will inform the King."

"You have little regard for the King's mistresses, Monsieur."

"I have always respected them, of whatever sort they be," replied Maurepas, venomously.[19] The Marquise boiled with anger. She immediately related this nasty exchange to the King. Meanwhile, Maurepas boasted of it conceitedly. At the Maréchale de Villars's, the minister proclaimed that the favorite's visit "would bring her bad luck." "I remember," he jeered, "Madame de Mailly also came to see me two days before being dismissed for Madame de Châteauroux; as you know, I poisoned her; I bring them all bad luck."[20]

Yet the King still could not make up his mind to dismiss this man who had been serving him for twenty years, and who knew how to entertain him. It was then that Richelieu came to rescue of the "grisette" whom he held in such contempt. Because he hated Maurepas, whom he blamed for keeping him away from the ministry, he came to see the Marquise and submitted to her a damning report on Maurepas's mismanagement of the Navy. (Indeed Maurepas held two positions concurrently, the Navy and the King's Household—the rough equivalent of what would later become the Ministry of the Interior.) Madame de Pompadour was delighted to pass the report on to Louis XV. It did not prevent the sovereign from inviting Maurepas to an intimate supper with Madame d'Estrades and Madame de Pompadour. Each person played his or her role to perfection and everything went smoothly. In the course of the supper, Jeanne-Antoinette pulled apart a bouquet of white hyacinths and the petals scattered all around her. This was an unimportant incident. But several days later, an offensive quatrain went around, alluding to an intimate ailment (a white vaginal discharge) the favorite suffered from:

> By your noble and frank ways,
> You enchant our hearts, Iris;
> You strew flowers in our footsteps,
> But they are white flowers.[21]

This time the culprit was unmasked. Only Maurepas could have composed those humiliating verses. On the evening of April 25, when she was alone with her lover in her château of La Celle, the Marquise succeeded in getting what she wanted from him. In the middle of the night, the King asked the Comte d'Argenson to take a letter to Maurepas giving him notice of dismissal: he was to leave for Bourges within the hour and not reappear at Court. He was not even allowed to reside in his château of Pontchartrain because it was too close to Versailles. His exile was to last until 1774, when the young Louis XVI would summon him as his mentor. Louis XVI made him the equivalent of Prime Minister without giving him the title.[22]

The dismissal was a bombshell. No one expected it, least of all Maurepas. The day before, at the King's *lever*, he had dazzled the sovereign with his witticisms. His favor had seemed undiminished. Before taking leave, Louis XV had urged him to enjoy Mademoiselle de Maupeou's marriage reception to which he had been invited. As soon as he received this *lettre de cachet*, Maurepas went secretly to say farewell to the Queen and the Dauphin, who were appalled by his being sent into exile. Marie Leczinska wept. Revolted, the Dauphin and his wife did not refrain from making the most disagreeable comments about the Marquise. The King found it necessary to tell his son that the charges against the former minister were very grave. "In a few years, I will show you my reasons and my proofs," he said to him. "He is fortunate that I merely exiled him; I could have done much more; he owes it only to my clemency."[23] There never was any follow-up to these mysterious remarks. The princely couple attached so little importance to them that it had no effect on their attitude toward the "*maman-putain*" whom they continued to abhor. Exasperated by their insolence, Louis XV kept his children in a state of semidisgrace and for a while refused to visit them.

Maurepas's dismissal was seen as the work of the favorite with whom the King still seemed infatuated. He spent most of his time with her, consulting her about practically everything. He appointed Rouillé, one of her protégés, to the Navy, the Comte de Saint-Florentin to the King's Household and gave Paris to the Comte d'Argenson. Though the latter was hardly a friend of the Marquise, far from it, he felt he should support the lieutenant of police (who was devoted to Madame de Pompadour) more actively than Maurepas had. As a result, several people were arrested: Monsieur de Pont-de-Veyle, the presumed author of the "*poissonades*" and Monsieur de Bazencourt, the King's *maître d'hotel* and a fanatically devoted henchman of Maurepas, a certain Caylus and several others who were suspected of being in the former minister's service.

However, these arrests did not put an end to the lampoons. Soon a new offensive poem appeared targeting Madame de Pompadour, with verses as follows:

> *Daughter of a leech and leech herself,*
> *Poisson, arrogant to the extreme,*
> *With no fear or terror, displays in this château*
> *The substance of the people and the shame of the King.*

Elsewhere, the favorite was denounced for making vulgarity reign at the Court:

In the past, good taste
Came to us from Versailles.
Today, the rabble reigns
And holds the high ground.
If the Court is lowered
Why be surprised?
Is it not from the market
That we get fish [poisson]?

Had Maurepas, in his exile, hired some versifiers? After a speedy investigation, a certain Chevalier de Rességuier was arrested and convicted for being the author of these insulting verses. He was sentenced to twenty years in prison. Shortly thereafter, the Marquise received a package that she found suspicious. She asked Quesnay to open it. The good physician found substances that presented no danger. It was a simulated assassination attempt, cooked up by Latude, a naïve youthful surgeon who hoped to make a fortune by exposing it. It cost him a prison term of forty years. The favorite had become merciless against her enemies. To Maurepas's brother-in-law, the Duc de Nivernais, who tried to intercede on his behalf by pleading Madame de Maurepas's poor health, she replied dryly, "I fully appreciate your situation with regard to your relatives; I sympathize with you and am aggrieved that I cannot help you on this occasion as I have on others."[24] She feared that she would be assassinated, so she bought a burial vault at the Capuchins, on the Place Vendôme in Paris. She had her mother's remains transferred there and erected a mausoleum. When the King asked her why she had made this purchase, she answered that it was for her mother and that "she would have herself buried alive there, if he ever left her."[25]

Whereas the Court for the moment was obliged to bow before the Marquise's triumph and her increasing power, public opinion did not abate. In a climate of financial crisis, people denounced the huge sums spent on building magnificent residences for her, intended for her pleasure. Improvements were being carried out at Crécy. It was for her that the château of Bellevue had been under construction since 1748. Beginning on March 10 of the same year, Louis XV had granted her the usufruct of land bordering the grounds of Versailles,[26] near the gate of the Dragon, where Lassurance had erected the pavilion she alludes to in her letter to Madame de Lutzelbourg. In Fontainebleau, Lassurance had constructed another hermitage, so that the favorite could escape from the burdens of the Court and receive the King quietly in the intimate ambience she was so adept at creating.

As usual, with the arrival of summer, the couple moved to Compiègne. Their time was filled with hunting, suppers, evening gatherings, balls and impromptu entertainments. That year a tent had been pitched near the Coras fish tanks, not far from the ponds in the forest. The King, Madame de Pompadour and several intimate friends went there for light refreshments. To vary their amusements, they sometimes arranged to meet at the Chinese summerhouse, a gift of the Grand Turk, erected between the road to Humières and the road of the Nymphes. Always afraid that her lover might be prey to boredom, Jeanne-Antoinette had scheduled several stays in the small châteaux. "She kept the King in such a volubility of movement that H.M. hardly had a moment for reflection."[27] The beautiful season ended in glory for the Marquise. Louis XV decided to take her to Le Havre. People said, nastily, that she wanted to see the ocean and eat fresh fish (*poisson*, again). In fact, the King wanted to carry out a propaganda tour in the provinces and demonstrate that he had an interest in his Navy and merchant marine fleet, both of which greatly needed to be expanded and modernized after the battles against the formidable British navy during the last war.

Once again, Madame de Pompadour was seen as the sovereign's favored female companion; he never considered inviting the Queen on this official trip. He appointed about twenty people to accompany him, among them the Duchesse de Brancas, the Marquise de Livry and the inevitable Comtesse d'Estrades. The Marquise de Vandières also accompanied the King and his guests.

When the King told the Archbishop of Rouen that he would be coming to see him in his residence in Gaillon, the prelate did not answer and merely bowed deeply. "Did you hear me? I will be coming to see you," the King repeated. He bowed again. After walking away from him, Louis XV turned around and said in loud voice: "No, Monsieur. I've changed my mind, I will not be coming to see you."[28] As the Queen's chaplain, Monseigneur de Tavannes wanted to impress upon the sovereign the scandalous nature of his escapade with his mistress. And as the official representative of the Church in Normandy, he was determined not to condone the King's behavior.

Louis XV decided that they would depart from Crécy on September 17. Madame de Pompadour and her friends took their seats in the coach that followed closely behind the monarch's. They made a stop at the Château d'Anet, where the elderly Duchesse du Maine[29] gave them a magnificent reception. It was hard to believe that this tiny dowager with a wrinkled face had once been a terrible schemer during the Regency. Tireless, Louis XV, who had hunted all afternoon in the Dreux forest, left Anet to have supper at the Château de Navarre,[30] which belonged to the Duc de Bouillon. They spent the night and the following day there before setting off for Rouen in the evening. The royal carriages wended their way all night along a road that was lit by burning fires every league of the way.

The cortege arrived in the city at eight in the morning. It was decked with banners, and the enthusiastic crowd gave the sovereign an ovation. Though they were exhausted by their nighttime travel, the ladies—and first among them the Marquise—were expected to smile and make a good impression while they admired the maneuvers from one of the bridges. They soon departed for Le Havre amidst an ecstatic population. The carriages advanced slowly. The King's loyal subjects wanted to kiss his hands, women held out their children and the security forces had to intervene to stop the most intrepid from hanging on to the doors of the coach. Finally, at six o'clock in the evening, Louis XV and his suite made their entry into Le Havre to the sound of the cannon being fired from the citadel. The Duc de Saint-Aignan, Governor of the city, was waiting for them, as well as the Duc de Penthièvre, Governor of Brittany and Grand Admiral of France; the Comte d'Argenson, Minister of War; and Rouillé, Maurepas's successor at the Navy. After driving through the city, which was lit up in his honor, taking a short walk and dining rather quickly, the King and his friends settled in the apartments that had been prepared for them in the town hall. These accommodations did not offer the women, who were completely worn out, the comfort they were accustomed to.

The following morning, however, the Marquise appeared refreshed and rested. After visiting the shipyard, she placed the first dowel in a ship christened *Le Gracieux* (The Gracious One) in her honor. This symbolic gesture made her presence by the sovereign's side official. She was still by his side in the afternoon, in exceptionally beautiful weather, as they watched maneuvers from the beach, the staging of a naval battle and the launching of three vessels. After that, they had to visit the rope and tobacco factories and the citadel. The King and his retinue gazed out on the panoramic view of the port from the hill of Ingouville. They left Le Havre on Sunday, September 21, at eight in the morning and arrived in Versailles two days later, after a stop at the Château de Bizy, which belonged to the Maréchal de Belle-Isles.

Madame de Pompadour was exhausted but delighted. She had been treated like a queen and returned from the trip convinced that Louis XV was still his subjects' *Bien-Aimé*. "You can't imagine," she wrote to the Duc de Nivernais, "how great was the adoration for the King and for everything surrounding him. . . . The Normans merely followed their heart."[31] It was most probably in memory of this happy trip that she bought the model of a vessel, with decks and eighteen cannon openings, from the dealer Lazare Duvaux.[32]

Twelve

"THE LIFE I
LEAD IS DREADFUL"

❦

At twenty-eight, in spite of appearances, the Marquise was a bruised and disenchanted woman: "I've seen so many things over the last four and a half years that I have been here, that I know more than a forty-year-old woman,"[1] she sighed. Though she was feared and the object of false flattery, people felt slighted at being indebted to her for favors, pensions, promotions and all the sinecures that she alone could obtain. Nothing could be done without her. The King was inaccessible and left most of the military, diplomatic and administrative appointments up to his mistress. "The consideration people show me doesn't surprise me.... Anyone might need my services.... This doesn't go to my head,"[2] she confided to her brother. She had understood perfectly well that it was self-interest alone that compelled most courtiers to grovel before her. By now she had penetrated the mysteries of this "detested"[3] Court and lost the bourgeois tone that people had so made fun of. She spoke haughtily with the greatest noblemen and indulged in semiconfidences only with a handful of intimates. She knew she had to play-act constantly and keep her thoughts to herself: "It's peculiar that this virtue [frankness] is punished in this country [the Court]. I experienced it and promised myself that I would never in my life tell the truth to anyone."[4] "I have looked and thought about things carefully since I've been here; at least I've acquired a knowledge of human beings.... They're the same in Paris, or in a provincial city, as they are at Court.

The difference in objectives makes things more or less interesting and makes vices more obvious."[5]

When the King gave her some respite, she aspired to solitude in those famous hermitages that were retreats for her. "Alone, I try to forget the human race and distract myself with gardening,[6] which is one of the things I like best."[7] She sometimes felt nostalgic for a bourgeois happiness with a beloved man and a close-knit family, underestimating a bit glibly her craving for pleasure and the ambition that had always consumed her. Though she had not cut her ties with the milieu of her birth, she no longer belonged to it. The Pâris brothers (as can be gleaned from Duverney's letters) talked to her with the greatest deference and dealt with her as one powerful person to another. Their relations were now confined to a respect for their mutual secret commitments. Madame de Pompadour was not any more intimate with Tournehem. Her only subjects of discussion with him were the architectural projects that were dear to her heart.

She maintained a steady, though distant, relationship with Monsieur Poisson, and did not hesitate to bring him back to reality when he became overly self-important and demanded more than his due. She had arranged to have honors showered on him, but knew how to curb his appetites. The very personification of the parvenu financier, in addition to being the proud father of the official favorite, he strutted about his estate of Marigny, established as a marquisate, and lived in grand style. Jeanne-Antoinette was not fooled by the consideration with which the former steward of the Pâris brothers was treated. When a courtier suggested that she arrange for her father to remarry, she replied dryly: "If the Poisson race were to die out, it would be no great calamity."[8] The elder Poisson adored his granddaughter Alexandrine, whom the Marquise sometimes took with her to Versailles or the other royal residences. Though some of Madame de Pompadour's biographers have been eager to commend her for her maternal feelings, she had hardly any time for her child. Doubtless she loved her, but she mainly dreamed of a glorious marriage for her, which would serve as a formal recognition of her own status. In the interim, as she searched for a husband with a lofty enough title, she placed Alexandrine in the convent of the Assomption,⁹ where little girls from the best families in France were brought up. Alexandrine was now her only remaining tie with Charles Le Normant, who had managed to come to terms quite well with his status of royally betrayed husband. The last thing Jeanne-Antoinette wanted was to be reminded of him.

Aside from her daughter, the only person she cared about was her brother, the Marquis de Vandières, who would be succeeding Tournehem. This was why she wanted him to go on what was called the "Grand Tour"—a long trip to Italy, homeland of all the arts—in preparation for his future position. She saw to it personally that the best guides accompanied him, those most capable of educating his taste—the architect Soufflot, the draftsman Cochin and the Abbé Le Blanc, unsuccessful candidate to the Académie Française in spite of her support. Madame de Pompadour was sad to part with him, for she was attached to him, as he had been her companion from childhood to her teens. She had sincere, almost maternal feelings of affection for him, and enjoyed his biting rejoinders. Louis XV showed the same interest in this subtle young man and used to invite him to the private apartments. This astonished Poisson: "That my daughter should dine with the King doesn't surprise me," he said, "since he sleeps with her, but as for Vandières, I can't get over it."¹⁰ Actually, Vandières suffered from the fact that he owed his advancement to his sister. He was also reluctant to follow all her advice. The Marquise felt intense sorrow at her little brother's departure ("*frérot*," as she called him). "You were right not to say goodbye to me," she wrote him, "for in spite of the usefulness of this trip for you and the fact that I've long wanted it for your own good, I would have found it difficult to part from you."¹¹ She felt very lonely after he left. She could hardly seek comfort in the friendship of the ladies in her entourage, since most of them cherished the hope of supplanting her with the monarch.

Since moving to Versailles, Madame de Pompadour lived only for her lover. "Except for the happiness of being with the King, which most certainly consoles me for everything, all the rest is a mere tissue of wickedness and platitudes, really all the wretchedness that human beings are capable of. Excellent matter for reflection, especially for someone as prone to reflection as I am."[12] She was constantly aware of the precariousness of her favored status. True, Louis XV needed her: she knew how to listen to him, reassure him, amuse him and draw him into a whirlwind of pleasures that she apparently knew how to renew ad infinitum. But she had no right to make a mistake, and no right to rest for an instant. With this Royal Highness, who expected everything from her and offered her only a pathological melancholy and valuable gifts, any slackening of her efforts could be fatal. If the capricious monarch grew tired of her presence, he would send her away without the slightest qualms. When people were out of sight, Louis XV forgot them so easily. Jeanne-Antoinette sought every possible way of binding him to her. She had to invent new sources of excitement, and remember to pay court to the Queen and the young members of the royal family. "The life I lead is dreadful," she said to Madame de Lutzelbourg. "I hardly have a minute to myself: rehearsals and performances and twice a week constant trips both to the little château and to La Muette, etc. Considerable, inescapable duties: Queen, Dauphin, Dauphine, . . . three daughters, two infantas,[13] judge for yourself whether I can breathe; pity me."[14]

The Queen still treated Jeanne-Antoinette affably, but her children remained united against her. In fact, their clan had been strengthened. The Dauphin had naturally triumphed over his wife's scruples and she modeled her behavior on his. The Maréchal de Saxe was no longer present to try to establish a *modus vivendi* between the two women. He was now living a luxurious existence in the château of Chambord, which the sovereign had granted to him for life in reward for his superior feats of arms.[15] Louis XV's daughters continued to voice their agreement with their brother and had rallied their younger sisters in their crusade against *"maman-putain."* Madame Victoire, who was just fifteen, had joined her elder sisters in March 1748. The youngest girls, Madame Sophie and Madame Louise, still really children, had come to live at the château on October 18, 1749. Lastly, for over six months, the Court had been home to Madame Henriette's twin sister, Madame Elisabeth (Madame Infante). She had come to visit her father, with her daughter Isabelle, for the signing of the treaty of Aix-la-Chapelle and to watch over her husband's interests. These two princesses were the delight of the King, who took great pleasure in Elisabeth's company, and spent so much time conversing with her that Madame de Pompadour felt offended. After Madame Infante's departure, Louis XV showed a renewed interest in his family, which gave his mistress cause for alarm. If the King were to enjoy his children's company, they might achieve their ends—they might convince their father to give up his mistress and return to a Christian way of life. The prospect was all the more frightening to Madame de Pompadour in that she knew her lover was very preoccupied by the hereafter and capable of sinking into religious devotion to expiate his free-and-easy private life.

Would she lead him on to the road of salvation or would she continue in the role that had been hers for four years? The Marquise had no preconceived plan. Her personal strategy was dictated by circumstances. Though she was very impressed by the example of Madame de Maintenon, she was not yet up to becoming religious out of love for the King. So she had no choice. She had to remain the magician who brought enchantment to his daily life. But her lover had already made great demands on her. With her failing health, her migraines, her coughing up blood, Jeanne-Antoinette was not always the voluptuous mistress that Louis XV expected. One night, pleading that it was too hot, he had preferred to sleep on his sofa. He occasionally complained of his favorite's coldness. She started to eat celery soup and truffles, drink chocolate perfumed with ambergris and buy aphrodisiac liqueurs that were more dangerous than effective. Appalled by this diet, Madame du Hausset, her Lady of the Bedchamber, thought it advisable to discuss it with the Duchesse de Brancas. Madame de Brancas, who was older than Madame de Pompadour, had a sincere affection for her and had never posed as a rival.

She came to see her and chided her. The Marquise burst into tears. "I'm afraid of losing the King's heart by ceasing to be appealing to him," she admitted. "Men, as you know, value certain things enormously and I have the misfortune of having a very cold temperament. I wanted to follow a diet that would warm me up to make up for this failing; and for two days this elixir has been doing me some good, or at least I think it has."[16] Madame de Brancas took the flask, opened it, sniffed it, grimaced and immediately threw it into the fireplace. "I don't like to be treated like a child,"[17] moaned the Marquise and she began to cry again. Then she confided that she was afraid that the King "would get sick of her, and take another mistress." "You won't avoid this by following your diet," replied the Duchesse, "and this diet will kill you. Make your company more and more valuable to the King through your gentleness; don't turn him away at other times, and let things take their course; the chains of habit will bind him to you forever."[18] Madame de Brancas promised that she would keep Madame de Pompadour's secret to herself, and the two friends parted with a kiss.

A short time later, the Marquise seemed calmer. "The master is more pleased with me," she confided to Madame du Hausset, "this is since I spoke to Quesnay, without telling him everything. He told me that to get what I wanted, I had to be careful to be well and to try to have a good digestion, and to exercise to improve it. I think the doctor is right and I feel like another person. I adore the King; I would like to be attractive for him. But, alas, sometimes he finds me cold and passive. I would sacrifice my life to please him."[19] This frigidity that obsessed the Marquise was probably due to the fact that she suffered from chronic leukorrhea, which must have rendered sexual relations painful. This was not really a secret at Versailles, since Maurepas had cruelly used it in his quatrain about "white flowers" and had thereby revealed her illness to anyone who might not have known about it.

Madame de Pompadour was finding it increasingly difficult to live up to her role. She knew that her body might betray her with the man whose passion she wanted to keep alive. Though her beauty remained intact and the men she met still found her seductive, this was not sufficient to reassure her. She was far too aware of her insurmountable intimate failings. All pretty women now aroused terror in her and she began to use every possible stratagem to keep them away from the King. For the moment, Louis XV had merely had insignificant dalliances, like the extremely brief affair that had just ended with the ravishing Comtesse de Forcalquier. But what if this blasé prince were to fall under the spell of a mistress who might have the gift of giving him a second youth? Madame de Pompadour could not imagine being dismissed as the poor Madame de Mailly had been. It is true that the latter had never had any influence over her lover and had not even known how to entertain him, but now more than ever, she should follow Madame de Brancas's suggestion and make herself essential to the monarch. But could the mistress become a friend? Could she keep her lover's heart and not have any physical relationship with him? This was a genuine challenge.

Madame de Pompadour did not yet give up her role as lover. Before doing so, she wanted to reinforce her position and be granted even more dazzling marks of official favor than in the past. In the autumn of 1749, the King gave her a new apartment at Versailles, the one that had been occupied by the Duc and Duchesse de Penthièvre, and Madame Infante during her stay in France. It was located on the ground floor of the château, under the King's State apartment, and was connected to it by a spiral staircase that Louis XV had been accustomed to using when he wanted to chat with his daughter.

Madame de Pompadour won it after a hard-fought battle with the King's daughters, who wanted to move into it. "Whether the Marquise lives above or below, my father the King will go there no matter what," said Madame Henriette. "He will have to go up and down, or down and up, just as much; whereas me, Lady of France, I cannot live upstairs in the small rooms."[20] The Penthièvres and the Comtesse de Toulouse were equally furious. The young couple had been relegated to out-of-the-way accommodations, and the Comtesse de Toulouse now had only two small rooms in which to entertain Louis XV when he came to chat with her. "They split things up, compromised, parceled them out, and everyone is dissatisfied," remarked the Duc de Luynes. The only one who was satisfied was Madame de Pompadour, and she claimed that the Penthièvres and the Comtesse de Toulouse were just as pleased![21] Before she took possession of her new domain, the Buildings service had to renovate it extensively to "alter it in the modern style."[22]

Much more spacious than her love nest (now promised to the Duc and Duchesse d'Ayen), the favorite's new lodgings—which gave out both on the northern flowerbeds and the terrace—had formerly been occupied by Madame de Montespan before going to the princes of royal blood. It included two antechambers, a large study with cut-off corners and light from three windows, a bedroom, a drawing room and a small study. On the side giving out on the inner courtyard and the passage of the Cour des Cerfs, there was a daybed, a bathroom, a wardrobe and a back study. A mezzanine was reserved for Doctor Quesnay and Madame du Hausset.

The Court wondered about the reasons for this change. "Madame de Pompadour knows the King," said the Duc de Luynes, "she knows he is religious and that his reflections and the sermons he hears might make him feel remorse and anxiety. She knows he truly and sincerely loves her, but that anything can surrender to serious thought, particularly since the matter is one of habit more than temperament. If he were to find in his family company that would gently and cheerfully attend to what might amuse him, then perhaps, having no violent passion to conquer, he would give up his present taste for his duty."[23]

In seeming contradiction to the comments the Duc de Luynes had written in the privacy of his study, Madame de Pompadour displayed enormous liveliness and energy with the King. She resumed the performances in the private apartments with more ardor than ever. She presented *Issé*, a pastoral in five acts[24]; *Le Philosophe marié*, a comedy by Destouches; *Le Médecin de village*, a ballet-pantomime by Dehesse; and *Les Fêtes de Thétis*, an opera in two acts,[25] in which she played the Dawn. She staged *Erigone* again and the premiere of an opera-ballet, *La Journée galante* by Laujon and Lagarde. That season, Madame de Pompadour made her debut in a new genre—tragedy; she performed in Voltaire's *Alzire*, which had been a great success at the Comédie Française in 1736. The author, who was invited to the performance, naturally complimented the actors, but he had the disagreeable experience of hearing the King criticize his latest play, *Oreste*, in a loud voice. This would turn out to be one of Voltaire's last appearances at Court.[26] He nonetheless composed some gallant verses for the Marquise, to congratulate her on her performance:

> *This perfect American* (Alzire)
> *Caused too many tears to be shed.*
> *Could I not console myself*
> *By seeing Venus at her toilette?*

Madame de Pompadour multiplied her comings and goings. During the year 1750, Louis XV spent only fifty-two nights at Versailles, and no more than sixty-three the following year. No one outside his circle of favorites could approach him any longer. The Marquise was delighted: "You can't imagine the extreme pleasure I derive from these trips," she wrote to her father. "My only regret is that they're so short. I could spend my life on trips."[27] The Prince de Croÿ has left an account of these private small sojourns.

"Life was lived with a great deal of freedom," he wrote during a trip to La Muette. "There was a big lunch, though supper was even more substantial, as it was the King's meal. He went for walks if the weather was good, or played cards in the drawing room after lunch. Then he worked or held council. At eight-thirty, everyone gathered in the drawing room; he came to play cards; at nine there was supper at a very large table for ten. Monsieur le Premier,[28] Governor of La Muette, served the King. . . . That day, starting from the King's left, the company included: the King, Madame la Marquise de Pompadour, the Prince de Soubise, the Duc de Luxembourg, the Marquis d'Armentières, the Marquis de Voyer, the Comte d'Estrées, the Prince de Turenne, the Comte de Maillebois, the Marquis de Sourches, the Marquis de Choiseul, the Comte de Croissy, Madame du Roure, the Duc de Boufflers, the Marquis de Bauffremont, the Duc de Broglie, the Prince de Croÿ, the Marquis de Pignatelli, the Duc de Chevreuse, the Duc de Chaulnes, the Duc de La Vallière, the Marquis de Gontaut, the Duc de Richelieu, Madame la Duchesse de Brancas, the Duc d'Ayen and Madame d'Estrades. Monsieur de Laval and Monsieur de Beuvron sat at a small table. This was a very merry trip. The Marquise was extremely lively; she did not like card games and played really to be naughty and to be seated and not out of fondness. She spends a lot of time with her flatterers, Monsieur de Meuse, Monsieur de Gontaut, etc. The King played two games after supper, for he liked high stakes and played very well and very fast, and he went to bed at two o'clock. This was the life in all the small châteaux."[29] It will be noted that there were far fewer women than there were men. According to the Prince de Croÿ, the King still seemed just as taken with Madame de Pompadour. Our chronicler was a bit disappointed to notice, however, that the conversation consisted mainly of "making fun of others and speaking ill of them."[30] "The Marquise went to great pains to raise the level of conversation."[31]

Louis XV continued to hold Council meetings during these trips, but according to d'Argenson, he attached very little importance to the affairs of the kingdom. He "lived a life of continual dissipation,"[32] devoting too little time to his ministers. "By giving little time to the affairs of government, they are generally strangled. Incapable of working hard, dividing his time between hunting and pleasures, he [the King] has no idea of what is meant by governing," asserted the Austrian ambassador, Count von Kaunitz.[33] Puisieulx complained of not having had any steady work with His Majesty for several months. Yet foreign policy was still a cause for concern, finances were in a state of crisis and Paris was seething.

In May 1750, there had been riots in the capital following the kidnapping of a number of children. The most insane rumors were spread. It was claimed, for instance, that a leprous prince needed to bathe in the blood of adolescents as a remedy for his disease! Was the Paris population prey to a collective psychosis or was their fear justified? The lawyer Barbier devotes several pages in his *Journal*[34] to these events without bothering to refute the most implausible speculations. The episode almost took on the proportions of an affair of State, for children had indeed vanished. Barbier accuses the henchmen of the lieutenant of police, who were usually in charge of arresting vagrants, of excessive zeal, motivated by an exceptional bonus offered for each arrest. At the time, young French people of both sexes were being arrested and transported to Louisiana, as well as to Mississippi, to join the silkworm manufacturing workforce. The police agents, wearing ordinary clothes, used a variety of tricks to pick up not only abandoned children, but also the sons of artisans and shopkeepers. Their indiscriminate overzealousness was such that there were several uprisings— in the Faubourg Saint-Antoine, the Place de la Croix-Rouge, the Faubourg Saint-Germain, the Porte Saint-Denis and near Saint-Roch, the neighborhood where Berryer, the police lieutenant, lived. His mansion was besieged by a threatening mob. Fearing for his life, he fled through a rear door and took refuge in the nearby Jacobin convent. Several patrol brigades, on horseback and on foot, had to be sent to protect his residence. It took them all day to break up the riot. Once order had been restored, several arrests were made and some hypothetical culprits were pursued, but the government did not seek to understand the deeper significance of the gravest revolt in Paris since 1720. The most sensible observers criticized Berryer for failing to give strict orders to his arresting officers immediately after the first kidnappings and for not taking measures to reassure the inhabitants of the city. But something even more serious had occurred. During the riots, which were without a doubt spontaneous, the King had been personally attacked with insults as violent and contemptuous as those once directed against Henri III by the Sainte Ligue. They were aimed not at the King's minions, but at his mistress, with whom he lived in outrageous luxury while the common people were squeezed for taxes. There was talk of burning down Versailles and the Château de Bellevue. Troops had to be posted to guard the Pont de Sèvres.

In the midst of all this turmoil, the Marquise underestimated the danger and almost fell victim to public abuse. She was on her way to Paris to visit the apartment that was being prepared for her daughter at the convent of the Assomption, when she was stopped by the Marquis de Gontaut, who had come expressly to meet her. He urged her to retrace her steps immediately, for a mob had already started assembling by the wall of the house where she was expected.

These events were disagreeable for the King and his mistress. However, what seemed to impress them was their monstrously anecdotal aspect. "Speaking of madness," said the Marquise to her brother, "you know about the Parisians. I don't think there's anything more stupid than their believing that their children were going to be bled to bathe a leper. I'm ashamed to admit that I thought they were less moronic."[35] Louis XV decided that he would avoid his capital city. "What!" he said. "I should appear before these wicked people who call me a Herode!"[36] So, in an attempt to frustrate the rebellious population, the King left for Compiègne on the night of June 6 without going through the capital.[37] "Neither the King nor any other member of his family went through

Paris so as to punish the inhabitants for their misbehavior,"[38] the Marquise wrote to her brother. Louis XV traveled down a road in the Saint-Denis plain, through fields of ripening wheat.[39] The trip had very much the appearance of a pitiful escape, but as d'Argenson pointed out, "It is fortunate to be away from a rebellious city."[40]

Thirteen

THE SHADOW OF
MADAME DE MAINTENON

Throughout the summer of 1750, Madame de Pompadour kept up the pressure on Tournehem to complete her Versailles apartment and her Bellevue château by the end of the stay in Fontainebleau. The Marquise's demands were especially hard to meet in that the same artisans and artists were working on both sites. Louis XV's passion for architecture was equal to his mistress's and he indulged his passion for building and renovation without restraint. The correspondence between Versailles's General Director of Buildings and the architect Lécuyer, his project manager, about the Versailles apartment, shows how much energy was expended to fulfill the favorite's wishes. The renovation had required tearing down walls and putting up new ones; creating bathrooms and kitchens; refashioning plasterwork and cornices; and delivering, adjusting, carving, painting and polishing wood paneling, with special care that the products employed be odor free. Workers had had to work around the clock. The decorators of the royal residences, Verberckt and Rousseau, had not had a moment's rest. And though overburdened with work, they had had to ask for their wages and then were paid only after a considerable delay.

While they were busily at work at Versailles, they were also putting the finishing touches on Bellevue. So the Marquise had christened the immense stretch of land on the hill of Meudon, overlooking the Seine and with a panoramic view of Paris. Before building the residence—on plans inspired by Madame de Pompadour and approved by Gabriel[1]—it had been necessary to work at the earth for a considerable period of time because of the slippery and sandy soil. The construction, begun after the signing of the peace of Aix-la-Chapelle, had been carried out at a very brisk pace. Over eight hundred workers had been needed, and it was rumored that seven million livres had been sunk into it. The actual expense (still considerable) was 2,600,000 livres. Louis XV was giving his mistress this little château in exchange for six houses she owned in Compiègne that he allowed her to continue using. Bellevue delighted her: "It is a lovely spot for the view," she said. "The house, though not big, is convenient and charming, and devoid of magnificence."[2]

The château was at the top of the hill. First you had to cross through gardens before entering the large main courtyard. In front was a two-story building with an attic; it consisted of a central pavilion flanked on both sides by slightly recessed wings. On the eastern facade, overlooking other gardens sloping down to the river, was a long terrace from which you could admire the view of Paris, which seemed at the same time far away and close.

The sobriety of the exterior contrasted with the splendor and refinement of the interior. The Marquise's personal taste was even more evident here than at Crécy. She had seen to every detail. Statues of Music[3] and Poetry[4] welcomed the visitor in the large entrance hall, which opened onto an antechamber that could be used as a dining room, and other rooms for entertaining. Madame de Pompadour had kept the ground-floor apartment for herself and installed the King's apartment on the first floor. The two lovers' bedrooms were one above the other and connected by an interior stairway. The Marquise had given hers an exotic character; there was a lacquered chest of drawers with pagodas and a painting by Carle Van Loo showing her disguised as a sultana, half stretched out on some pillows, and a black servant bringing her a cup of coffee. It seems likely that on the small rosewood tables she displayed the two Indian magots, the Chinese porcelain roosters, the Japanese monkeys and the Nankin fans, purchased from the dealer Lazare Duvaux in May 1750. And she must have found a place to hang the gauze lantern from India. In the bathroom, Boucher had painted *La*

Toilette de Vénus[5] and *Vénus Consolant l'Amour*.[6] Next to the bathtub was a bidet covered with a rosewood marquetry of floral patterns.

The monumental stairway, with its mythological scenes painted by Brunetti, recalled a Palladian villa. It led to a hall whose general design had been conceived by the Marquise—garlands framing a series of panels by Boucher. The panels above the doors in the dining room were by Oudry, the ones in the music room by Pierre and those in the formal drawing room by Carle Van Loo, who had also painted the panels in the King's apartment. Bellevue, like all châteaux, had a chapel; and the altarpiece, *L'Adoration des Bergers* (The Adoration of the Shepherds),[7] was by Boucher. Madame de Pompadour, of course, had also had a theater built, an extremely unusual one, with Chinese decorations, and the remarkable feature that it could be expanded or reduced in size as desired.[8] It was draped in blue satin with a solid silver foliage pattern and could hold up to five hundred people.

Garnier d'Isle designed the gardens, giving the place of honor to a statue of Louis XV, a masterpiece by Pigalle that was destroyed during the Revolution. Pigalle also made a group statue, *L'Amour et l'Amitié* (Love and Friendship), and shortly thereafter he sculpted Friendship, a statue with the Marquise's features, draped in a flowing robe, a hand on her heart. An Apollo by Guillaume de Coustou enlivened the grove of the Arts.

Madame de Pompadour regarded Bellevue as her personal creation. People said that the King would be spending several days a week there with her and a select group of friends, and so would not be inconvenienced by his family. However, the inauguration of the château on November 25 turned into a catastrophe, to Jeanne-Antoinette's despair, for she had staked her honor on everything being perfect. At the last minute, she cancelled the illumination and the fireworks. She had just been warned that, once again, she was in danger of being cruelly jeered in song by the Parisians, who could not forgive her luxury and expenditures. It was a cold and humid night. The fireplaces, which were being used for the first time, began smoking in all the rooms. It was impossible to serve supper in the château, so the favorite had to arrange to have it served at Brimborion, a small pavilion erected during the

Regency that had fortunately been integrated into the Bellevue estate. The King looked grumpy, though he stayed at Bellevue for the night. The guests lacked enthusiasm, and they felt that the purple velvet uniforms embroidered with gold, chosen by the new chatelaine, were not very becoming.

Louis XV's obvious boredom deeply distressed the Marquise and she suddenly fell sick with a dreadful migraine. Yet she refused to be demoralized; she invited the King to stay with her again and the following visits went as she had hoped. To her great relief, the sovereign acquired the habit of coming to this new residence and soon felt comfortable in it. Being included in the trips to Bellevue soon became a mark of supreme favor. The Marquise performed her role of hostess with tact and gaiety. She now gave her theatrical performances in her own residence, since Louis XV had put an end to the ones in the private apartments as a cost-saving measure. "The King wants to reduce his expenses in all sectors," she said to Madame de Lutzelbourg, "though this isn't a significant expense, the public thinks it is, so I did it to humor public opinion and set an example."[9] The privileged guests who were usually invited to her performances now came to see them at Madame de Pompadour's. She inaugurated the new theater on January 27, 1751, with a comedy written for her by La Chaussée, *L'Homme de fortune*, and an allegorical ballet, *L'Amour architecte*, for which the machinery used for the scenery operated perfectly. Amidst rumbling thunder, the château of Bellevue, all lit up, could be seen rising out of a mountain, and around it, a host of busy dancing male and female gardeners. However, the Marquise did not have the success she had expected. The audience was bored by the ballet. As for La Chaussée's play, it was judged mediocre, and this was compounded by the fact that the actors had several memory lapses. The troupe made up for this failure on February 20 with Quinault's *La Mère coquette* and Dancourt's *Les Trois Cousines*. The King enjoyed himself, to the relief of the Marquise.

The Marquise took possession of her princely apartment at Versailles just as her relationship with Louis XV was taking on a new cast—love was gradually changing to friendship. She might have agreed with Madame de Staël's definition of glory "as the mourning for happiness in splendor." But this lovely coquette, in whom mind and heart always waged a merciless battle, had succeeded in exercising so much authority over the monarch that, for a long time already, he could not do without her presence. By no longer sharing his bed, she became more than ever his companion, partner and adviser. Her influence would continue to grow uninterruptedly. After captivating him, she had literally captured him. This was a change for which she had been preparing for a year, since she saw it as inevitable. Humiliating as this might be to her female pride, at least she had the satisfaction of keeping all the prerogatives of an honorary mistress and the authority of a queen.

At her morning toilette, she always received the most important State personalities—ambassadors, princes and a large number of courtiers. "She decides, she arbitrates, she looks upon the ministers as hers,"[10] d'Argenson seethed. "The ministers tell her ahead of time whatever they have to say to the King. He himself wants it that way,"[11] asserted Count von Kaunitz, the Austrian ambassador. She talked with the representatives of foreign powers and informed them of the sovereign's intentions. No one hesitated in comparing her power to that of a Prime Minister. "She has a quality that makes her highly qualified for government; she is capable of impenetrable secrecy. This is how she acquired the King's trust, so much so that as soon as something happens, he has the need to tell her every important thing that's been said to him,"[12] added Kaunitz. In March 1751, the Marquis de Puisieulx worked with the King in the Marquise's presence. According to Baron Le Chambrier, the Prussian ambassador, Madame de Pompadour was "delighted by this, probably in order to show herself to advantage in the mind of the King of France, displaying talents that he had previously not thought her capable of. Here she is then, within earshot of the most important affairs of government."[13] He further added that the favorite, who had hitherto not been very interested in politics, might have felt "that she had to make herself essential to the King of France in his primary concerns, *in order to make up for the fact that he no longer needed her as much for his pleasure*[14] and that by attaching himself to her in this manner he would find it more difficult to dismiss her."[15]

In her own way, Madame de Pompadour seemed to want to follow the example of Madame de Maintenon, whose fate had made a striking impression on her. Louis XIV's morganatic wife had founded Saint-Cyr, an educational establishment for impoverished girls of the nobility. Louis XV's mistress, Madame de Pompadour, wanted to gain immortality by creating a royal military school. It was to provide lodgings, food and military training for five hundred young noblemen between the ages of eight and eleven whose fathers were still serving in the military or had died on the battlefields. This idea, which conformed to the latest conceptions of specialized and efficient schooling, had been given to the Marquise by Pâris-Duverney, who was very familiar with the army's needs. She adopted it with an enthusiasm that matched her ambitions. They plotted together before discussing the project with the King, who was not hard to convince. Over the year 1750, Louis XV and his favorite consulted with Duverney, Montmartel, Tournehem and Gabriel in great secrecy. "The King is very eager for this project to be realized." Madame de Pompadour wrote to Duverney on April 4, 1750. "He would first like to know how much money would be needed for this residence so that it can never be dismantled. H.M. does not want to use exceptional funds for this building."[16] On September 18, she was deeply moved by a visit to Saint-Cyr. "I can't tell you how touched I was by that establishment and everything I saw there. They all came to tell me that they would like to set up a similar one for men. This made me want to laugh, for when our venture becomes finalized, they'll think the idea came from them."[17] Duverney urged the Marquise to induce the King to promulgate the edict founding the establishment. He thought this would help the sovereign regain his popularity, as he was greatly in need of doing at the time.

As the project was taking shape, new ties were created between Louis XV and Madame de Pompadour. "I was enchanted to see the King go into detail," she said to Duverney. "I'm burning with impatience sometimes to see the thing become public, because then it will no longer be possible to reverse course. I'm counting on your eloquence to win over Monsieur de Machault [Comptroller General of Finances], though I believe he's too fond of the King to stand in the way of his glory. Finally, my dear Duverney, I'm counting on your vigilance to let the world know about it soon."[18] The fruit of her shared efforts with the sovereign, she hoped it would contribute to his glory, and at the same time, she wanted to bask in some of the glory herself. Great was her disappointment in January 1751 when her name wasn't mentioned in the edict that created a "Royal Military School." Nevertheless, she never lost interest in this undertaking, which she had inspired and instigated.

The construction work, financed by a new tax on playing cards, began the following May, on a huge plot of land near the Seine, in the Grenelle plain, not far from the Invalides. When a lack of funds threatened to halt the construction in 1755, the Marquise offered to pay the workers out of her own pocket. "I will not allow an establishment that is supposed to immortalize the King, make his nobility happy, and inform posterity of my attachment to the State and to H.M., die in its tracks."[19] The first boarders moved in in 1756, but the building, whose plans had to be revised by Gabriel, was only fully completed in 1773. By then the Marquise had been dead for nine years.

In early 1751, in spite of her growing power, Madame de Pompadour feared her opponents. She had to fight against the usual courtiers, intrigues, the women who wanted to supplant her as royal favorite, and she had to confront the will of God as expressed by the pope. That year the Supreme Pontiff, Benedict XIV, was celebrating his jubilee. A plenary indulgence was promised to all those who submitted to a certain number of devotional exercises. This was the opportunity for great sinners to make a show of repentance. As adulterers, Louis XV and Madame de Pompadour were certainly sinners in the eyes of the Church.

The Marquise, at that time, hardly thought about religion, though she went to mass every morning. Not attending the holy services would have seemed scandalous, even if this Court was not known for its austere morals. Madame de Pompadour kept up appearances and conformed to custom, but she didn't feel at all guilty about the life she led. This was not true of the King, who had remained deeply religious and attached to the holy precepts that had been inculcated in him in childhood by Cardinal Fleury. Since the famous scenes in Metz, in 1744, Louis XV had avoided the sacraments. He preferred not to confess to sins for which he lacked the desire or will to repent. He felt that shammed contrition was worse than sin. Yet he remained racked by remorse. One evening, early in their affair, he had wanted to read a sermon by Massillon to Jeanne-Antoinette. She had laughed off the suggestion and, to her astonishment, he had returned to his own quarters downstairs, leaving her in tears. She understood that with a lover like him she should not show too much religious indifference. Most contemporaries believed that it was only a matter of time before he would turn to the Church. Would the King and his mistress "do their jubilee"? This was the question on everyone's lips and it gave rise to the most contradictory rumors.

Though it should have been a strictly religious issue, it was complicated by politics. Indeed, for two years, fiscal matters had pitted the clergy against the royal government. In May 1749, Machault d'Arnouville had made the King promulgate an edict establishing a new tax called "*le vingtième.*" It was to apply, without distinction, to the three orders regardless of income, whether from land ownership, personal or movable property, commercial income or legal practice. Louis XV had been obliged to hold a solemn parliamentary session to compel his parliament to record the measure, for it threatened many privileges. During its five-yearly assembly, in May 1750, the clergy, whose custom it was to vote what was called the "*don gratuit*" (free gift), reminded the King that its contributions had always been voluntary. However, that year, though the sovereign did not make the clergy pay the *vingtième*, the sovereign had taxed them with an additional contribution. This led to a general outcry. The assembly presented remonstrances to the monarch and he proceeded to dissolve it. The Court immediately divided into two parties. Machault's party was supported by Madame de Pompadour, the financiers, the Maréchal de Noailles and the Maréchal de Richelieu. The religious party (the *dévots*) led by Monseigneur de Beaumont, Archbishop of Paris, was supported by the Comte d'Argenson, Minister of War; Boyer, keeper of the profit register; and Cardinal de Tencin, State Minister. The royal family, of course, was completely behind the *dévots* and Louis XV tried in vain to maintain a balance between the two clans.

In 1751, passions were exacerbated by the jubilee. The clergy was not disposed to any compromise with the King, and the *dévots* hoped to launch their final offensive against the great woman sinner who was held responsible for the monarch's shocking behavior. The Queen and her children were overcome with such ostentatious piety that d'Argenson described it as akin to "bigotry." They performed penance and self-mortification, and had masses held for the King's "conversion." They even indulged in weird practices, such as meditating in front of skulls trimmed with ribbons. Marie Leczinska even claimed to own the skull of the famous seventeenth-century lady Ninon de Lenclos, nicknamed *la Belle Mignonne* (the Pretty Darling).

Though she feared the influence the confessors might have on the sovereign, the Marquise, "more mistress than ever," behaved "with a boldness and temerity"[20] that astounded her enemies. She did tremble, however, upon learning that the Holy Father had sent a brief to the Archbishop of Paris ordering him to put an end to the scandal of the royal love affairs. Louis XV met with the prelate, but the substance of their discussion was never disclosed. People had it that the King, finally touched by grace, was going to banish his mistress to the convent of the Assomption and "do his jubilee."

For once, the Marquise was probably reassured by her lover's weaknesses. With great discretion, Louis XV had been entertaining several venal young beauties recruited by his valet Lebel. Apparently, at the time, he had "recovered his virile strengths thanks to his new dishes,"[21] and this hardly appeared to be a prelude to the jubilee. Yet at the beginning of Lent, the King seemed overcome with religious fervor. He attended all the services assiduously and cancelled some hunting expeditions so he could listen to the sermons of the Reverend Father Griffet, who had come to preach before the Court. The Jesuit, unembarrassed, devoted his homilies to the subject of the adulterous woman. Louis XV listened without flinching. The Marquise was so upset that she developed a fever—"jubilee fever," as it was sarcastically called. The *dévots* were pleased to note that the King went less often to see the favorite at her morning toilette, and that he was spending more time with his family. Moreover, throughout the entire period of penitence he didn't stay away a single night. He sometimes went to La Muette or Bellevue for supper, but returned to Versailles to sleep. This does not mean he stopped seeing Madame de Pompadour. He had conversations with her every day and worked in her company, and she continued to host her little suppers, still showing all the qualities that the King found attractive.

On April 1, 1751, the death of Madame de Mailly, his first mistress, plunged Louis XV into a state of grief. The unfortunate Countess had spent the last years of her life expiating the excesses of her youth, though it could hardly have been called turbulent. She wore a hair shirt, observed austere practices and paid off all her debts, which left her nearly penniless. By the time she died, she had almost acquired an aura of saintliness, and she asked to be buried among the poor, with a simple wooden cross on her grave. Since she had never asked the King for anything, her humility was inevitably compared to the Marquise's haughtiness. However, Jeanne-Antoinette succeeded in consoling the King and preventing him from sinking into a deep melancholy. "Madame de Pompadour is the King's best physician and she watches over him, but she's a bad physician for the purse."[22]

She was essential to the monarch and he wanted to keep her by his side. Since he had given up all carnal relations with her, he thought he could now receive the sacraments and do his jubilee. But Father Griffet and Father Perusseau, whom he consulted, remained adamant. They demanded that the Marquise be banished to make amends for the scandal. The King tried other avenues. He arranged for consultations at the Sorbonne and even in Rome. Several years later, Madame de Pompadour would write to the Holy Father explaining that Louis XV had told his confessors and the Doctors of the Church that she "was necessary for his happiness and for the good of his political affairs, and that she was the only person who dared speak truthfully with him."[23] The sovereign received the same answer from all the religious authorities[24]: he could only be granted the Church's forgiveness if he dismissed the favorite. In spite of all the pressures exerted on him, Louis XV did without Easter and the jubilee.

Madame de Pompadour felt relieved, but now she feared she would have to pretend to be religious to keep the King's friendship. "It's not a wild conjecture to suggest that the Marquise's model in her plans is Madame de Maintenon. If the Queen were no more, she would soon become devout and the King would not feel that his following the example of his great-grandfather would be an expensive price to pay for a clear conscience,"[25] said Kaunitz. For the time being, however, the Marquise had to continue to entertain her beloved. She did so by organizing many small trips. On September 13, 1751, the birth of the Duc de Bourgogne seemed to bring her serenity. The Dauphine, who had had several miscarriages, had finally produced an heir to the kingdom. Madame de Pompadour shared the happiness of Louis XV and the royal family. "You can imagine my joy, *grand-femme*,[26] given my feelings for the King. My emotions were such that I fainted in Madame la Duchesse's antechamber. Fortunately, I was pushed behind a curtain and my only witnesses were Madame de Villars and Madame d'Estrades. Madame la Dauphine is doing marvelously. And so is Monsieur le Duc de Bourgogne. I saw him yesterday: he has his grandfather's eyes, which is clever of him."[27] A few days later, she lured the King off to Crécy prior to their stay in Fontainebleau.

At Court, people rejoiced over the Prince's birth. At Bellevue, the Marquise presented the King with a fireworks display in honor of the event. But during the celebrations held in Paris, the public was very cold toward the sovereign. There were hardly any cries of joy when they exited from Notre-Dame after the *Te Deum*. And when Louis XV came out on the steps of the Hôtel de Ville to show himself to the crowd, there were no cheers at all. This hostility deeply affected Madame de Pompadour. She wanted to go to Paris, but was persuaded to stay away. She was loathed. She was considered responsible for the people's poverty. And when the Dauphin and Dauphine went to Notre-Dame for the churching ceremony, the mob that lined the streets along the way demanded bread and yelled curses against the favorite: "Send away the harlot who is governing the kingdom and causing its death; if we could get our hands on her, there would be nothing left with which to make relics."[28]

Fourteen

1752: THE YEAR OF LIVING DANGEROUSLY

The celebrations for the birth of the Duc de Bourgogne at Versailles, at the end of December 1751, left a mood of sadness. In the evening, an icy north wind blew out the illuminations, and the coaches arrived at the château in semidarkness. Inside, it was freezing and though the hall was brightly lit, the chandeliers were placed too high and shed a harsh light on people's faces. The guests noticed that there were far fewer women than men. Still fearing that the King might single out a pretty woman, the Marquise had gone over the guest lists and eliminated potential rivals. And the Parisian bourgeoises, who usually attended these kinds of festivities, had not been invited. This was the King's way of showing his resentment of the capital city for its hostility, and the favorite had done nothing, of course, to contest the measure! That evening, Louis XV looked somber, the Dauphin and Dauphine uttered not a word and Mesdames were bored. The Queen alone exhibited the air of contentment that was expected in such circumstances. The courtiers carried out the sovereign's will by wearing magnificent new suits, but they regretted that they had had to incur the expense for such a dreary reception. Though she looked beautiful in her formal gown and jewels, the Marquise lacked her usual graciousness. The King had turned his back on her when he saw her. Yet she took her seat at his table when he played *lansquenet*.

Louis XV had no reason to rejoice. Since the disconcerting peace of Aix-la-Chapelle, his people had turned against him. The obsessive fear of food shortages, due to a succession of bad harvests, had further added to the discontent. As he himself put it, the *Bien-Aimé* (Much Loved) had turned into the *Bien-Haï* (Much Hated). Satirical tracts conjured the shades of Jacques Clément and Ravaillac (assassins of Henri III and Henri IV, respectively) to bring the reign of the "tyrant" to an end. The King, who was accustomed to adulation—not to say adoration—was shattered by the growing tide of hatred against him and felt powerless to contain its poisonous onslaught. All the old rancor against financiers and tax collectors was aimed at Madame de Pompadour, and her dismissal might have been a calming gesture, but the King had no more intention of yielding to the threats of the populace than to the will of the priests. He made absolutely no effort to regain his lost popularity. He had too much pride and was steeped in the principles of absolute monarchy that the *philosophes* were beginning to challenge. Instead, he chose to withdraw into himself, make himself inaccessible and keep distant from the French, whom he regarded as ungrateful. However, he had serious problems that needed to be solved urgently. He had to restore a balanced budget and assure the livelihood of an angered population. He had to find solutions to the religious issues that were taking on political implications with the revival of Jansenism. He had to subdue a rebellious parliament that was grasping for power; and he had to keep a close watch over a literature that threatened the very foundations of a supreme authority.

A pernicious atmosphere reigned at Versailles. A pseudo murder attempt against the Duc de Bourgogne brought the sovereign's bad temper to a climax. While he was attending the changing of his grandson's swaddling clothes, Madame Sauvé, a chambermaid, discovered a mysterious package in the Prince's cradle which she immediately handed to the Duchesse de Tallard, Governess of the Children of France. Not daring to open it, the Governess gave it to the Comte de Saint-Florentin. The minister found it contained powder and a lock of hair wrapped in a sheet of paper on which an insolent message had been written for Louis XV and his favorite. In the late afternoon, Madame de Tallard, "looking very troubled," went to see the King three times, and Madame de Pompadour, who never paid her visits, stayed with her for an hour. "We sus-

Madame de Poisson, Madame de Pompadour's mother, was considered a great beauty in her youth. (Adélaïde Labille-Guillard)

Le Normant de Tournehem, generally acknowledged as Madame de Pompadour's father. (Louis Tocqué)

The Château d'Etiolles.

Jean-Marc Nattier painted this portrait of Louis XV about the same time the King made
Madame de Pompadour his mistress.

A young Madame de Pompadour, surrounded by various objects designed to emphasize her role as patron of the arts. (François Boucher)

An event in the Hall of Mirrors.

The ball given by the King to celebrate the Dauphin's marriage. (Charles-Nicolas Cochin)

Madame de Pompadour's only child, Alexandrine Le Normant d'Etiolles, who died at the age of ten in 1754.
(François-Hubert Drouais)

The Marquis de Marigny, Madame de Pompadour's younger brother.
(Jean-François de Troy)

The Cardinal de Bernis, friend and adviser to the royal mistress.

A secret staircase linked the King's apartments with those of his mistress, both at Versailles (shown above) and at Madame de Pompadour's châteaux.

The Duke de Chouiseul Stainville, Minister of State.
(Louis-Michel Van Loo)

The Château de Bellevue, viewed from the gardens. The painting bears the arms of Madame de Pompadour.

Madame de Pompadour, painted in 1755, again emphasizing her role in supporting the arts.

(Maurice-Quentin de La Tour)

A later portrait of Louis XV, painted in 1748. (Maurice-Quentin de La Tour)

The "Belle Jardinière" portrait of Madame de Pompadour.

(Louis-Michel Van Loo)

pected that some great event was taking place."[1] On the following day, no one aside from the servants was allowed in to see the Duc de Bourgogne. The incident became known. Who could have been capable of such criminal audacity? Tongues wagged. Several days later, Madame Sauvé was imprisoned. Minimizing the incident, Madame de Pompadour encouraged the belief that Madame Sauvé was so "deranged" that she had placed the package in the child's bed and made it look as if she had saved his life when she sounded the alarm. Presumably, she had hoped to make a fortune for herself and her family.[2] However, no one believed in the guilt of the accused for long.[3] People were convinced that she had seen the guilty person and had kept silent for fear of reprisals—which led to the supposition that the potential "regicide" was a person of high rank.[4] The Marquis d'Argenson suspected the Duchesse de Tallard. He thought she might have staged this incident in order to "insult the King about his mistress,"[5] in the hope of getting her dismissed. The truth was never known.

Whether innocent or guilty, Madame de Tallard belonged to the religious party that now included Madame d'Estrades, the favorite's close friend. Though Madame d'Estrades had been an intimate of Madame de Pompadour since her presentation at Court, she was jealous of her and had tried to seduce the King. She even boasted of having yielded to him one night in a gondola on the grand canal, while the ailing Marquise was resting in her quarters. This one-night stand (if it had indeed taken place) had had no sequel. On the other hand, Madame d'Estrades's affair with the Comte d'Argenson could be a cause for alarm. Jeanne-Antoinette knew that every single thing she said or did was reported to the Minister of War, a man who wanted her demise and had an influence over the King. When Madame d'Estrades fell gravely ill, people unashamedly whispered that the Marquise had tried to poison her. Fortunately, she quickly recovered her health.

Madame de Pompadour had to be constantly on her toes, by the side of this capricious monarch who was prey to chronic depression. However, on February 2, 1752, he was not overly worried on learning that his daughter Madame Henriette was running a high fever. After a sleigh ride, she had coughed up blood, but had made Madame Adélaide swear not to tell anyone. The fever persisted the following day, along with an alarming cough. She was bled twice and suffered suffocating shortness of breath. The King and Queen went to see her several times. Her conditioned worsened. Louis XV, who had cancelled his trip to Bellevue, never left his daughter's side. On February 7, feeling that she was approaching death, Madame Henriette confessed and received communion. The King called off the formal dinner, but his hopes were raised again when he saw that his daughter seemed calmer. He left her sitting up in bed, a fan in her hand. But the following morning, he was wakened at seven: Madame had lost consciousness. Her death was imminent. The sovereign was respectfully advised to remain in his quarters and spare himself a painful sight. Surrounded by his wife and children, all of them in tears, he waited for the fatal news in his bedroom, while the courtiers milled about the Oeil-de Boeuf antechamber.

When Madame Henriette died, the Dauphine decided that the Court would move to Trianon. The King was too dispirited to take any initiative. The Court never remained at Versailles after the death of a member of the royal family. As soon as he arrived in the small château, the monarch closeted himself in his quarters with his children, while the Queen took up residence in the adjoining Trianon-sous-Bois.[6] The Marquise was extremely worried: the King had not asked her to follow him. She did not hesitate for long and went to join him. He welcomed her into his quarters with complete naturalness and gave her the Queen's apartment. Her bold gamble had succeeded.

For several days, Louis XV languished in a deep depression. Nothing seemed to pull him out of it. He stopped working, lost his appetite and grew thin. He "looked like a man racked by grief" and knew that the populace was muttering, "See what happens when you offend God and impoverish your people! God takes away your beloved daughter."[7] The *dévots* thought that they would finally see their prayers answered. In his great distress over the Princess's death, the King would surely repent and get closer to his children. He was often seen with Madame Adélaide, and seemed to become attached to her. She was now referred to as "Madame," as she had become the King's eldest daughter.[8] When he offered to move her into an apartment that was adjacent to the Marquise's and had an interior stairway he could use to come down to see her, people assumed that the royal family had finally prevailed over the favorite. This was underestimating Jeanne-Antoinette. Her relationship with the King was as tender as ever, and she did everything to try to soothe his grief. She would stop at nothing to retain his affection, even becoming religious along with him, if necessitated by circumstances. The fact that he was drawing closer to his children no longer worried her, as long as the royal family was considerate to her. In her desire to master the situation, it was she who had suggested to the monarch that he give Madame the apartment.[9] Obviously, she hoped to benefit from the arrangement. It was her way of showing the King that she didn't resent his family and she might also have thought that she would win the good graces of the Princess, who still called her "maman-putain."

After the Lent sermon preached by Father Dumas, in which he alluded to David and Bathsheba and "brazenly inveighed against the King's love affairs," the life of the monarch and the Marquise resumed its customary routine, punctuated by the usual small trips and distractions. The King never parted from his favorite. Throughout the entire winter, he was seen at Versailles only on Sundays.[10] On August 2, while he was resting at Compiègne, he received a letter from the Dauphine at Versailles informing him that the Dauphin had been taken ill with a violent fever. Louis XV dashed off at six in the morning to join his son.

The Prince had suddenly felt sick after eating a large quantity of pastries and taking a walk in the bright sunlight along one of the ornamental lakes of Versailles, "la pièce d'eau des Suisses." At first, it was thought that Louis-Ferdinand was suffering from one of his chronic bouts of indigestion. But then the physicians diagnosed smallpox, the illness most feared at that time. The greatest specialists, the physicians Ponce and Dumoulin, had rushed to the Prince's bedside and decided to bleed him. For fear of contagion, the sovereign was not allowed to get near his son. The Dauphin was told that his father could not come because he had sprained his knee. On the other hand, defying all restrictions, the Queen did go to see him and the Dauphine never left his side. Though she had never had the dreadful disease, the Dauphine kissed her husband constantly and acted as his nurse. She convinced him that he had the measles and a special issue of the *Gazette de France* was printed for him reporting this.

For three days, everyone feared the worst. Semiconscious, the Prince was delirious, sang and wanted to confess even though he had just received absolution. The King and the royal family were in dreadful anguish. It was impossible not to worry about the future of the dynasty. If the Dauphin were to die, the only person left to assure the survival of the family line was the little Duc de Bourgogne, who was not even a year old! While the King could still have children, the Queen was too old for childbearing. The Orléans branch of the royal family would surely try to assert their claim to the throne, and it was not implausible that the descendants of Philip V of Spain, who had never accepted the partitioning of Utrecht, would do the same. In other words, one foresaw a long succession of conflicts. The physicians decided to risk all. In spite of the patient's high fever, they proceeded to bleed him again, and administered an emetic and enemas. The smallpox "was driven out." On August 8, he began to suppurate, which was a reassuring symptom. Hopes were raised. By August 14, the Dauphin was out of danger.

On the day before, with respectable hypocrisy, Madame de Pompadour confessed to the Duc de Croÿ how worried she had been for the Dauphin. She had no tender feelings for this prince who loathed her, but she would surely have been repudiated if he had died. For had such a misfortune struck Louis XV right after his daughter Henriette's death, he would surely have interpreted the successive bereavements as the expression of divine wrath. Undoubtedly he would have decided to atone for his dissolute private life and tried to behave like a responsible family man, at least for a while. Madame de Pompadour would have borne the brunt of his resolution. For the present, her situation had not changed at all. "I thought the Marquise held her own very well," assured the Duc de Croÿ. "However, I think the King was bound to her primarily by habit. People constantly tried to amuse him and distract him."[11] Indeed, the Dauphin's recovery became the occasion for a number of celebrations—at the Prince de Soubise's, the Duc de La Vallière's, the Duc d'Ayen's and the Duc d'Orléans's. The Marquise was always by the King's side. She threw a large reception at Bellevue that ended with fireworks.

She still benefited from the same favor. However, in spite of her being more on her guard than ever before, she had no idea that Madame d'Estrades and the Minister of War had concocted a plan against her that could seriously threaten her position. "A great crisis and great changes are expected at Fontainebleau . . . people are convinced that the Marquise will be dismissed,"[12] wrote d'Argenson, on September 21, 1752. Everyone knew that the King liked pretty women and readily succumbed to their charms. For over a year, he had noticed the young Comtesse de Choiseul-Beaupré, a beauty who was anything but shy. Dufort de Cheverny compared her to the young Fontanges, who had been loved by Louis XIV, but the future minister Comte de Choiseul-Stainville thought she "looked like a kept woman who had great familiarity with society."

She was the Comtesse d'Estrades's niece and the Marquise's distant relative, and thanks to her she had made an advantageous marriage to a disgraced offspring from the illustrious Choiseul family.[13] The wedding had been celebrated at Bellevue, on April 25, 1751, and the young couple went to live at Madame d'Estrades's, just when she became the mistress of the Minister of War. Thanks to the Marquise, the Comte and Comtesse de Choiseul-Beaupré entered into the sovereign's intimate circle. A military man who lacked both intelligence and fortune, the Comte de Choiseul-Beaupré obtained the envied position of *menin*, or nobleman, to the Dauphin while his wife was given the position of supernumerary Lady-in-Waiting to the princesses. These titles made people talk. It was proof, once again, that the favorite's mediation was something that no one could oppose. However, Louis XV had needed no coaxing: he had a great fondness for Madame de Choiseul. D'Argenson sniggered at the thought that the Marquise "might be fooled despite her knowledge in the art of ruling over the monarch."[14]

The Choiseul-Beaupré couple were now included in all the revelries, trips and suppers. The Comte, who was considered "stupid" by everyone, was promoted to Inspector of the Infantry. This was when the courtiers understood the Comtesse d'Estrades's scheming. "She's acting as procuress so the Marquise de Pompadour will be sent packing, while the Marquise would like to send her packing, and some of our ministers are involved because they want to free the State from this ambitious leech [i.e., Pompadour],"[15] prophesied d'Argenson.

Now the center of attention of Versailles, Madame de Choiseul-Beaupré acted the paragon of virtue. She said repeatedly that she would never be unfaithful to her husband and that she wasn't interested in any of the young men at Court. But this pseudo ingenue postured and claimed that she would not be able to resist the King. This was a common refrain. According to some, she had already yielded to the monarch. In order to throw people off, she flirted provocatively with the Dauphin, who was not impervious to her advances. Devout as he was, he had no compunctions about cuckolding a wife whose behavior was exemplary.

Her affair with the King (or its beginnings) worried the Marquise. But the trust the King showed her, the fact that he assigned her the place of honor next to him and his attentiveness calmed her in her moments of doubt. The young Choiseul-Beaupré was merely a dalliance that had to be tolerated. In early 1752, Count Kaunitz, a shrewd observer of the French Court, alluded to the King's infatuation for this tender young creature (she was under twenty). He said, "A new passion might have frightened the Marquise, but the feelings the King had for her were based on friendship and trust and these were made even more solid."[16]

Madame Henriette's death, the period of grief that followed and the Dauphin's illness seemed to have subdued the King. But since he did not indulge in religious devotions, it was reasonable to assume that he would feel the need for new pleasures. Madame d'Estrades saw this as the opportune moment to attain her goal. She lectured the young Choiseul girl at length. At Fontainebleau the young woman was to ask the monarch to make her his "official mistress" and demand the dismissal of Madame de Pompadour. D'Argenson and Madame d'Estrades worked out the scenario, and Madame de Choiseul performed the first act to perfection. Thanks to Richelieu, who played the part of the go-between, a correspondence began between the beauty and the sovereign.

A tryst was arranged. Everyone's fate depended on Madame de Choiseul's talent—Madame d'Estrades's, the Comte d'Argenson's and, of course, Madame de Pompadour's. The minister and his accomplice anxiously awaited the return of their protégé. Doctor Quesnay and Dubois, d'Argenson's secretary, witnessed the scene.

"After a rather long wait, Madame de Choiseul arrived, tousled and untidy, a sign of her triumph. Madame d'Estrades ran up to her, with open arms, and asked her if it has taken place. 'Yes, it has,' she replied, 'I'm loved; he's happy. She'll be dismissed; he gave me his word.' This news provoked an explosion of joy. Quesnay was the only person not to be excited. 'Doctor,' said d'Argenson, 'nothing will change for you, and we hope you'll remain with us.' Quesnay rose and said coldly, 'Monsieur le Comte, I was attached to Madame de Pompadour in her prosperity, I will remain so in her disgrace.' He left the room immediately, but no one distrusted him. 'I know him,' said Madame d'Estrades, 'he's not the kind of person to betray us.'"[17]

Though the King said nothing to her, the Marquise soon learned of the misfortune that was threatening her. In tears, she confided her misfortune to the Marquis de Gontaut, one of the first confidants of her love affair with Louis XV. Nothing could have distressed this nobleman more, for as ill luck would have it, he himself was at the origin of this misfortune. A year earlier, he had been so eloquent in pleading Choiseul-Beaupré's cause to Madame de Pompadour that she had taken it into her head to marry him off. And she had personally chosen the young woman who was now demanding her dismissal! Gontaut left his unfortunate friend in a state of despair. He blamed himself for being the unwitting cause of her downfall and, seeking a way to rescue her, recounted the story to his brother-in-law, Choiseul-Stainville.

Cynical, witty, dangerously intelligent and the darling of all the women—though his ugly looks might well have made his wit go unnoticed—the future minister listened with a knowing smile. He already knew the whole story from salon gossip and from the betrayed husband who had come to him to vent his rage. Choiseul-Stainville had nothing but contempt for this boastful dolt, who bragged that he would set fire to the Château de Fontainebleau but was actually so spineless that he would go along with anything that would serve his interests. Contrary to what he claims in his *Mémoires*, Choiseul was not concerned with saving the honor of his family when he advised his cousin to take the Countess, who was in the early stages of pregnancy, away from the Court. He knew that the young Madame de Choiseul-Beaupré would not be able to supplant the Marquise for very long. This young couple with no future therefore had to be banished as quickly as possible, and the power of a woman who had ruled over the monarch for seven years strengthened. Choiseul didn't know Madame de Pompadour very well and their relations were rather cold. The favorite was wary of his caustic wit, while he was hurt at being spurned and had neither admiration nor sympathy for her. Yet he understood that she had to be helped if he wanted to benefit from a course of action that would cost him nothing. For the Marquise was not reputed to be ungrateful.

Choiseul assured Gontaut that he knew how to allay the Marquise's fears. And on his brother-in-law's urgings, they went together to see the favorite, who was still weeping. "Moved by her tears, I could no longer contain myself," says Choiseul. "I told her that I knew that Madame de Choiseul would be leaving Fontainebleau in two days and wouldn't be returning to Court until after her confinement."[18] He did even more. By a ruse he succeeded in getting Madame de Choiseul-Beaupré to give him the letters she had received from the King and he gave them to the Marquise. We know nothing of what went on between Madame de Pompadour and the King. But she came out of it victorious and more powerful than ever. Louis XV made her a duchess. Her rival had been permanently ousted.[19]

Fifteen

A DUCHESS HIGH AND LOW

On October 17, 1752, Madame de Pompadour, presented by the Princesse de Conti, took her duchess's stool in the King's chamber.[1] No feelings were aroused "in this country" by the new presentation. None, at any rate, compared to those aroused by the lovely Madame d'Etiolles seven years earlier. The King was confirming as official the prerogatives of "a necessary friend,"[2] a friend who was now thoroughly familiar with all the customs of the Court. The distinction brought very little joy to either Louis XV or Jeanne-Antoinette. It was merely a "reconciliation gift"[3] in a love affair where passion had died out. A platonic love, which would have suited Madame de Pompadour, was not something she could hope to share with the sovereign. He was too sensual, too capricious, too avid for new sensations and not sentimental enough to be satisfied with that kind of love. But the dream of the little Poisson girl, "fit for a king," would not die out. It would live on, under new guises; it was up to her to invent them. She would remain the mistress, even if she no longer reigned over the senses of the man she loved. She wanted to keep him under her domination, a domination made of tenderness, sincerity and gaiety, but founded on an inflexible authority. The King yielded to her as he might to an excessively loving mother. This somewhat timorous submission is the only way to explain Louis XV's disgrace of the Comtesse de Choiseul-Beaupré, to whom he had promised that he would be dismissing the Marquise.

At thirty-one, Madame de Pompadour played a novel role in the French Court. As a second queen, she continued to usurp the part of the legitimate Queen, while being excluded, like the latter, from the pleasures of the royal bed. She accorded her true love only passing, carnal affairs. She thus encouraged him on the road to dissoluteness, while depriving him of the pleasures of the chase. Procurers were in charge of recruiting young female bed companions. She knew that the King hardly ever behaved like a conqueror. Narcissistic, sadly enamored of himself, he was convinced that all women would yield to him without his having to pursue them. Bachelier and Lebel, his valets, scoured Paris to find young beauties who could revive his languid senses. The King didn't have the insatiable sexual needs long attributed to him by legend. A melancholic man, whose sexual desire was easily blunted, he needed to be perpetually astonished, excited, intoxicated. His desperate pursuit of pleasure could lead to fiascoes. There was a well-known incident involving a *Fermier général*'s attractive wife who had offered herself to him. After having fondled her for a quarter of an hour "with such free and cavalier manners that she was astounded," he whispered to her: "Madame, you must excuse me. I'm no longer young. I'm sure you deserve all the attentions of a gallant man; but the truth is, the King is no manlier than any other, in spite of the best intentions and great desire. It's three o'clock; if you wait till dawn, you might run into an indiscreet person. The shortest follies are the best; I'll never forget your kindness. Get dressed and I'll walk you to the mirrored door of the hall."[4] Such disappointments were unimportant with very young women. The less experience they had, the more they reassured the King about his virile talents. And with virgins he didn't have to fear for his health. Madame de Pompadour was convinced that she could not be dethroned by these girls and that they presented no danger for her.

The King thus became accustomed to erotic trysts in Lebel's bedroom, which they called the *trébuchet* (bird trap) because young girls were taken there. It was there that in late March 1753 he first beheld a masterpiece of nature whom he had wanted to meet after having admired her on a miniature. She had a fiery gaze, a small, innocent-looking rosy face and an uninhibited, voluptuous body. The young Murphy (or

O'Murphy), nicknamed "Morphise," was under fourteen and a virgin. Her mother, who sold clothes and trinkets, peddled the virginity of her daughters as soon as they became nubile. The eldest lived with a Monsieur Melon, professional gambler; the second made beads for costume jewelry; and two others were members of the Opera, seraglio of all sensual delights. The youngest one, who was being offered to Louis XV, had just had her first communion. She worked for a seamstress-madam and posed for painters in the nude.[5] When he first met her, Louis XV asked her if she had already seen him. "Yes, on the six-franc écu," she replied with a laugh. The King arranged to give her mother ten thousand livres and appointed himself master of the damsel. He soon moved her into a bourgeois house in Versailles with a governess. This comfortable, discreet residence in the neighborhood called the Parc-aux-Cerfs[6] is mentioned by both the lawyer Barbier and the Marquis d'Argenson.[7] The monarch used to seclude himself there for hours. Only his valets knew where to find him. The Marquise was perfectly aware of these escapades—people even suspected her of being Lebel and Bachelier's accomplice. She was convinced that if he were exhausted by Morphise the King would no longer look at the ladies of the Court and that he would always come to her to enjoy the pleasures of friendship and calm the torments of his anxious mind. However, Louis XV's strong sexual passion for Morphise made it seem as if he were neglecting his great friend. Even the papal nuncio recounted the jealous scenes that the Marquise reportedly made to the King. D'Argenson promptly proclaimed that the hour of her demise was at hand. Contemptuous of the endless Court gossip, the Prince de Croÿ prudently noted: "All of this is probably not very reliable, the truth in such matters is not easily known."[8]

When he went to see the Marquise at her toilette, he found she had "more influence than ever and was still extremely pretty."[9] She still expressed herself with the same commanding grace and often used the royal *we*. "There will be many Tuesdays when the King will not be able to see you, Messieurs, for I hardly think you will come looking for us at Crécy,"[10] she had recently said to the ambassadors. She ordered the ministers not to have long conversations about serious matters with the monarch: distressing news was too devastating to His Majesty; it affected his bilious humor. The sovereign, who "abhorred work" and distrusted his ministers, looked very unwell at the time. He laid down his burdensome problems at his favorite's feet. She would listen without interrupting him and never seemed weary of hearing him repeat the same things.[11] While he went hunting—for she had long stopped going with him—she educated herself in politics. She had read the Marquis de Torcy's[12] manuscript attentively and could discuss the consequences of the Utrecht peace treaty. Indoctrinated, probably by Machault, who wanted to reform the fiscal system, she spoke to the King about his people's hardships.

Madame de Pompadour had added the ducal drapery lined with ermine to her coat of arms and the velvet calotte to her coach. Granddaughter of an obscure Burgundian weaver, daughter of a questionable financier, her ascension seemed unbelievable, but she had asserted her power with such force that it no longer astonished anyone. Having arrived at the highest rung of a complex, extremely hierarchical society, Jeanne-Antoinette was bent upon a brilliant marriage for her daughter Alexandrine. The child would be a strange match for anyone. By birth she belonged to the world of finance, but being brought up by the King's favorite she could aspire to an enviable alliance. The Marquise-Duchesse's ambitions knew no bounds, so great was her need to be recognized and highly regarded. Her background adhered to her in spite of the aura of glory she had now had. Her daughter's marriage, which she regarded as a personal apotheosis, would make her a permanent part of the nobility. Matches at Court were often concluded between families when the future spouses had just barely reached the age of reason. The young couple's personal qualities were irrelevant. These were alliances between two families and two fortunes; nothing else mattered.

With her romantic streak, Jeanne-Antoinette thought of marrying her daughter to the Marquis du Luc,[13] Louis XV's son with Madame de Vintimille, who had died shortly after giving birth to him.[14] The child had been legally recognized and brought up by the betrayed husband, but his resemblance to the King was so striking that he had been nicknamed the "*demi-Louis*." Madame de Pompadour arranged to have him come to Bellevue with his tutor one day and acted as though she were accidentally running into them in the garden. She asked his name and admired his good looks. With perfect timing, like in a stage play, Alexandrine showed up just then, and the Marquise led the two children into a copse of fig trees where she waited for the King. Louis XV wanted to know the child's name and seemed embarrassed when told. "They would make a beautiful couple," said the favorite. "The King played with the demoiselle, and seemed not to pay attention to the boy, whose bearing and gestures as he ate figs and brioches so resembled those of the King that Madame was truly astonished," according to Madame du Hausset, Lady of the Bedchamber. "'Ah!' she said, 'Sire, look . . .' 'What?' he said. 'Nothing,' said Madame, 'except that he's just like his father. . . .' 'I had no idea,' said the King, with a smile, 'that you know the Comte de Luc so well.' 'You should kiss him as he's very handsome.' 'I'll start with the demoiselle,' said the King, and he kissed them very coldly with a constrained look." This detached attitude struck Madame du Hausset. "'That's the way he is,' said Madame de Pompadour with a sigh. 'But don't the two children look like they were made for each other? Louis XIV would have made the child into a Duc du Maine. I don't ask for as much. Just giving his son a position and a royal warrant as duke. But because he's his son I prefer him to all the little dukes at Court. My grandchildren would resemble their grandfather and grandmother and this combination, which I hope to see, would make my happiness one day.'"[15]

The Marquise abandoned her fantasy very soon, for it was doubtful that the King would give his consent. She therefore had to choose one of the "little dukes" at Court. To everyone's surprise, she set her heart on the Duc de Fronsac, son of the Maréchal de Richelieu. It was a surprising blunder for a woman of such discernment. Did she want to test the limits of her power, or challenge a nobleman who had always shown contempt for her? We cannot say. Her audacity, however, did not provoke the gibes that might have been expected, for she asked Louis XV himself to make the proposal.[16] Richelieu responded with remarkable presence of mind: since his son's mother belonged to the House of Lorraine,[17] he was under the obligation of asking the

Emperor's permission before marrying him off. Madame de Pompadour did not pursue the matter. But since she wanted to avoid another disappointment, she showed less haste and drew closer to the Duchesse de Chaulnes.[18] After several months of discreet negotiations, in August 1752, an agreement was reached for Alexandrine's marriage to the young Duc de Picquigny.[19] Alexandrine was eight years old and the duke, eleven. They were to be united two years later. Immediately after the ceremony, the young bride was to return to the convent and her husband was to complete his education with his tutor until they were both old enough to live as a married couple.

The Marquise had no concern for her daughter's happiness. "I find she's getting much uglier," she said; "as long as she's not shocking-looking, I shall be satisfied, for I'm far from wishing her an exceptional face. It only turns the entire female sex against you."[20] The only thing that mattered was the rank Alexandrine enabled her to have at Court and its countless ensuing advantages. This union and her own elevation to the title of Duchesse strengthened Madame de Pompadour's position "in this country," for till then she had always been dependent on the King's whim.

Madame de Pompadour maintained the relationship she wanted to have with the monarch, even if Morphise took up much of his time. She kept informed of everything that concerned France. She already pictured herself Prime Minister without the title. Indeed, most contemporaries credited her with considerable political influence. This became apparent during the parliament's exile from Paris, in May 1753.

The Parlement de Paris and the provincial parliaments had always made it a point of pride to fight against the royal authority. Louis XIV had crushed their pretensions by almost completely eliminating their governmental functions. However, ever since the Regent had needed them to annul the late King's last will, they had reasserted their power. The parliaments were courts of justice and they were in charge of registering royal edicts, but they wanted to establish themselves as representatives of the nation. The members of parliament, who purchased their positions and were in a sense nominated by the entire body of magistrates before sitting among them, constituted a homogeneous social group. Family ties uniting almost all of them for generations reinforced their strength and cohesion. Concerned with preserving their acquired privileges, they had developed a critical attitude. The magistrates criticized the monarchy's administration and denounced the very principle of royal absolutism—usually in its financial policies. This had recently been the case for Machault's *vingtième*. The King had had to hold a *lit de justice*, a special session of the Parlement, and order the registration of this tax in person. Now the Jansenist crisis was exacerbating tensions between the King and his parliaments.

The quarrel between the Jansenists and the Molinists,[21] which had seemed to have died down, was rekindled under the pressure of a number of prelates who wanted the rigorous application of the principles of the papal bull, *Unigenitus*.[22] In the hope of achieving this end, several bishops, starting with Monseigneur de Beaumont, Archbishop of Paris, forbade the clergy from administering the sacraments to anyone who could not show a certificate of confession signed by a *constitutionnaire* priest, in other words, a priest supporting the principles of the bull. The fact that several people had been refused the sacraments caused great agitation in Paris, and the victims brought the matter before the Parlement, whose members were often favorable to the Jansenists. After a series of remonstrances, on April 17, 1752, the parliament finally obtained recognition by the King of the judges' right to intervene in religious affairs. The magistrates wanted to take advantage of this unquestionable political victory immediately. On the very next day, they promulgated a ruling prohibiting priests from refusing the sacraments just because a person was unable to show the required certificate of confession. This caused so much commotion that the King's Council annulled the ruling the following November 21. Furious at being dispossessed of its rights, the parliament presented remonstrances to the King and denounced the Church's control over the monarchy.[23]

The issue was becoming dangerously political. At Court the royal family, loyal to its Jesuit confessors, sided with the Molinist clergy. Up to then, Louis XV had tried to moderate the excesses of both the Molinists and the Jansenists. But this time, the parliament was going too far. The King vented his displeasure at Madame de Pompadour's, in the presence of Madame du Hausset. "One day," she writes, "the master arrived all fired up. 'What's wrong?' said Madame. 'The big robes[24] and the clergy are perpetually at daggers drawn; I'm upset by their quarrels. But I hate the big robes much more. Deep down, my clergy is attached to me and loyal; the others would like to put me under their tutelage.' 'Firmness alone can silence them,' said Madame. 'Robert de Saint-Vincent[25] is a firebrand whom I wish I could banish; but that would create a dreadful uproar. On the other hand, the archbishop[26] is a quarrelsome diehard. Fortunately there a few people in parliament whom I can count on; they act very tough but they soften when the time comes. It costs me a few abbeys, a few secret pensions. There's a certain V . . . who is useful to me, though he acts fanatical.' 'I know about him, Sire,' said Madame. 'He wrote to me yesterday, claiming to be my relative and asking me for a rendezvous.' 'Well!' said the master. 'See him, let him come; this will be an excuse for granting him something if he behaves.'[27] At that moment, Monsieur de Gontaut arrived. The King was pacing restlessly; then suddenly he said: 'The Regent was very wrong to give them back the right to make remonstrances; eventually they'll cause the State's downfall.' 'Oh, Sire,' said Monsieur de Gontaut, 'you're too strong to be weakened by little lawyers.' 'You have no idea what they're up to and how they think,' said the King. 'They're an assembly of republicans. That's enough. Things as they are will last as long as me. You can chat about it, Madame, on Sunday with Monsieur Berryer.'"[28]

Louis XV was completely free in expressing his thoughts in front of Madame de Pompadour. She did not approve of Monseigneur de Beaumont's intransigence, nor did she support the parliamentary pretensions that threatened the King's power. She came down against the magistrates and encouraged the monarch to stand firm. Louis XV decided to clamp down and sentenced the members of parliament to exile. "Do whatever you want, but I want to be obeyed,"[29] he said to his ministers at the end of a Council meeting.

He was dining at Bellevue at his favorite's when he was told that the gentlemen had been escorted *manu militari* to different cities in the kingdom.[30] Leaning toward the Marquise, he whispered the news to her and she applauded it immediately. That evening the King was in a charming mood; he supped gaily, even whistled and sang, a sign of exceptional exhilaration in his case. He didn't care that people had shouted *Vive le parlement*. He had made a show of authority.

Far from being threatened, the favorite still had a dominant position at Court. The firmness she encouraged in the King with regard to the magistrates earned her the gratitude of the royal family and they began to treat her with greater consideration. The Duc de Croÿ was pleasantly surprised to learn, during a stay at La Muette, that the Queen, the Dauphin, the Dauphine and the princesses took part in all the festivities organized by the Marquise. The King seemed very relaxed, but "spoke only to people whom he found amusing."[31] When Jeanne-Antoinette fell ill with one of her dreadful migraines and retired to her quarters, the monarch's children were seen, one by one, inquiring after her. "It was very pleasant to pay court in these circumstances; we were very much at ease,"[32] adds the memoirist. During these trips, Louis XV was always by the Marquise's side, he spoke less of hunting, never discussed politics and gambled for high stakes. Madame de Pompadour continued to reign. Not just "important matters, but even details, were cleared with her," adds the Duc de Croÿ. "I saw . . . how skillfully she behaved with the corps of first duchesses; she was polite with them when she took her seat at the formal dinner, in the presence of the Queen and all the children of France; but they all treated her with consideration and she behaved well."[33]

Sixteen

PATRONESS OF THE ARTS

All-powerful at Versailles, Madame de Pompadour was nostalgic for Paris. She wanted to walk around the city incognito, shop in luxury stores like all the grand ladies of her day, and visit Alexandrine at the convent of the Assomption. She was no longer content with the apartment the King had made available to her at the Hôtel des Ambassadeurs. She wanted to have her own residence in the capital. The opportunity arose when the heirs of Henri-Louis de La Tour d'Auvergne wished to sell a mansion that was very well located on the Faubourg Saint-Honoré. The Marquise purchased it on December 24, 1753, for 730,000 livres. The mansion (which is today the Elysée palace, the residence of the French president) was built in 1718 by the architect Molet for the Comte d'Evreux; it included two stories and a mansard roof. On the north side, it faced a courtyard flanked by two protruding buildings ending in pavilions; on the south side, it looked out onto a large garden that extended to the Champs-Elysées. Only the ground floor, made up of two apartments, one large and the other small, could be lived in. The first floor could only be reached through a back stairway.

The Marquise immediately hired Lassurance for extensive renovation work. The large apartment was completely redecorated with paneling by Verberckt, fireplaces by Trouard, paintings by Boucher and Van Loo and a huge Gobelin tapestry in the large drawing room. The small apartment was converted into an antechamber, a dining room, a bathroom and several wardrobes.[1] These rooms were now ready to be furnished. Lassurance made very few changes to the outside of the building. He built a parapet along the mansard roof in order to give the illusion of height to the somewhat austere facade. Since the Marquise required an open perspective on the gardens, the trees on the Champs-Elysées between her mansion and the Cours-la-Reine were cut down, which infuriated the Parisians, who liked to cool off in the leafy shade. Everyone talked about the "palace of the queen of courtesans."

Ever since she had been living at Court, the favorite had been encouraging creativity in all its forms. As the official mistress, she commissioned quantities of works for her many residences and even, occasionally, for royal dwellings, and she reigned over the artists and artisans of the kingdom. She never refused to meet those who were introduced to her as young talents. She was also presented with jewelry, watches, engraved gems, pieces of silverware and gold work, sculptures and so on. She admired objects made with very different techniques and in very different styles, and had the wisdom not to impose her taste on the creators. She always left them free to express their talents as they wished, thereby stimulating their genius. She cared about details and demanded perfection, which helped the craft industries in Paris and the art of Versailles reach their apogee. Like the King, she purchased things from the art dealer Lazare Duvaux, whose shop, Au Chagrin de Turquie, was on the rue Saint-Honoré. Duvaux traded with the Far East and dealt with the best cabinetmakers, silversmiths and bronzesmiths. The most valuable and unusual objects could be found in his store. Not only did he supply Louis XV, the Marquise, the princes and the *Fermiers généraux*, but foreign sovereigns as well. The journal book he left affords an interesting survey of the taste of his time.

Madame de Pompadour liked furniture, fabric, bronzes, paintings, sculptures and china for the immediate, sensual pleasures she derived from them. She didn't hesitate to mix objects from different periods and civilizations—as is clear from her infatuation with lacquer and porcelains from China. When she was very young, she had frequented the French artistic elite at Le Normant de Tournehem's, and her tastes had grown even more discriminating since then. Boucher, who had introduced her to painting, greatly contributed in developing her innate sense of what is today called interior design.

As the mistress of a monarch who enjoyed the pleasures of intimacy, she had succeeded in creating an atmosphere of refined luxury in all her residences—environments expressing a princely art of living and differing completely from the previous century's conceptions of royal art. It has sometimes been said, with a touch of contempt, that she contributed to the birth of an excessively mannered *Pompadour art*. In fact, the Marquise understood that she was living in a period of artistic change. She liked the elaborate shapes of the *rocaille* style, with its curves, seashells and abundant flowers; this is apparent in the wood paneling, the framing of the tapestries, the marquetry, the bronzes and the porcelains. Her favorite cabinetmakers, Pierre de Migeon and Oeben, are among the most prestigious representatives of this school. (Oeben made Louis XV's celebrated cylinder desk at Versailles, now considered a masterpiece of French furniture.) With his erotic charm, Boucher— very unjustly lambasted by Diderot in his "Salons"—also expresses the aristocratic style of life of the first half of the century. The Marquise's predilection for the *rocaille* style did not prevent her from ardently supporting Soufflot, Gabriel and Cochin, who were outspoken opponents of this aesthetic. She protected David's precursor, Vien, and approved of the Comte de Caylus's archaeological theories. She convinced Louis XV to accept Soufflot's plans for the construction of the church of Sainte-Geneviève, known today as the Panthéon. The architect's aim was "to combine the lightness of construction of gothic buildings with the purity and magnificence of Greek architecture."[2]

Spurred by her love for Louis XV and the glory she dreamed of for him, Madame de Pompadour sought a renewal of royal art, regarded as too solemn and outdated since Louis XIV's death. Grandiose artistic conceptions, like those imposed by the Sun King, were rejected, as they no longer corresponded to the preoccupations of the period. New means of expression had to be found to exalt the sovereign's grandeur. A debate had started on the role of art in society: it seemed right for art to be put in the service of the nation. The founding of the Ecole Militaire, a project inspired and desired by the Marquise, fulfilled that requirement.[3] The point of view of the Enlightenment bourgeoisie was never better expressed than by Pâris-Duverney in a letter to Gabriel: "The point is not so much to build an edifice to the King's glory as to create one that is useful to the State and conforms to our ideas for educating the five hundred young people for whom the building is intended. There should be no wavering between the beautiful and the useful when the two cannot be combined."

In the Department of Buildings, Le Normant de Tournehem adopted the same work philosophy. Concerned that the French should have an idea of what would later be called their national heritage, he asked Bernard Lépicié to draw up a detailed catalogue of the King's paintings. On September 14, 1750, a free, permanent exhibit of the royal collections opened at the Palais du Luxembourg; it included a great many canvases that had been forgotten in storage and were just barely saved. Tournehem reformed the stagnating Royal Academy of Painting and Sculpture and oversaw its teaching activities, insisting that students be required to have a perfect command of drawing, perspective and anatomy. As a creative impetus, he appointed a jury of specialists, with himself as president. They selected the works that would be shown every year in a salon and be exposed to the criticism of the public and specialists. Tournehem was very eager for the French school of painting to be seen again as an heir to antiquity and the Italian masters. As Buildings director, he wanted to add to the beauty of Paris, as did the King and the Marquise. When, after the peace treaty of Aix-la-Chapelle, the tradesman from the Six Corporations[4] decided to build a monument to the monarch's glory, he organized a competition for the design of the future Place Louis XV (today the Place de la Concorde). More than a hundred architects took part in the competition. The King chose Gabriel's plans. Tournehem died in 1751, so it was his successor, Madame de Pompadour's brother, now Marquis de Marigny, who presided over its realization.

The Marquise had long lamented the fact that France didn't have a porcelain factory and had to buy its porcelains from Meissen, the famous factory in Saxony that flooded Europe with its objects. On Machault's advice, she encouraged the Vincennes factory to develop processes capable of rivaling the Germans'. Their main production was sculptured flowers. Over time they succeeded in making decorative pieces representing mythological or pastoral scenes that achieved a degree of commercial success. The Marquise encouraged Lazare Duvaux to order important pieces from them. On his favorite's entreaties, Louis XV agreed to transfer this experimental workshop to Sèvres, near Bellevue. A number of painter-decorators, specializing in landscapes, birds, flowers or genre scenes, were then hired. They helped bring about changes in the style of the porcelains, but the participation of Boucher, and later of Falconet, both of whom supplied the artists with models, gave an exceptional quality to these new creations. At the same time, they worked on colors. In 1749, they had achieved a Chinese-like blue with a cloudy highlight, followed by a turquoise called "celestial blue." In 1753, they developed a "jonquil yellow." An apple green and a pink, called "Pompadour pink," appeared in 1756 and 1757. Madame de Pompadour bought the first table service created at Sèvres, with bouquets of flowers against a white background. Vases and trays soon made their appearance. On February 11, 1754, after an intimate supper, Louis XV unwrapped a blue, white and gold service in front of his guests. "It was one of the first masterpieces," says the Duc de Croÿ, "from that new porcelain factory that intended to surpass that of Saxony and bring it down. . . . The clay and the white seemed to me very beautiful and comes close to that of Japan."[5]

At the end of each year, the King made it a habit to exhibit the most beautiful Sèvres pieces in his apartments and the courtiers rushed to buy them. Designated as a royal factory in 1759, the firm soon became the leading porcelain factory in Europe. When the sovereign wanted to honor a foreign monarch, he would send him a Sèvres porcelain, an object of royal propaganda. Thus Empress Maria Theresa received a service with a motif of green ribbons, famous to this day, and the Elector Palatine, a service with a checkered pattern. Sèvres porcelain was considered as the most refined in Europe and orders poured in from everywhere.

Aware of the importance of her patronage, both directly and through the Buildings Department, Madame de Pompadour never refused to pose for the greatest artists of her time. In 1748, Nattier, who was very fond of mythological allegories, made her portrait as Diana. She probably found it too academic. It was Boucher, though his calling was not that of a portraitist, who painted her as she wished to appear. He multiplied the image of the "Idol" in every kind of costume and attitude. In 1750, she is the slender young mistress wearing a tight-fitting, moon-colored "Spanish-style" taffeta dress, with one hand skimming the keys of a harpsichord, and spread out at her feet a learned jumble of books, manuscripts, maps crushed by a globe; objects that were deliberately chosen to evoke the role she wished to play as patron of the arts, sciences and letters.[6] Oddly, it was when her beauty was beginning to fade, and she was no longer the King's lover, that Boucher painted the canvases that show her at her most radiantly seductive. The most famous one, of 1756, exhibited at the salon of 1757, shows her in the same décor as in 1750, except that the harpsichord has vanished. This time, the Marquise is half stretched out on a sofa, next to a writing case laden with papers. She is wearing a sumptuous green silk dress, dotted with mauve bows and flowers, and negligently holding a book, as though her reading had been interrupted. Her gaze, lost in reverie, is not that of a coquette but of a sensible woman, absorbed in thought.[7] Two years later, Boucher portrayed her sitting at her toilette, with an open neckline; thrown over her shoulders is a white muslin negligee tied with a pink ribbon, and on her wrist, a bracelet with a cameo of the King as clasp.[8] The academic style of this portrait is surprising in the Marquise's favorite painter. She surely preferred the one where she is seated among her books, in a shady copse, dressed in a simple high-necked dress trimmed with satin bows. She gave the most beautiful version of this painting as a gift to her dear Abbé de Bernis, whose works are among the books surrounding her, along with those of Voltaire.[9] Madame de Pompadour is shown with quite different features in 1759, in the Bellevue gardens under Pigalle's statue *L'Amour et l'Amitié*; she is with her favorite pug, a tiny lapdog, in awe before this sublimely elegant woman wearing a pale pink taffeta dress trimmed with lace and pearls.[10]

She willingly let herself be painted as Friendship by Pigalle, as Music by Falconet, Abundance by Adam, Diana by Tessart and Pomona by Lemoyne, but the capricious Quentin de La Tour had virtually to be begged to paint her portrait. The Marquise felt that he, better than anyone else, would give her the look of a woman patron, with no affectation. The negotiations conducted by the Marquis de Vandières dragged out for months. The artist, who was probably very tired, was reluctant to paint the favorite. When his terms (which were, by the way, exorbitant) were accepted, he made himself comfortable with his illustrious model and asked her if he could work in comfortable—i.e., slovenly—attire in her presence.

The pastel, which aspired to the status of a great historical portrait, was exhibited in the salon of 1755 without receiving the expected acclaim. The reflection on the glass did not show it to advantage, and the public preferred to sigh over the posthumous portrait of Madame Henriette. Yet the Quentin de La Tour let the viewer admire an extremely elegant grand lady, wearing a formal court dress with a leafy blue-and-gold pattern, apparently taken by surprise while consulting a score—and before having completed her toilette, since she has not had time to put on jewelry. She has a lively, cheerful gaze, and her lips seem ready to speak but not of frivolous matters. Her mind is taken with the books that are lying on the table—Buffon's *Natural History*, Montesquieu's *Spirit of the Laws*, Voltaire's *Henriade*, *Pastor Fido*,[11] a volume of the *Encyclopedia*, from which the plates illustrating the *Carpenter's Art* fall carelessly over a large portfolio bearing the Pompadour arms. Among these prestigious books is a more modest volume entitled *Pierres gravées* (engraved stones). This is a collection of Madame de Pompadour's own works. The Marquise enjoyed engraving in her spare time. She had a lathe at Versailles to engrave fine stones as well as a printing press. Under Guay's[12] supervision, she handled the burin quite well, usually choosing subjects that exalted her lover's glory or mythological scenes. She left sixty-three engravings; the originals are at the Bibliothèque de l'Arsenal. She also amused herself printing several pages of Corneille's *Rodogune*.

By then Jeanne-Antoinette had given up theater. She was too busy and too tired to learn new parts. Besides, the Bellevue performances had not had as much success as those at Versailles. Other diversions had to be found. The last theatrical season, in 1753, had ended on a splendid note with *Le Devin du village* (variously translated as The Village Diviner, Village Soothsayer or The Cunning-Man), by an author who was not well known at Court, Jean-Jacques Rousseau. He had written both the libretto and the music of this short opera, which had been given its first performance at Fontainebleau.[13] The Marquise had liked it so much that she had wanted it performed again at Bellevue. Rousseau, however, had refused to accept the invitation of the King, who—unbeknownst to him—had wanted to give him a pension. The idea of being performed by the favorite and her friends hardly struck him as a godsend: "As it will be performed at Court by noblemen and noblewomen, I expect it to be sung out of tune and mangled, so I won't go," he wrote to Madame de Warens. "Besides, since I didn't want to be presented to the King, I don't want to do anything that could make it seem like I'm looking for another opportunity."[14] Nevertheless, after the Bellevue performance, Louis XV, who had very much liked his work, had sent him a hundred louis and Madame de Pompadour, fifty. This earned her a convoluted compliment from the inveterate misanthrope.

Several months later, the King and his favorite would have refrained from performing Rousseau's *divertissement*. He was attracting attention for his strong stand in what was called the "war of the Bouffons" (Comedians), a strident polemic between the partisans of French opera and those of Italian opera. One group was faithful to the tradition of Lulli and praised the work of Rameau, whereas the other believed the traditional art was stiff, unnatural and outdated, a symbol of an absolutist regime. They wanted pathos and sensibility. The presence of a troupe of Italian comedians, Les Bouffons, performing Pergolese's *La Serva Padrona* (The Servant as Mistress), was dividing Paris into two camps. There was "the King's corner," the traditionalists who gathered near the sovereign's box, and the "Queen's corner," a group of innovative spirits that happen to cluster under the Queen's box—men such as Diderot, d'Alembert, d'Holbach, Grimm and Rousseau. In his *Letter on French Music*, published in November 1753, Rousseau treated French music as beneath contempt and attacked Rameau with a virulence that was very nearly insulting. It created a general outcry. Rameau, who was legitimately considered the greatest composer of his day, had his supporters. But since they all belonged to the antiphilosophical party, the *philosophes* felt obliged to support Rousseau. And so a technical quarrel, which should have concerned only specialists, immediately took on political overtones; it fed into the grievances of the traditionalists, who were opposed to the new philosophical spirit and the *philosophes'* great work, the *Encyclopedia*.

Had Madame de Pompadour remained Madame d'Etiolles, she would surely have espoused the cause of the *philosophes*, championed Italian opera and been an ardent supporter of the *Encyclopedia*. But her position with Louis XV put her in a predicament as far as her true tastes were concerned. Knowing the King's aversion for the "philosophical sect," she found herself obliged to champion the French school, and she commissioned an opera from Mondonville, who had to compose *Titon et l'Aurore* in great haste.

Defending the *Encyclopedia*, whose publication she had encouraged, was infinitely more perilous than taking sides in the war of the Bouffons. It will be recalled that the Marquise used to see Diderot and d'Alembert—who were not admitted at Versailles—at Doctor Quesnay's house. Their projected work, a compendium of all human knowledge, had immediately appealed to her. The first two volumes were published in 1752. But when Monseigneur Boyer warned the King of the work's suspicious tendencies, and told him that it tended to "destroy the royal authority, establish a spirit of independence and rebellion, and lay the foundations for error, skepticism and the corruption of morals and religion in obscure and dubious terms," Louis XV banned its publication. Malesherbes, director of all publications in the realm, saved the enterprise by keeping in his house all the unpublished manuscripts that were supposed to be seized and burned. It is likely that Madame de Pompadour knew about this. Diderot begged her for help. She answered firmly, leaving no doubt as to her loyalty to the King's policy, yet she was also quite clear about her contempt for the religious party. "I can do nothing in the affair of the *Dictionnaire encyclopédique*," she wrote him. "They say the book contains maxims that are contrary to religion and royal authority. If true, the book should be burned; if untrue, the slanderers should be burned. Unfortunately it is the clergy that's accusing you and they never want to be wrong. I don't know what to think of the whole thing, but I know what to do—and that is not meddle in any way. The priests are too dangerous.

"However, everyone has said good things to me about you. You are held in high esteem for your merit, and honored for your virtue. On the basis of these testimonies that are a tribute to you, I believe you're innocent and it would be a pleasure for me to oblige you in everything. The banning of the *Encyclopedia* is a settled matter based on the deposition of the *dévots*, who are not always just and truthful. If the book is not as they say it is, I can only pity you and maintain my loathing for hypocrisy and false zeal while I wait for you to give me the opportunity to be useful to you."[15] She secretly encouraged Diderot[16] and d'Alembert to continue their work, but advised them to be prudent on the subjects of religion and royal power. They answered her without mincing their words that writers could not accept self-censorship.[17] In select company, Madame de Pompadour openly praised the merits of the *Encyclopedia* to Louis XV, stressing its practical aspect. Weary of fighting, the King finally gave in and publication resumed, though he continued to harbor the same suspicions about the *encyclopédistes*. When Marmontel recommended d'Alembert to the Marquise for a pension, she replied: "He's a hothead. . . . He became passionate about Italian music and sided with the Bouffons."[18] Marmontel reminded her timidly that d'Alembert was first and foremost the author of the *Encyclopedia* preface. D'Alembert never received a pension. The favorite knew that Louis XV would have been unyielding on this score.

The Marquise tried discreetly to get her old friend Voltaire back into good graces, after she had seen Madame Denis who came to plead her uncle's cause. But the *philosophe*'s long stay with Frederick II made it hard to mollify the sovereign, who was already prejudiced against his former historiographer. Richelieu, too, tried to prevail upon Louis XV, but in vain. The Marquise continued to follow the great man's career, and the inclusion of *La Henriade* as one of the books on de La Tour's pastel shows that he remained one of her preferred authors. Montesquieu was luckier, but then he came to her with a more modest request. He solicited the Marquise's help in suppressing a book still in press, by *Fermier général* Dupin, that was a refutation of *The Spirit of the Laws*. Being a great admirer of Montesquieu's work, Madame de Pompadour promised to intervene and Dupin's little book was never published.

After her dear friend the Abbé de Bernis was appointed ambassador to Venice with her help, the Marquise only received two men of letters regularly in her home—Pinot Duclos and Marmontel. The latter, author of *Contes moraux* (moral tales) and, more interestingly, of very spicy memoirs, was considered her literary adviser. She encouraged him in his work and arranged for him to receive a sinecure at the Buildings Department under the directorship of her brother, the Marquis de Marigny. When Marmontel came to thank her, she said to him, not without haughtiness, "Mentally, men of letters have an egalitarian system that sometimes makes them ignore proprieties. I hope, Marmontel, that when it comes to my brother, you will never forget those proprieties."[19] Marmontel was quick to understand that this young man had to be treated tactfully because of his "pride, which made him anxious, easily offended, excessively sensitive. . . . He feared that he was not held in high enough esteem, and that people might be talking, maliciously and enviously, about his birth and fortune; his anxiety was so great that if, in his presence, someone whispered in someone else's ear, be became extremely alarmed."[20]

The Marquise loved literary works and was also a bibliophile. She read a great deal and remembered the essentials of what she read. This allowed her to speak with ease and without pedantry in all circumstances. She had already built up a library at Etiolles and she continued to add to it constantly, buying regularly from book dealers. She sometimes acquired entire libraries, such as Godart and Beauchamps's collection, specializing mostly in theatrical works. By the end of her life, she had collected over four thousand volumes, which were auctioned off individually.[21] The collection consisted primarily of literature and history, with editions from the seventeenth and eighteenth centuries. There were mainly novels and theatrical works, including the monumental edition of Pierre Corneille, illustrated by Gravelot. She had supported that publication project, which had been suggested by Voltaire in order to provide Corneille's descendant with a dowry.[22] Consistently refined in her tastes, the Marquise had commissioned bindings from Padeloup, Dubuisson, Douceur, Bisiaux and Derôme in red, blue, green and lemon Morocco leather; a few had checkered patterns, but most were very sober.

Seventeen

THE TEMPTATION
OF POLITICS

Though discreet, Louis XV's "love affairs" were upsetting and humiliating to the Marquise. Morphise was pregnant and her child was due very soon. Whereas Jeanne-Antoinette had dreamed of becoming pregnant and giving the King a child, it was instead this cobbler's daughter who was about to give birth. It was rumored at Versailles that the sovereign was going to recognize the illegitimate baby and "declare" the mother as his mistress. This made Madame de Pompadour anxious, though she didn't miss any opportunity to assert her power. No one questioned the influence she had over the sovereign, but her jealousy (for that was indeed what it was) could easily have driven her to make serious mistakes. When she discussed the affairs of the kingdom with the monarch, particularly the problems relating to the parliament, she had no compunctions in being acrimonious, contending that his subjects would hold him in contempt if he didn't show greater firmness with the magistrates. She was always intent on arousing his sense of sovereign grandeur, a quality he possessed to a high degree, but which was all too often numbed by his natural indolence. The King remained unpopular. On the pedestal of the Bouchardon statue that would later be erected on the Place Louis XV, someone had scrawled: "This resident of the woods has retired here, outside the city, and outside the hearts of his subjects."[1]

Father Laugier, who preached at the Court during Lent in 1754, didn't spare the sovereign at all. "Faced with having to do everything, he did nothing," he said. He upbraided the ministers, who "did everything and abused their power." He expressed pity for "a population that was forced into disobedience, for it was being asked to give what it no longer had, having already given away everything," and indignation that money could "flow in huge quantities for buildings and useless things."[2] No one discussed the sermon, nor did Louis XV make any comments. However, the Marquise was implicated only for her spending, not for imposing a dissolute life on the monarch. And there was no mention at all of Morphise.

The beautiful creature gave birth in May. It was claimed that Madame de Pompadour had volunteered to bring up the child. "Following the example of the illustrious Maintenon,"[3] said d'Argenson mockingly. Whether true or not, nothing came of it. The King did not recognize his love child and Morphise soon vanished from his life. Some people said that the Maréchale d'Estrées had contacted the young mistress—it is not known how—and had suggested that she ask the King to dismiss his old Marquise. It was speculated that Morphise had been naïve enough to do so and Louis XV had dismissed her. He married her off, with a handsome dowry, to a young, penniless nobleman, Jacques de Beaufranchet, an officer in the Beauvais regiment. He dreamed of a brilliant future, but was killed in 1757 in the battle of Rosbach.[4]

Louis XV's lack of interest in his illegitimate child calmed Madame de Pompadour. She was enjoying a peaceful stay at Bellevue when news came, on June 15, 1754, that her daughter Alexandrine had suddenly died at the convent of the Assomption. She had had an attack of convulsions and dreadful abdominal pains, and had passed away after four hours of suffering; the physicians had been unable to do anything to save her.[5] Alexandrine's father had been warned in time and had been present when she breathed her last. The Marquise was devastated. She lost consciousness and had to be bled. For two days she was thought to be on the verge of death. The King rushed to her side and stayed at Bellevue; he spent hours trying to comfort her, for her grief was unexpectedly violent for a woman who was accustomed to mastering her emotions. The Queen sent her a page to express her condolences. The ex–future Duchesse de Picquigny had already been laid to rest in the choir of the chapel of the Ladies of the Assomption, but her mother remained disconsolate.[5] Her grief was aggravated by the death of Monsieur Poisson ten days later. However, Madame de Pompadour had an indomitable spirit. She decided to live for the King—the choice she had made ever since she had started to share his life.

Overcoming her sorrow, she returned to her former ways at the Court. Alexandrine's death had occurred several days before the marriages of three girls in her family, unions instigated by her and which she had decided to celebrate at Bellevue. Everyone thought that the weddings would not take place; instead, the Marquise postponed the ceremony. Her two nieces, Mesdemoiselles de Baschi, were married to Monsieur de Lugeac and Monsieur d'Avaray; Mademoiselle de Chaumont-Quitry, a distant cousin, was married to Monsieur d'Amblimont. They were three little girls; the eldest was barely thirteen. Though she was too dispirited to accompany them to the parish of Versailles for the religious ceremony, she received the young couples and their families at Bellevue for a feast. That very evening the new brides returned to their convent, just as the unfortunate Alexandrine would have done had she lived another year.

By early July, Madame de Pompadour was dining again in the private apartments with the King and their circle of close friends. And, like every year at that time, she left for Compiègne. The Prince de Croÿ visited her during her toilette, where she was in the habit of receiving ambassadors and courtiers. "I saw the Marquise for the first time since the loss of her daughter, a dreadful blow that I thought had completely crushed her," he said. "But because too much pain might have harmed her appearance and possibly her position, I found her neither changed nor downcast, and by one of those Court miracles that are not unusual, I found her neither worse nor affecting a more serious air. However, she had been terribly shaken, and was in all likelihood just as unhappy inside as she seemed happy on the outside."[7] In the evening, he saw her bantering gaily with the King. However, her grief was still extremely intense. "For me happiness has died with my daughter," she used to say.

During the following months, the Marquise lived like an automaton. Often ill, she would isolate herself in her bedroom and think of leaving the Court; then she would suddenly summon the energy to appear, as in a dream, gracious and relaxed, before the King and the courtiers. As usual, she organized all the Fontainebleau entertainments. But she was often on the verge of exhaustion. "My nerves have been in a very bad way for ten days. I feel better right now. . . . The head has too much authority over the body and produces dire effects,"[8] she wrote to Richelieu on December 12, 1754.

Her love for Louis XV and her concern for his glory are what kept her alive. She therefore continued to follow the affairs of the kingdom with great attention and they were very alarming. The parliamentary rebellion tied to the religious quarrels was still a major preoccupation. On August 20, 1754, after extended negotiations conducted by the Prince de Conti, the King finally called back the exiled parliament members. They returned on September 4, to cheers from the populace. That same day, the magistrates registered a somewhat sibylline royal declaration. It imposed "silence" on both parties "with regard to matters that had been the object of the latest divisions"—i.e., the proofs of confession—and enjoined parliament "to take action against the offenders, in conformity with the ruling." These men did not hide their satisfaction, for this "law of silence" could be interpreted as favorable to their Gallican pretensions. The opportunity arose very soon. When the priest of Saint-Etienne-du-Mont refused to minister to a woman who was a former "convulsionary," they denounced the matter to the King. He immediately referred it to Monseigneur Beaumont, who supported his priest. After hearing first the prelate and then Monsieur de Maupeou, President of the Paris parliament, Louis XV ruled in favor of the latter. In order to prevent the parliament from starting proceedings against the Archbishop, the King sent him a *lettre de cachet* forcing him into exile in his house in Conflans.

The parliament rejoiced and there was great excitement when Maupeou published the King's letter. "I showed my discontent to the Archbishop of Paris," said Louis XV, "by punishing him in a manner that lets him know my firm determination to maintain peace in my kingdom."[9] The Parisians were jubilant; the King had dared "punish" the Archbishop. "The King's firmness is admired," wrote the lawyer Barbier, "and he is being praised as much as he was denigrated for two years."[10]

It was said that the King had written his letter while he was at the favorite's and that she was behind it—that Madame de Pompadour, friend of the *philosophes*, had seized the opportunity to take revenge on the priests for their hostility to her. However, everything leads us to think that she had been very cautious. Now that she was no longer sleeping with Louis XV she hoped that even if she was unlikely to gain the *dévots'* support, she could at least stem their resentment of her. She thought she should disarm her old enemies, which would strengthen her position with the monarch and allow her to enjoy the political power that fascinated her increasingly. In her eagerness to solve the seemingly endless conflict between the parliament and the clergy, she had arranged to have the Comte de Choiseul-Stainville—the man who had saved her from disgrace at the time of the Choiseul-Beaupré affair—appointed ambassador to Rome.

A steady correspondence had started between the two.[11] "I would like you to find a way of speaking to the pope alone," she wrote to him during Monseigneur de Beaumont's exile. "Attend tirelessly to the important matters entrusted to you as I am determined you should succeed," she wrote several days later. Choiseul had a very difficult mission to fulfill with the pope even though His Sainthood Benedict XIV professed tolerance. Since most of the bishops in France had shown solidarity with Monseigneur Beaumont and had appealed to the Holy Father, the latter, it was feared, could interfere in the kingdom's internal affairs—which is exactly what Louis XV wanted to avoid at all costs. Choiseul had received very strict instructions on this point. He was to assure the Supreme Pontiff of his Very Christian King's great esteem, but make him understand that the King would be settling his conflict with part of his clergy on his own and without any outside arbitration. However, the order that sent the Archbishop of Paris into exile, followed shortly thereafter by similar orders against a number of other prelates, suddenly aggravated the crisis.

During this crucial period, the Marquise encouraged Choiseul in his negotiations; she kept him informed of events at Court, though her letters dealt primarily with the relationship between the clergy and the parliament. We sense from this correspondence that she admired the ambassador and would keep him in mind for a key position in the near future. Meanwhile, she continually reminded him that he would have to prove himself. She had instantly understood that he was a man whose political intelligence was far superior to that of the standing ministers. Clearly she saw him as the future great man whose career she wanted to shape and on whom she dreamed of relying.

As far as religious affairs were concerned, the Marquise remained very moderate, condemning both the religious party's excesses and the parliament's bellicose ardor. She favored a middle ground that would restore domestic peace yet show consideration for the Supreme Pontiff's authority. "There's too much fanaticism here. I won't comment on the conduct adopted; I moan and remain silent," she wrote to Choiseul on April 21. The parliament had just reopened the conflict even though it might have seemed settled, after the King had decided, with an assembly of twenty-six bishops, that the proofs of confession would no longer be required from people requesting the sacraments. But on March 18, the parliament, seeing itself as ruling over ecclesiastical discipline, had adopted a decision stipulating that the *Unigenitus* bull had neither the "character" nor the "effects of a rule of faith." It was immediately annulled by the King, who reproclaimed the bull "the law of the Church and the State." Madame de Pompadour was worried, of course, about the pope's reaction. She counted on Choiseul's skill to get the Supreme Pontiff to accept the need to temporize and allow the King to act alone in this matter. "You know from my last letter how distressed I am by the behavior that has been adopted," she wrote him on April 28. "Time and the support of religion, of which we are so full, will bring the remedy to our present troubles. You can nevertheless emphasize that the King loves the Church and will always love it, and will support it no matter what. . . . Build up your courage and your attachment to the Holy Father; try to keep his favor, strengthen it if possible, and you can be sure that the court of Rome will not lose out."[12] She again encouraged the ambassador some ten days later: "Whatever lengths the King and other concerned people go to to arrange matters, the monsters always set up an obstacle. . . . Honest people are in despair. I would very much like it if you could perform an important service for the King. My friendship for him has not left me idle as far as he's concerned. I'm of the same opinion as you regarding the parliament and the clergy: a deadline cannot be set. With time, the blindfold will fall from their eyes."[13] When she learns that Benedict XIV approves of Louis XV's attitude, she is thrilled: "I love the Holy Father madly. I would like my prayers to be effective and will say some every day for his benefit. . . . Your services seem to have brought satisfaction. . . . I took every precaution to be informed of the welfare of the State."[14]

The assembly of the clergy, meeting in Paris in May 1755 under the presidency of Cardinal de La Rochefoucauld, immediately split into two camps, so the prelates solicited the pope's intervention. At Versailles it was feared once again that, to resolve the conflict, the pope might make a decision that would plunge the kingdom into turmoil. Choiseul, on the King's orders, had to negotiate again to prevent Benedict XIV from becoming the arbiter in an internal French conflict—for, though it revolved around religious questions, the stakes were essentially political.

During this new crisis, the Marquise sided resolutely with the moderate clergy—as did the pope—against the magistrates. "The parliament is showing off its importance. The King will stand firm. These little republicans will have to yield to an authority founded on justice. . . . The insurgents against the treaty, the members of parliament—nothing will shake my courage. Set your mind at rest and remain fond of me. You know, little excellency, that I deserve it."[15] Madame de Pompadour wanted to put an end to this protracted quarrel—particularly dangerous at this point, since the kingdom was threatened with war. She ardently wished the pope would publish an encyclical repealing the *Unigenitus.* "Whatever difficulties you encounter, I'm certain of your success. You'll know how to use the persuasiveness you've acquired, the Holy Father's friendship, the subtlety and magnetism of your character and above all your attachment to the King, to his peace of mind and to the welfare of the State. . . . It is very true that you contribute greatly to my peace of mind. I can't attain it so long as the King is tormented and the kingdom is in ferment. Consider the obligation I'll have to you. It shall not be a burden for me, Monsieur. The friendship I have for you will lighten it."[16]

Choiseul was astute in his negotiations and in January 1756, thanks to the Marquise, he was received into the order of the Holy Spirit. But it was not until the following October that he convinced the Holy Father to issue an encyclical that conformed to Louis XV's wishes. It upheld the *Unigenitus* bull, but stated that the proofs of confession should no longer be required. This was not enough for the parliament; the parliamentarians resumed their struggle shortly thereafter.[17]

Never had Madame de Pompadour been so closely involved in French politics. To avoid importuning Louis XV in their private conversations, she wrote him long letters. Their frankness astonished the Abbé de Bernis, to whom she showed copies when he returned to France in the spring of 1755 after a three-year term as ambassador to Venice. She opened her heart to the Abbé. He had guided her first steps "in this country," a place that now disgusted her and which she sometimes thought of leaving. Or so she confided during their initial conversations; she told him about Madame d'Estrades's scheme to oust her and elevate Madame de Choiseul-Beaupré to the rank of official mistress. She also gave the Abbé copies of her letters to Louis XV requesting his permission to retire from the Court. Bernis did not feel that they "showed a firm resolution to withdraw from society."[18] On the other hand, he found her political letters "admirable" and was astounded at the Marquise's ability to "tell the King the truth with so much energy and eloquence."[19] He urged her to continue her work as a secret adviser. Having noted that she was admirably well informed on all matters, he deplored "the disorder in finances, the general insubordination and the King's loss of authority."[20]

Because in earlier times they had been close, Bernis was in a position to give his friend some judicious advice. Since, in the strict sense of the word, she was no longer the King's mistress, she should stop subjecting him to jealous scenes. She had to try to make the sovereign enjoy "her pleasant company," so that he could listen to her calmly. The Abbé further suggested that she draw closer to the Comte d'Argenson and help mend his relationship with Machault, for Bernis considered their disagreements harmful to the government. At first, Madame de Pompadour recoiled at this suggestion, but he soon convinced her; he promised her that he would bring about the reconciliation. He was unable to do so, however, because of d'Argenson's obstinacy.

Finally, Bernis tried to calm the Marquise's hostility toward the Prince de Conti. His confidential conversations with Louis XV were a great source of irritation to her. The King told her nothing: he excluded her from the secret diplomacy that he was conducting with a group that was not a part of the official cabinet. The Prince de Conti was one of the foremost members of this group.[21] Like one of Bluebeard's women, Madame de Pompadour was dying to know the substance of the conversations between the King and his distant cousin. She had become fiercely jealous of this haughty nobleman and wanted to estrange him from the King. Bernis put her on her guard. He suggested that she simply say to Louis XV, "If you want to put him in charge of governmental affairs, make him a member of your council. If you don't trust him enough to give him that position, return the control of government—which the Prince has usurped—to your ministers."[22] The Marquise took Bernis's advice and greatly benefited from it.

While Madame de Pompadour was following developments with the clergy very closely, the international situation had become very serious, for the peace accord of Aix-la-Chapelle had never been anything more than a truce. The conflicts between the great powers were still unresolved. British-French rivalry had worsened in the colonies; on the Continent, Austria wanted to take its revenge on Prussia, while Prussia's overriding aim was to rule Germany. At the slightest incident, war could once again break out both in Europe and the overseas territories.

Louis XV, whose navy was very inferior to England's, had no intention of provoking this long-standing enemy, who sought to chase the French from North America, the West Indies and India. The King dreaded a confrontation; he much preferred negotiation. As for Madame de Pompadour, she had been convinced for a while that there was nothing more to fear from England. She had welcomed the English ambassador graciously and, through him, she had maintained very cordial relations with the Duke of Newcastle.[23] She was far from suspecting the Court of St. James's true intentions. The French ambassador had failed to detect them as well, probably because the cause of the conflict was located very far away, in Canada, where the frontiers between the French and British possessions were not clearly drawn. The French had made their way from Quebec to the Great Lakes and had taken possession of Louisiana, thereby ruling over huge, though underpopulated, territories. The British, who were there in much greater numbers than the French and owned thirteen colonies along the coast, accused the French of blocking their westward expansion. The British settlers wanted to destroy the French domination and were pressing this demand on their home country. The main strategic concern was the Ohio River, which represented the shortest distance between Louisiana and Canada. Incidents near Quebec and Montreal, on the banks of the Saint Lawrence River, grew in number, and in October 1754, the English sent a squadron, under the command of Admiral Boscawen, with the mission to capture and destroy the French vessels carrying troops or munitions. Versailles adopted a wait-and-see attitude. In June 1755, the English, without declaring war, unexpectedly attacked the French. But the news had not yet reached France when the Court left for Compiègne in the beginning of July 1755.

Eighteen

SECRET NEGOTIATIONS

In Compiègne the summer promised plenty of amusements. The King went hunting as usual, and Madame de Pompadour had the pleasure of discovering the new hermitage, Louis XV's addition to the grounds, near the river. It was almost an exact duplicate of the one at Fontainebleau. She inaugurated it by holding a dinner with the sovereign and their close circle of friends. The days went by peacefully—they played *paume* (an early version of tennis), took walks, socialized in small groups and admired the work on the terrace that was supposed to be completed the following year. The ladies were very moved by the young Prince de Lamballe, who had come to take his oath as Master of the Royal Hounds. He was only eight years old and had just lost his mother, the pious Duchesse de Penthièvre. There were performances organized every evening to keep the Court agreeably entertained. Unlike Versailles, a sense of freedom reigned, although the King continued to work with his ministers and receive the ambassadors.

Suddenly, on July 18, 1755, the atmosphere changed. There were alarming, unconfirmed rumors: the English navy had attacked the French fleet. Apprehension turned to dismay the following day with the news of the capture of two French vessels, *Le Lys* and the *Alcyde*, with eight hundred men aboard. The next day, "the prevailing feelings were anger and a desire to kill,"[1] though the King looked sad and the ministers wore suitably grave expressions. The Marquis d'Argenson scribbled a few irate remarks that are a good illustration of the Court's bellicose mood: "Those arrogant, ambitious, usurping British—like the Algerians, they declare war and attack, unlawfully, on the basis of usurping claims. Our war is just, theirs is like the war in Algiers, the wolf against the lamb."[2] Though there was no further news, armed conflict seemed inevitable. Councils and committees met constantly and everyone wondered anxiously how the European powers would react since, in principle, Austria was allied with England and Prussia with France.

The King feared waging war against his enemies on both land and sea, with the kingdom unprepared. The cabinet was divided. Machault preferred negotiating, at least to gain time, whereas d'Argenson and Rouillé—only recently appointed in Foreign Affairs—recommended invading the Netherlands, in order to intimidate the English and defeat Austria, France's age-old enemy. The Prussian King's representative, Baron Knyphausen, urged the French to intervene and promised help from Frederick II.

Though he took some emergency measures, Louis XV remained cautious. He withdrew his ambassador to London, the Duc de Mirepoix, granted the British two weeks to leave the kingdom and had a long meeting with the Maréchal de Belle-Isle. He had given orders to increase the size of the cavalry, the infantry and the Navy, and to arm the warships. Superior officers, noblemen who wanted to go into the service, plenipotentiary ministers and financiers all hastened to Compiègne. Soon it became known that major construction was being undertaken in Dunkerque to make room for a larger number of ships. Meanwhile, the King was advised to cut back expenses and complied without flinching. He willingly agreed to reduce his travel and entertainment expenses, sell some horses and curb his taste for new buildings, but he wouldn't hear of dismissing the Marquise, who was perceived to be a leech on the State. Jeanne-Antoinette thought that in giving up her trips to Crécy she was setting a good example. She missed them, but felt this sacrifice had "the hauteur that was suitable to a good Frenchwoman."

While everyone was in suspense waiting for news, Louis XV decided to spend a few days at La Muette, where he naturally took the favorite and a few intimate friends, including Madame d'Estrades. On August 7, Madame d'Estrades requested permission to go to Paris and asked the Marquise at what time she should return for supper. "At the usual time, Comtesse," Madame de Pompadour replied graciously. Several minutes later, a courier stopped Madame d'Estrades's carriage and handed her a *lettre de cachet* from Monsieur de Saint-Florentin, Minister of the King's Household. She was told to surrender her position as Mesdames' Lady-in-Waiting and never to reappear at Court. This unexpected disgrace, three years after the Choiseul-Beaupré affair, caused quite a stir. When he heard the news, the Comte d'Argenson fainted. He was terrified that he was about to suffer the same fate as his mistress, but he escaped with a mere scare.

Madame de Pompadour's revenge on this woman for betraying her came when she least expected it. But no one suspected the real reason behind the harsh measure. People talked about the incompatible personalities of Madame Adélaïde and Madame d'Estrades—an incompatibility that was indeed quite real; they believed that Madame de Pompadour had taken advantage of this enmity to get her scheming cousin dismissed. In fact, the favorite had higher motives. She was preparing to play a secret diplomatic role. This meant that all indiscreet individuals had to be sent away, starting with Madame d'Estrades, who spied on her for the Minister of War. Her disgrace had become a necessity.

Madame de Pompadour had never belonged to what was called the "Prussian clan," which considered Frederick II to be the model Enlightenment ruler and refused to see him as a despot. He was admired for his genius, his government and even his conquests. To most enlightened minds, the alliance with the "Solomon of the North" had to be maintained. The policy dictated by Cardinal de Richelieu in earlier times, which consisted of weakening the House of Hapsburg with the support of the Protestant German princes, was considered a maxim of State that should remain unchallenged. However, the world scene had changed in the last century. The Bourbons were firmly established in Madrid and the Austrian Empire, undermined by internal problems and directly threatened by Prussia, no longer represented a danger for France. Underestimating her weakness, Empress Maria Theresa wanted to reconquer Silesia, which she had lost at Aix-la-Chapelle, and she thought she could inflict a bitter defeat on Frederick II. He in turn dreamed of substituting Prussian rule for Austrian rule over the whole of Germany. In the unending struggle that loomed between the two States, Maria Theresa needed a powerful ally. She knew she could not count on England, for England had everything to lose and nothing to gain from war on the Continent. France alone could come to her assistance. But to arrive at such a "reversal" of alliances required admirably well-informed secret services and extremely skillful diplomats. Maria Theresa had these assets and she had long been planning this dramatic diplomatic coup with her Chancellor,[3] Count Kaunitz, who had been her ambassador to France from 1750 to 1753.

A prodigal, worldly, very cultured aristocrat, Kaunitz had been very well received at Versailles. Louis XV "had spoken to him with great kindness and the familiar air of an old acquaintance that had surprised everyone."[4] He had paid court to Madame de Pompadour and noticed that "she had been very appreciative" of it. He realized very quickly that "the thoughts and opinions of the King's mistress were a very serious matter in this country,"[5] so he became twice as attentive to her and "made polite gestures" to all her friends. He was eager to convince the favorite of the Empress's peaceful intentions; he assured her that she wanted to maintain peace in Europe. Flattered by Kaunitz's interest in her, the Marquise lapped up his words. "If Madame de Pompadour were involved in foreign affairs, I have reason to believe that she would not serve us badly,"[6] he wrote in 1751. This was the period, in fact, when Madame de Pompadour was helping the King work with the Marquis Puisieulx. Kaunitz, encouraged by the favorite's affability, informed her of Maria Theresa's desire to ally herself with France.[7] Madame de Pompadour remained guardedly noncommittal. However, when the ambassador left for Vienna, in 1752, she assured him that "the King not only liked H.M. the Empress, but . . . had always considered her a friend and had the highest esteem for her."[8] These are remarks that the Marquise would never have been so bold to make unless Louis XV had wanted them repeated to Maria Theresa. Indeed, he had allowed Jeanne-Antoinette to inform Kaunitz that he had very little confidence in

Frederick II.[9] His alliance with the King of Prussia was beginning to weigh on him, since Frederick had repeatedly been tactless about him. He criticized Louis XV's government openly, commented cruelly on his private life and nicknamed the favorite "Her Petticoat Majesty."[9]

As soon as the British attack on the French ships was officially announced, Maria Theresa and Kaunitz felt the time was ripe to begin negotiations with Louis XV. But knowing France's hostility to Austria, they wished to enter into secret negotiations with the King and they wondered who was the best intermediary—the Prince de Conti or Madame de Pompadour? Kaunitz wrote a letter to each and let Count Starhemberg,[10] the Empress's ambassador to Versailles, decide which of the two he felt was most capable of carrying out the mission.

Starhemberg decided on Madame de Pompadour and gave her Kaunitz's letter. "Madame, I have often hoped I would have the opportunity of reminding you of my existence," he wrote her. "I now have such an opportunity, which, knowing your feelings, should not be unpleasant for you. . . . Monsieur le Comte de Starhemberg has extremely important proposals to make to the King but of the kind that can only be handled through someone who has the honor of His Very Christian Majesty's complete trust and whom H.V.C.M. would assign to Count Starhemberg. Our proposals, I think, will not make you regret your effort in asking the King for someone to negotiate with us; on the contrary, I flatter myself that you will be grateful to me for having given you a new mark of my attachment and respect thanks to which I have the honor of being, etc."[11] The Marquise hastened to hand the King a rather laconic note from Maria Theresa: "I promise, on my word as empress and queen," she wrote, "that none of my proposals made to the Very Christian King by Count Starhemberg will be divulged and that these matters will be kept in the deepest secrecy forever, whether or not the negotiations succeed; it is assumed that the V.C.K. makes the same declaration and promise in exchange. Written in Vienna, August 21, 1755."[12] Maria Theresa was not shocked, as Starhemberg had somewhat feared, that he had chosen Madame de Pompadour over the Prince de Conti. "She has the King's complete trust," was her reply to him. "It might have been very harmful to exclude her."[13]

The Court was completely ignorant of this overture. The ministers knew nothing. Of a common accord, Louis XV and Madame de Pompadour designated the Abbé de Bernis as the person who would hear the Empress's proposals. He had always been beyond reproach for his trustworthiness, loyalty and discretion. And as he was about to leave for Madrid, where Louis XV had just appointed him ambassador, no one would suspect that he was in charge of another mission. When the Marquise informed him of his new responsibility, Bernis was taken by surprise, but hid his anxieties about Austria's diplomacy. He had doubts about Maria Theresa's sincerity and warned Madame de Pompadour of a possible trap. The Empress could be pretending to negotiate in order to gain time and establish ties with other powers to better isolate France. And if she was acting in good faith, she would inevitably drag the King into war with Prussia. He warned that Louis XV, who would certainly have to fight England, no longer had great generals and that the kingdom's finances would not allow him to engage in a long and unpopular conflict.

Just as Bernis was concluding his talk, the King came in to join the Marquise. Bernis advanced the same arguments in his presence. The sovereign looked irritated. "Well," he replied a bit emotionally, "then we should thank Monsieur de Starhemberg politely and tell him that we're not interested in any proposals."

"I don't feel that way, Sire," said the Abbé. "Your Majesty has everything to gain by finding out the Viennese Court's intentions, but we should be cautious in our answer."[14] Louis XV seemed relieved and decided that Bernis would meet the ambassador in Madame de Pompadour's presence, in the Babiole pavilion at Bellevue. When the Abbé suggested to the King that he at least let the Minister of Foreign Affairs in on the secret, he was met with a categorical refusal. The King demanded absolute secrecy. When Bernis was alone again with Madame de Pompadour, he "congratulated her on the flattering trust shown to her by the Viennese Court"[15] and reassured his old friend as to her future with her former lover. She was now too intimately involved in his politics for him to consider separating from her.

The first interview took place, in the utmost secrecy, in early September. Starhemberg and Bernis arrived discreetly, each on his own. The Marquise and the Abbé had mutually agreed that they would remain impassive while the ambassador stated the Empress's offer. They did well, for as he read his statement, the diplomat could not guess what impression he was making. Under the guise of apparent frankness, the Austrian report was awesomely clever. Maria Theresa assumed Louis XV was weary of his alliance with Frederick II and annoyed that Frederick was negotiating with the Court of St. James. Madame de Pompadour and Bernis, who knew nothing of these negotiations, kept their sangfroid, thereby letting the ambassador think that perhaps the French cabinet already had this information. On the basis of her suppositions, the Empress suggested a treaty of alliance between Austria and France. She said she was prepared to concede part of the Netherlands to Don Philippe, Louis XV's son-in-law, providing she could reclaim possession of the Italian duchies that she had lost. She added that she would not be opposed to the Prince de Conti's acceding to the Polish throne, as Louis XV wanted.

Perplexed, Bernis warned the King against a hasty rapprochement with Austria. First they needed confirmation of Vienna's allegations concerning the Anglo-Prussian negotiations, for they had no prior knowledge of it. In the meanwhile, he suggested that Louis XV inform Maria Theresa that he was ready to unite with her to defend the European peace accord. This declaration couldn't possibly harm French interests. The King told the Empress that being "loyal to the rules of honor," he could not cast doubt on the good faith of his allies and "believe them capable of disloyalty or betrayal." Disappointed by this delaying tactic, the Empress hoped that the King would himself suggest a common plan of action.

While the sovereign was sending the Duc de Nivernais as ambassador extraordinary to Frederick II to find out what his intentions were, he asked Maria Theresa whether she was willing to give up her alliance with England. Louis XV dreamed of forming a continental coalition that would isolate his principal enemy. The talks continued for several weeks in complete secrecy. Bernis, however, was beginning to feel very isolated compared to Starhemberg, who had the support of the Viennese cabinet, and he finally managed to get the King to agree to his being helped by several ministers. Rouillé, Séchelles, the Comptroller of Finances, and Saint-Florentin were the only ones informed. Offended that Bernis had been chosen over them, they started out with feelings of veiled jealousy toward him and this hardly simplified his task.

Though she did not take part in the discussions, the Marquise was kept abreast of all the negotiations. The Court was still ignorant of what was being said at the favorite's, but there was much talk of the Abbé de Bernis as Rouillé's successor in Foreign Affairs. "The Marquise will have been responsible for that choice," said d'Argenson. "She seems in every way the Prime Minister of France and the King wants it that way, even as far as outward appearance is concerned. Certainly it's nicer to see a beautiful, erect nymph at the helm than an ugly hunched monkey like the late Cardinal de Fleury; but these beautiful ladies have the temper of white cats. They're pleasing at first in some ways, but then they have a sudden whim and they bite you and scratch you."[16]

Madame de Pompadour followed the diplomatic mission of her friend the Duc de Nivernais. Frederick II received him as a great friend, kept him in the dark for as long as possible and finally told him the truth at the end of January 1756. He had indeed allied himself with England through the Treaty of Westminster, concluded two weeks earlier. The King of Prussia used his wiles to persuade Nivernais that this alliance would have no effect on the relationship between France and Prussia. Meanwhile, he tried to cajole the favorite through his ambassador, to find out if there was a rapprochement between Austria and France. "Try to flatter her and see if she will lose her self-control and reveal out of effusiveness what the ministers are hiding out of wisdom,"[17] he wrote to him. But the Marquise remained completely self-possessed. She even went so far as to declare publicly that the Westminster treaty was to the kingdom's "advantage." Frederick II tried another tactic. One of his brothers, Prince August Wilhelm, hypocritically requested a copy of the favorite's portrait by de La Tour, "in the hope that the patron muse of painting would not refuse this portrait to posterity."[18] The Prussian representative to Versailles was furious that he was coming up against the all-powerful favorite's impassiveness, though she gladly received Starhemberg. "In the Council," he wrote, "no resolution of any importance is made, in external or internal affairs, without her being informed or forewarned."[19]

Even after the Anglo-Prussian alliance was officially announced, Louis XV hesitated a long time before committing himself to Maria Theresa. Their interests were opposed. The King of France, who was going to declare war on England,[20] wanted to maintain peace on the Continent. After endless discussion and a bit of blackmail on the part of the Empress—she threatened to take up again with her old British allies—Louis XV followed his mistress's insistent entreaties and called a formal meeting of his ministers. He explained the situation to them and requested their advice. D'Argenson, Minister of War, boldly said that he anticipated the beginning of a conflict that could ignite all of Europe. But after he had spoken, Bernis reached into his portfolio and took out a letter from Kaunitz that Madame de Pompadour had just given him. It described an attempted Anglo-Austrian rapprochement. Could France fight England with all the major European powers united against her? The ministers, who realized that the King's mind was already made up, decided to support the alliance with the Empress.

On May 1, 1756, a treaty was signed between France and Austria, in Jouy, in one of Rouillé's properties. Known as the First Treaty of Versailles, this "masterpiece of wisdom and politics,"[21] as Bernis put it, answered two contrary wishes—France expected it to bring peace and Austria, war. Austria agreed to total neutrality in the French-British conflict, and France agreed to respect the territories that belonged to Maria Theresa, particularly the Netherlands. However, in article VI, the two powers pledged to aid each other with a military corps of 24,000 men should either side be attacked by a third power.

"Madame de Pompadour is delighted," said Starhemberg, "with the conclusion of what she regards as her work and she assured me that she would do her best so that we could continue. . . . She let me know that whenever I wished to send something directly to the King, I could request a meeting with her and that she already had permission to see me in private whenever I wanted."[22] Several days later, he added the following revealing lines to Kaunitz: "It is from her that we should expect everything in the future. She wants to be held in esteem and indeed she deserves it. I will see her more often and more privately when our alliance is no longer a secret, and then I would like to have things to say to her that would flatter her personally."[23]

Without dispelling the mystery that had surrounded those negotiations, the Marquise let it be known that she had played an essential role. Yet she knew that this "reversal of alliances" was severely criticized at Court. The Prussian party was unrelenting and held her responsible for a treaty that was seen as against the kingdom's interests. The monarch was blamed for having been the favorite's plaything, while being called "my cousin" or "my princess" by the Empress had gone to the favorite's head—this was the rumor spread by the King of Prussia and his agents. However, a large part of the public approved of the treaty. It was believed that the "union of the two greatest powers would command the respect of all of Europe."[24] The Marquise was convinced of this. "I hope the justice of the cause will bring us luck," she wrote to Choiseul, "and that we will make that fierce nation repent for mistaking as weakness what was actually the wisest and most refined policy. I have not concealed from you how pleased I was about our treaties with the Empress. The public, though unable to measure just how advantageous they are, responded to them with great joy. It is a double satisfaction to those who took part in it."[25] As a way of immortalizing an event as significant as this, she had an onyx stone engraved by Guay, based on her own design: "France and Austria hand in hand at the altar of loyalty, trampling the mask of hypocrisy and the torch of discord."

Nineteen

ARRANGEMENTS WITH
THE POWERS ON HIGH

Madame de Pompadour constantly astonished Versailles. The revelations about her political role were less surprising, however, than her nomination as one of the Queen's Ladies of the Palace, the highest position to which a woman could aspire at Court. This was Louis XV's way of showing his gratitude toward his favorite, whose devotion and discretion he alone was aware of. The Queen welcomed her rival affably. Like the favorite, Marie Leczinska was skilled at controlling her feelings. She knew that the two former lovers' days of passion were long gone and had been persuaded that "it would be a heroic act on her part to forget the past."[1]

This advancement fulfilled the Marquise's greatest wishes. Though she did not govern France, as d'Argenson claimed, she was the monarch's secret adviser and confidante. However, at the whim of the King, her favor could abruptly come to an end. The position she had just been given protected her from disgrace, which was always a possibility with someone as unpredictable as Louis XV. As the thirteenth Palace Lady she now had an official role. Designated as supernumerary, she was to keep the Queen company and serve her when one of her companions was unable to fulfill her functions.

The King had wanted her to be included in the Queen's Household for a long time, but consideration had had to be shown for the devout Marie's feelings; she refused to have in her entourage a woman who was known to be living in sin. In the late summer of 1755, Machault and the Prince de Soubise had advised their friend Jeanne-Antoinette to return to the bosom of the Church. After mature reflection, she had made up her mind. Securing a position with Marie Leczinska and retaining the esteem of the Austrian Empress, who was notoriously pious and intransigent with regard to morals, were well worth a conversion of sorts.

At the end of September, Madame de Pompadour met Father de Sacy, a brilliant Jesuit, apparently less stringent than Father Pérusseau. She told him of her desire to return to the fold. Now that she and the King were merely friends, she hoped to receive absolution and eventually take the sacraments, which she had avoided ever since the beginning of her liaison with Louis XV. Father de Sacy began by reminding her that she was married and that her presence at Court remained scandalous, since it wasn't justified in any way. If she wanted to save her soul, she had to return to her husband. Under the Jesuit's dictation, she wrote a faultlessly humble letter to Monsieur Le Normant. She confessed the error of her ways, begged his forgiveness and asked him if he would accept to resume conjugal life with her, in spite of her past affronts to his honor. Though this might have hurt her pride, she knew she was running no risk. Le Normant had found wonderful consolation with the prettiest actresses in Paris, and had set up house with Mademoiselle Raime, a dancer at the Opera, maliciously nicknamed "*Rem publicam*" (public object, i.e., a prostitute). However, to ensure that Jeanne-Antoinette would be taking no chances, the Prince de Soubise brought the letter to Le Normant personally and clearly hinted that the King would be angry if he accepted his wife's offer.

Monsieur Le Normant, who had no intention of living with Jeanne-Antoinette ever again, took the luxury of writing her an extremely ironic and well-phrased rejection: "Madame, I have just received the letter in which you tell me of the soul-searching you have undergone and the intention you have of devoting yourself to God. I can only be edified by this resolution. I'm not surprised that you would find it difficult to be in my presence and you can easily appreciate the difficulty I would feel. I would like to forget that you offended me; your presence would only remind me of it more vividly. Therefore the only course of action, for us both, is to live separately. Whatever cause for displeasure you gave me, I want to believe that you guard my honor jealously, and I would consider it compromised if I were to take you into my house and live with you as my wife. You know yourself that time has no effect on what honor prescribes. I have the honor of being, respectfully, Madame, your very humble and very obedient servant."[2]

Recovering quickly from wounded pride, the Marquise was delighted to hear her spiritual director advise her to secure a position at Court in order to rectify her situation and finally make it proper. To fulfill her wishes, she had merely to draw inspiration from Madame de Maintenon, whose example guided her more and more with every passing day. Her conversations with Father de Sacy continued, while she told her friends Madame de Mirepoix and Madame de Villars that her husband had refused to take her in and that she sought to save her soul. The Queen's intimate friend, the dour Duchesse de Luynes, was soon let in on the secret. Under these circumstances, Marie could no longer object to accepting the Marquise in her Household. And Louis XV could now require that his wife appoint his former mistress as one of her Palace Ladies. Very moved, Madame de Pompadour said to Madame de Luynes, modestly, that she had never asked for the position, "that she had been required to take it and that she had just acted on the advice of her confessor."[3]

On the day of her new presentation to the Queen, February 8, 1756, Madame de Pompadour "declared herself devout" and radically changed her habits. She gave up her public toilette, and now received courtiers and ambassadors seated in front of her tapestry frame. She read religious works and could be seen at mass in the Queen's retinue, with lowered headdress, deep in prayer. She talked about religion, said she feared divine retribution and went so far as to not eat meat on Fridays in the private apartment—something she had never done before. She arranged to have an apartment for retreats at the Capuchins of the Place Vendôme in Paris. People expected her to give up makeup and her beautiful clothes and jewels, but she didn't. She remained just as elegant and continued to preside over all the Court amusements.

This sudden "conversion" was even more puzzling than her recent promotion. There were those who were indignant that she sought to save her soul at Court, insinuating that she should have retired to a convent. There were others who believed that her conversion was a prelude to the King's conversion. Several devout ladies came to her without any scruples and requested her protection. Some speculated about the implications of the old saying "Arrangements can always be made with the powers on high, God is merciful, if you find an understanding priest." Those who were wisest abstained from passing judgment and tried to explain the surprising turnaround. "Since she has never seemed at all deceitful . . . , it would seem she was in good faith," said the Prince de Croÿ.[4] The Duc de Luynes, too, thought she was sincere: "She herself admits that she doesn't have as much attraction and taste for devotion as she would like, and that she hopes to attain grace through fervent prayers. . . . She is in poor health and has many ailments. God often uses such expediencies to bring about conversions."[5]

The Duc de La Vallière, who knew Jeanne-Antoinette well, seemed more skeptical. He confided his impressions to Voltaire, from whom she had requested a translation of the Psalms of David. "She's been brightened by a ray of grace, but devoid of ecstasy; and there are only a few small changes," he wrote to Voltaire. "She no longer attends theatrical performances, and refrains from eating meat three days a week for the whole period of Lent, but only as long as she's not inconvenienced. . . . In other respects, it's the same life, the same friends—and I flatter myself that I'm among them—and she's as kind as ever and has more influence than ever. This is the position she's in and the reason why she would like your version of the psalms. She knows you, admires you and would like to read you again."[6] Voltaire, who was sending around his clandestine edition of La Pucelle, had no desire to undertake that kind of assignment. He may have missed an opportunity to get back into favor.

Jeanne-Antoinette felt she should justify herself to Choiseul, who was still in a difficult position with regard to the Holy Father. "The fact that I chose religion, after much mature and extended deliberation, means that accusations of cleverness, skillfulness, foresight and even duplicity will be leveled against me," she wrote to him the day after her nomination. "Yet I'm just a poor woman who has been seeking happiness for ten years and who thinks she has found it. I wrote to my husband on Father de Sacy's orders. He replied wishing me all the very best, but saying that he never wanted to see me again. The reverend father then insisted that I take a position at Court for the sake of propriety. The King was kind enough to write to the Queen and she made me a supernumerary in her palace. I would have been very distressed to be titular, for I can't perform assiduous services because of my palpitations and I requested as much. Your friendship for me will make you find all these dull details interesting."[7] The "poor woman" then went on to discuss the Jansenist quarrel, which was still dividing the clergy, and begged Choiseul "to restore peace in the Church" by following the moderate path advocated by the King.

Was Madame de Pompadour sincere or was she playing an admirably staged part with the complicity of the King and a few faithful friends? Had Father de Sacy been summoned to find the necessary arrangements between the powers on high and the Court? No one can say. But when Madame de Pompadour was appointed Lady of the Palace, the Jesuit refused to give her absolution. She would subsequently meet a less intransigent priest who let her receive the sacraments without requiring her to leave Versailles. "One day she informed me of this religious intrigue and apologized for having concealed it from me," said Bernis. "I had the courage to tell her that this farce didn't impress anyone; that she would be thought of as false and hypocritical; that since it wasn't heartfelt, religious devotion would eventually bore her; that she would look ridiculous becoming a *dévote*, and even more ridiculous if she gave it up out of boredom. My prediction did not please her; but she carried it out to the letter and gave up the part after the Duc de Choiseul's return."[8]

For the time being, the Marquise, at the height of favor, almost forgot about the King's young mistresses, and put all her energies into the great political issues that were being discussed in her quarters. She spent most of her time with the monarch, though she had walled up the interior stairway that connected their apartments. Louis was somewhat annoyed that he now had to cross a large drawing room filled with people in order to join her in her boudoir. In the evening, she dined gaily in the King's private apartment, where she still had the role of hostess. "All of this made for a most singular combination," remarked the Prince de Croÿ.[9]

Madame de Pompadour's mind was occupied by several matters at once: the war with England, the conflict between the parliament and the clergy, and Choiseul's negotiations with the pope. France was about to fight the British navy. On December 21, 1755, Louis XV had sent the English Foreign Ministry an ultimatum requesting that the captured vessels and their crews be restored to France. Since the English had rejected the ultimatum, the King considered that he was at war with England. He appointed the Maréchal de Belle-Isle Commander on the coasts of the Atlantic and the English Channel, and the Maréchal de Richelieu Commander on the coast of the Mediterranean. In April he decided, in Council, to organize a landing on the island of Minorca, a British possession since the Treaty of Utrecht in 1713. He hoped to take his enemies by surprise, return Minorca to Spain and secure Spain's alliance in exchange. While the Maréchal de Belle-Isle made several sorties off the coast of the English Channel to intimidate the British, an expedition left from the islands of Hyères, under Richelieu's command, on April 12, 1756.

The Marquise was very excited by these developments. After supper one night, she told the Prince de Croÿ that she feared the English might make a landing in Aunis; "that the Mahon expedition had started under the best auspices; that the Navy's preparations were admirable; that those who declaim that we're lacking in everything when this isn't true should be hanged. Finally, as her attachment to Monsieur de Machault was as great as her enmity for Monsieur d'Argenson, the Navy had every advantage! She also said that we shouldn't lay down arms until we had crushed the English; that respect was the most important thing for a great power; that it was better that we all perish rather than allow it to be undermined. . . . In sum, she spoke very forcefully and with much dignity and had a loftier spirit than might be expected."[10]

The Court was staying at Compiègne when news came that Minorca had fallen to the French. The squadron, under the command of Monsieur de La Galissonière, had reached the island on April 18; 12,000 men had disembarked and laid siege to Fort St. Philip, which overlooked Mahon and was reputed to be impregnable. On June 27, the French captured the fort in spite of an attack led by Admiral Byng; he was forced to retreat to Gibraltar.

The King and his favorite were elated. Everyone at Compiègne rejoiced and the sovereign ordered the celebration of a *Te Deum* service. Good news from Canada, where the French had won several victories under Montcalm's command, and the occupation of fortified towns in Corsica helped contribute to the general euphoria. Madame de Pompadour invited the Court and the foreign representatives to her Compiègne hermitage, where she threw a big fete, ending in fireworks. She went around the brightly lit grounds distributing ribbons to the ladies and sword knots "à la Mahon" to the men.

She had maintained a regular correspondence with Richelieu during the siege, and naturally wrote a letter of congratulations to him. Their ambiguous relationship can be felt in the tone: "I'm sure you know that I'm pleased to call you my *Minorquin* [Minorcan]. We are all brimming with joy, particularly given the way the fort was captured. It couldn't have been more dazzling for the nation and the general! You must admit that you have a lucky star and that it has never failed you. . . . I could upbraid you for having approached other people instead of me for this interesting matter. I'll keep my grudge until you're happy, but then I'll let you know how far trust should go in friendship when one has received so many proofs of it and I'll teach you, old bore that you are, that you can never be too tactful on that score. Goodnight *Minorquin*, this word makes me forget Richelieu's wrongs."[11]

Meanwhile, Bernis, isolated in the Duc de Penthièvre's apartment with Starhemberg, was all alone, fighting against the machinations of the Austrian Court. Maria Theresa's ambassador was trying to change the defensive alliance between the two States into an offensive alliance. The Abbé, whose position was extremely awkward, since he was still negotiating in secret without consulting the Minister of Foreign Affairs, consented to offensive actions only if Frederick II were the first to violate the peace of Aix-la-Chapelle. Madame de Pompadour was pleased when informed of the details of these deliberations: "We are beginning to take revenge on the perfidiousness of the English in a brilliant way," she wrote Choiseul. "I hope that the justice of our cause will always bring us luck and that we will make that fierce nation repent for having construed the effect of an extremely wise policy as weakness. . . . I didn't conceal from you how pleased I was about the treaties with the Empress."[12]

However, the atmosphere was darkened by news from Germany. On August 29, without declaring war, Frederick II had invaded Saxony, forced August III's[13] weak army to capitulate, and was threatening Bohemia. This energetic offensive put an end to the hesitations that had been tormenting Louis XV and Bernis for months. Though France was already at war with England, she had to send troops to assist Maria Theresa. Instead of the 24,000 men spelled out in the treaty, France sent 45,000 men, because of the entreaties of the Dauphine, whose family had been gravely affected by the disaster. Louis XV assigned the command of the troops to the Maréchal d'Estrées, though the Marquise would have preferred the assignment to go to the Prince de Soubise, who had only one division under his orders.

Kaunitz thanked Madame de Pompadour, and she was flattered once again by the Viennese Court's consideration. "I am extremely touched by the justice rendered to me by Their Imperial Majesties and the kind consideration with which they honor me. This would add to my zeal if such were possible, but as you know from the proofs I've given you, Monsieur, it could not be added to."[14] Kaunitz appealed to the favorite once again, stressing that the defensive treaty should be changed to an offensive one.

Unfortunately, the King needed money to support the war effort. In July 1756, an edict restored the *vingtième* and instituted a second tax. Since the parliament was opposed to registering the measure, Louis XV had to do so by holding a solemn parliamentary session (called a *lit de justice*) on August 13. The parliamentary revolt had started up again with greater intensity than ever. The publication of the controversial encyclical—which upheld the *Unigenitus* bull but abolished the requirement of proof of confession for receiving the sacraments—had once again given the magistrates the opportunity to challenge the King's power. They used as an excuse the fact that the encyclical had been published without a printing permit and without the printer's name to prohibit the bishops from quoting or circulating it. All the parliaments in the kingdom sided with the Paris Parlement, on the basis of the "theory of classes" whereby the individual sovereign courts were all part of the same corps.

At a time when Louis XV would have liked to devote his energies to diplomatic negotiations and military preparations, he kept struggling with a rebellious magistracy. On December 13, 1756, he had to impose his will again by holding another solemn parliamentary session. He rode through Paris, where the prevailing mood was silent hostility. The magistrates listened impassively as the King's Chancellor read out three declarations. First, he reconfirmed the *Unigenitus* bull as a law of the State; secondly, he prohibited the magistrates from delaying the exercise of the law; thirdly, he abolished sixty secular advisory positions in the parliament. These announcements were greeted with astonishment, which quickly turned to indignation. Most of the gentlemen were incensed by the royal proclamations and handed in their resignations at once. News spread like wildfire through the capital, where the population sided wholeheartedly with the parliament. The King was violently criticized. The verses that people mumbled to one another now invoked his death:

> *You go to Choisy, you go to Crécy,*
> *Oh that you would go to Saint-Denis!*[15]

Twenty

THE ASSASSINATION

ATTEMPT

Gloom pervaded the beginning of the year 1757. The weather was cold and humid. The Marquise, like most of the courtiers, had a dreadful cough. Madame Victoire's cold was so bad that she could not follow the Court to Trianon and had to stay in her quarters at Versailles. On January 5, the King came to see her. Her condition was not alarming. After spending a short time with her, Louis XV intended to leave again for Trianon, where he was supposed to celebrate the Epiphany. At a quarter of six, he was about to board his coach when a man cut through the ranks of his guard, came right up to him and then ran away. The King took two steps forward, faltered, grasped the Duc de Montmirail, turned toward the Dauphin and the Duc d'Ayen and mumbled, "I've just been given a nasty blow." He then put his hand to his chest and found it was covered with blood. "I've been assassinated," he said. "It's that man there. Don't hurt him."[1]

While people seized the culprit, the King was led to his bedchamber, which wasn't ready to receive him since his servants were at Trianon. His attendants seated the wounded monarch in an armchair, as comfortably as they could, and found only two handkerchiefs to stem the flow of blood from his wound. "I've been stabbed! I won't pull through!" mumbled Louis XV and then fainted. People ran here and there in a panic. His Majesty's surgeon, La Martinière, was sent for immediately. As they waited for the expert, those present disagreed as to whether it was better to let the blood flow from the wound or not.

They decided just to undress him and lay him out on his bed, directly on the bare mattress. When he regained consciousness, he asked for a confessor urgently. The chaplain serving at that time received his first confession and gave him absolution. At this juncture, the Queen's surgeon and the Dauphine's first surgeon arrived, but they did not dare examine the wound in La Martinière's absence. As for Bouillac, physician to the Children of France, he decided the wounded man should be bled (though he had certainly already lost sufficient quantities of blood!).

The royal family had just been told of the assassination attempt. Madame la Dauphine rushed over first and immediately sent for sheets and a shirt from her husband's quarters. The Queen, deathly pale, remained prostrate at her husband's bedside. Mesdames, who had been summoned without being forewarned of the misfortune, fainted at the sight of their father soaked in his own blood. The Dauphin was in a state of shock and sobbed loudly when the King handed him the key to his writing desk, saying, "My son, this now concerns you. May you be happier than I was. I'm leaving you the kingdom at a very critical moment. I hope you'll have enough insight to govern for the best." The Dauphin took his father's hands, kissed them and mumbled, "Would to God that I had received the blow!" "That would have been far more painful for me!" replied Louis XV. Then he asked for his confessor again.

When La Martinière finally arrived at the illustrious victim's bedside, he examined the wound and announced that it was not dangerous. In her joy, the Queen flew into his arms and kissed him. But there was still cause for worry—the weapon might have been poisoned. Frightened and anguished, Louis XV became short of breath. He was bled again, four hours after the first bleeding. Somewhat calmed, the sovereign confessed a second time and stayed alone with Father Desmarets for over half an hour. The holy oils were brought in, but since Cardinal de La Rochefoucauld was not present to administer them, the ceremony of Extreme Unction was postponed. Believing that his final hour had arrived, Louis XV made honorable amends; he asked the Queen and his children to forgive him for his scandalous past, and said that he felt serene leaving the kingdom in hands as qualified as those of his son. Silence reigned, interrupted only by the royal family's sobs.

Overwhelmed by the news, Madame de Pompadour had fainted as well. She had to be revived and bled. In spite of her weak state, she had insisted on being taken immediately to her apartment at the château, where she waited for news of the King. Bernis, who had arrived at Versailles before her, went down to see her. "She threw herself into his arms, weeping and sobbing," and even her enemies would have been moved. The Abbé begged her to "summon all her inner strength, to be prepared for anything, and to submit to Providence."[2] But he added that she should not listen to people who might advise her to leave. As the friend of the King and the possessor of State secrets, she should only obey the monarch's orders. Admitted into the sovereign's bedchamber, the Abbé "came back to console her at all hours of the night."[3]

The following morning, the physicians were fully heartened. At midnight La Martinière had "lifted the device" and noted that there was no sign of poisoning. The King had slept, and there was every reason to believe he would make a rapid recovery since the wound was very superficial. In spite of the surgeon's assurances that the wound was not serious, the King continued to think he was in mortal danger. He asked the Dauphin to preside over the Council. Gripped once again by his recurrent morbid fears, Louis XV sank into a state of deep melancholy. He behaved like a person who was seriously ill. Prostrated behind the curtains of his bed, he hardly moved or ate. His family did not leave his side. On the ninth day, the physicians exhorted him to take a few steps.

As soon as they had recovered from their initial fright, the courtiers became more interested in Madame de Pompadour's fate than the King's. Would she be sent away? Would she leave of her own free will? People recalled the unforgettable scenes at Metz that had brought about Madame de Châteauroux's disgrace. The King's confession and his repeated conversations with Father Desmarets suggested that the reign of the priests could be following upon the reign of the favorite. The Queen and her daughters focused their minds on the sovereign's conversion. "All eyes were on the Dauphin; he was the rising sun. . . . The drawing room outside the King's bedchamber was a true arena where people whispered to each other, putting on airs of great serenity."[4]

Under the pretext of so-called friendship, "people called on the Marquise to see the expression on her face."[5] They drifted in and out of her apartment as if it were church during Holy Week. The unfortunate Jeanne-Antoinette did nothing but weep, and sometimes she fainted. Though Quesnay, who saw the King five times a day, kept assuring her that he was almost fit enough to attend a ball, she could not set her mind at rest. If the monarch was in such satisfactory condition, why didn't he get in touch with her? The only person the Marquise trusted was Bernis. He had promised that he would faithfully tell her whatever the King might say about her. However, the Abbé had also told her frankly that if the sovereign were to ask his advice on what conduct to follow with her, he would recommend that he "put an end to the scandal, by no longer living on familiar terms with her."[6]

As she waited anxiously for news, Jeanne-Antoinette never left her apartment and tried to put on a valiant front for her visitors. But she was very distressed: the King seemed to ignore her. The royal family thought they were in a strong enough position to force her to leave Versailles. The elderly Comtesse de Toulouse informed the Abbé of their wish. He responded with polite indignation. As the possessor of the monarch's secrets, he said, Madame de Pompadour had to wait for the King himself to express his wishes. Frustrated by this irrefutable argument, the royal family turned to Machault. They flattered and cajoled him. They convinced him that it would be admirable to help the sovereign reach a decision—a painful one, but necessary for his inner peace. They insinuated that, afterward, he would have a very good chance of being appointed Prime Minister.

Though Saint-Florentin and Rouillé had come by to see the Marquise several times, Machault had not yet visited her. Madame de Pompadour had an uneasy presentiment on seeing him walk into her small drawing room for the first time a week after the attempted assassination. They were left alone. When the minister walked out, she burst into tears. "I must leave, my dear Abbé," she said to Bernis as he came in. After drinking some orange blossom tea—with great difficulty for her teeth were chattering—she gave the order to prepare for her departure to Paris. She then retired to her drawing room with her confidant and asked that no one be allowed in except her intimate friends and the ministers.

Soon the Maréchale de Mirepoix was announced. "What are all these trunks for?" she cried out. "Your servants say you are leaving." "Alas, dear friend, it is the master's will, Monsieur de Machault told me." "And what is his opinion?" "That I should go at once. . . ." "He wants to be the master, your Lord Chancellor, and he is betraying you. He who quits the game loses it," exclaimed the Maréchale.[7] The Prince de Soubise, the Abbé de Bernis and Marigny came in to see the Marquise shortly after Madame de Mirepoix. They spoke among themselves for almost an hour and persuaded their friend not to leave Versailles. Marigny slipped away to warn Madame du Hausset. "She's staying," he said, "but mum's the word! We will make believe she is going so as not to rouse her enemies. It is the little Maréchale who convinced her; but her guard (this was her nickname for Monsieur de Machault) will pay."[8] The Marquise regained her composure and on the eleventh day after the assassination attempt, her hopes were raised, for at last she received a note from the King."[9]

Louis XV was beginning to get up and walk around his bedroom, leaning lightly on his cane. He continued to look sad and weary. His family never left his side. The Dauphin followed him even into his private cabinet. The Queen and the princesses came by to pay court, before and after mass, and stayed until he made a sign that they should leave. They came up to him one by one and kissed his hand before being kissed by him. One afternoon, at around two o'clock, when almost everyone had left for lunch, the King, who was still in his dressing gown and nightcap, signaled to the Dauphine that it was time to leave and told the Dauphin not to follow him. He came up to Madame de Brancas as she was leaving. "Please give me your mantelet," he said. Without showing any surprise, the Duchess handed him her mantelet, which he threw over his shoulders. He took leave of her and went down to see Madame de Pompadour. "It was like the Deity in the Opera who was brought in by stage machinery to allay all fears."[10]

When he returned, at around four o'clock, he was a different man. He smiled, talked affably and even jested about the short cape he was wearing. The following day, he dressed, went hunting and resumed his normal way of life. In a very short time, Jeanne-Antoinette had succeeded in comforting him and reviving his taste for life. Though she knew very little about the assassin, she assured him that he was a madman who had acted alone; his sword had not been provided by either the Jesuits or the magistrates.

In one hour, Madame de Pompadour had reasserted her influence over the monarch. The Court was amazed, the schemers disconcerted, the Dauphin agitated, the Dauphine petrified. The Marquise, however, had recovered her serenity. Everyone returned to pay court to her. It was now clear that her reign would last for a long time to come. "I will say only one word concerning all the horrors that took place in the King's bedchamber," she wrote to Choiseul. "Imagine the second part of Metz, except for the sacraments, which he was not in a position to receive. . . . Have no fear that these events will weaken my courage. Only the loss of the King could do this. He's alive, and I don't care about anything else. Cabal, humiliations, writings, etc., nothing will scare me and I will serve him no matter what happens to me, as long as I'm in a position to do so."[11]

While an anxious public opinion wanted to know who had armed the assassin and sought to unravel the reasons behind this great crime, the King's immediate entourage followed the Marquise's example and decided to characterize the criminal as a madman or fanatic. As soon as he was arrested, he was put in the Guard Room, stripped of his belongings and left stark naked. Anyone could go see him and talk to him freely. He was almost an attraction. The man, whose name was Damiens, admitted his crime, but refused to say whether he had accomplices. "Beware of Monsieur le Dauphin," is all he said. A conspiracy was feared and this led to several arrests. Transferred to the Versailles prison on Machault's orders, Damiens endured a first form of torture; his feet and calves were burned with red-hot irons to make him talk. He struggled as best he could, but informed against no one. While waiting for him to be tried and sentenced, there was endless speculation. Some people attributed his crime to the parliament, others to the Jesuits, with each side blaming the other for the ignominious act. Every day insults to the King were posted on walls in the capital and even in Versailles, on the walls of the château. The sovereign, who wanted to be kept apprised of everything that was being said about him and all the plots against him, demanded complete candor from his ministers. For years, copies of private correspondences had been sent to him as a matter of course; they were opened in the offices of the *Intendant des Postes*, Jeannelle, and skillfully resealed before being forwarded to their addressees. This institution was called the *Cabinet noir* (Black Cabinet), and it was not always used solely for political ends, for Louis XV also loved knowing about his subjects' love affairs.

Madame de Pompadour often resorted to Jeannelle's services. Given the seriousness of the circumstances and the King's depressive state, the Marquise insisted that special precautions be taken. The *Cabinet noir* was to avoid giving him letters that alluded to criminal plots against him or letters saying dreadful things about him. Jeannelle forwarded her orders to d'Argenson, who was in charge of the Paris sector. He refused to abide by them. Profoundly annoyed by an attitude that she regarded as damaging to the monarch, Madame de Pompadour retaliated against the minister. This became the perfect opportunity for her to get rid of an enemy who had been feuding with her underhandedly for years. He seemed to be the only person not to have grasped that she had recovered her former prerogatives. She had tried, on Bernis's advice, to get closer to him, but d'Argenson had seen these attempts as "the desperate efforts of a drowning person grasping at straws."[12] The Marquise's resentment of him had grown even greater. She arranged to be taken to see him and addressed him aggressively. "Monsieur," she said, "these abominations must be concealed from the King. He cannot sleep and is worried. Continue to watch over his safety, but do not speak to him about it." "Madame," he replied, "no one is more eager to do so than I. Please ask the King—in one of those moments of kindness and intimacy when he can't refuse you anything—not to question me further. I would be only too happy and glad to respect a silence that might be useful and necessary to the King's health; but I can't if and when he questions me." "I understand," Madame de Pompadour resumed with resentment, "you prefer to see him unhappy and pose as the good servant. But, Monsieur, these letters are quite extraordinary. It is odd that Berryer,[13] who controls the entire police force, fails to find any letters, whereas your small staff, which is not looking for them, always finds them."[14] The minister's phelgmatic response had exasperated her. Bernis found her at home, leaning on the fireplace, still in her coat, her hands in her muff. "You look like a lamb lost in dreams," he said to her. "A wolf is making the lamb dream,"[15] she replied and then burst into tears. The King walked in just at that moment. Seeing her upset, he put some Hoffman drops into a glass of water and handed it to her. She drank it, kissed his hands and regained her composure.

On the following day, the Court learned of the dismissal of d'Argenson and Machault. Their removal had been decided by the King and Madame de Pompadour. Louis XV did not sacrifice d'Argenson just to appease his favorite's rancor. People had persuaded him that d'Argenson, with his cabals, had a way of fanning the flames of discord in Paris and Versailles. But d'Argenson was a man of experience, and with the start of a war that was, to say the least, disquieting, he was someone who would have compelled respect from the military command. His nephew and successor, Monsieur de Paulmy,[16] though a perfect gentleman, seemed very young to be taking on such responsibilities.

Machault's dismissal was even more surprising. He had been very close to Madame de Pompadour. He was criticized for his accommodating attitude toward her, his authoritarian ways, his dryness and haughtiness. But the King resented him for having made him hold the last solemn session of the parliament and not predicting that this would bring the parliament's rebellion to a head, a rebellion that might even have inspired the assassination attempt.[17] Machault was known to have a genuine political intelligence and an invaluable knowledge of the Navy, which he managed along with the position of Lord Chancellor. Now, given the parliamentary crisis and the coming armed sea conflict with England, his replacement had to be, if not superior to him in intellect and knowledge, at least his equal. But this was not the case of Monsieur de Moras, who was given both Finances and the Navy, and immediately complained that the double assignment was too burdensome. When Choiseul asked her why she had made "such laughable choices," the Marquise answered that she thought the former ministers should be replaced by men who held subordinate positions in their departments. Choiseul pointed out that "this might have been a cogent reason for her personally, nonetheless on this occasion, the beginning of a war that was terrifying in scope and in all its ramifications, it was not in the best interests of the State."[18]

"With the confidence of a child," Madame de Pompadour was convinced that "with her help everything would go well," writes Bernis. "I didn't see things the same way, nor did our allies. Given the circumstances they regarded the dismissal of the two ministers as a major error."[19] The all-powerful Marquise, who had appointed Bernis Minister of State, gave Choiseul a gracious welcome when he returned from Rome. She saw to his appointment as ambassador to Vienna to protect the interests of the alliance, which she considered as being primarily her handiwork. Moreover, she intended to help the King bring his recalcitrant parliament to heel. She was experiencing the giddiness of power.

However, some of her friends warned her against possible impending dangers. "As long as Messieurs d'Argenson and de Machault were at their posts, the public blamed them for the misfortunes of the State," the Comte de Sade wrote her.[20] "Their exile exposes the King, and you too, Madame. Everyone knows the confidence he has in you; he loves you, talks to you, and listens to you. What a glorious moment for someone who loves the King and the State. Don't let yourself be seduced by bad advice. Don't listen to those who tell you that the population is capable of bearing new taxes. . . . I think that the King has only one resource left for finding money—to get it by reforming his Household. No one is so unjust as to want him to cut back on his pleasures, but he should end the abuses and thieving that don't contribute to the magnificence of his Court, or its splendor, or its pleasures. . . . The reform I'm suggesting, though dreadful for a minister, is a simple thing for a King who is loved. Let him punish harshly the first person who dares grumble, or let him convince him through gentleness; let him make everyone aware of the situation he is in, and the poverty of the people; let him hold out hope that he will restore things in happier times, and grant other favors. There is no Prince, no great noblemen who will not comply with the demands of the moment.

"Since no one is suspicious of me, I hear everyone's complaints; the grumbling is universal. I'm too attached to you to flatter you and too truthful to hide things. The parliament business causes countless misfortunes that would move you if you could see them clearly before you. A kingdom cannot be left without law for such a long time. A mediocre person might tell me that the King must not back down. But, Madame, you don't think this! Is it backing down to concede to the tears of an entire people kneeling before him?

"Truth is always listened to when it is spoken by the graces. You might find my initiative very bold, but it comes from a citizen who loves the State and is attached to you, from a man who has no fear in taking it because he knows you."[21]

The Marquise replied: "I know I have enemies, I know who they are, I did nothing to attract them and I have contempt for them."[22]

The young Marmontel wrote her a letter, expressing the same sentiments as the Comte de Sade. "Now that the ministers have been dismissed and that the men who are replacing them have no power or influence, be aware, Madame, that eyes are riveted on you and that from now on reproaches and complaints will be leveled at you, whether ill fortune continues or public blessings, whether you bring a remedy or end it. In the name of your glory and peace of mind, Madame, make haste in bringing about this happy change. Do not wait until necessity commands it or another person does it; you would lose the praise and be accused of an evil for which you would not be responsible. Everyone who is attached to you has the same anxieties and the same wish as I." Madame de Pompadour answered that she "had courage and that she wanted her friends to have courage for her as well."[23]

Twenty-one

THE GIDDINESS OF POWER

Madame de Pompadour liked the monarchy as much as the King. The state of depression that had come over Louis XV since the assassination attempt contributed to bringing him even closer to a female companion in whom he could confide freely and openly. She gave him the strength he lacked and needed in order to take on the heavy responsibilities of government. His insatiable need for her reassuring presence gave this perpetually ailing woman indomitable strength. In spite of the exhortations of his confessor and those of the royal family, he and his former mistress continued to form an apparently indissoluble couple.

Madame de Pompadour was intelligent and had a great fund of knowledge, but she was not qualified to take on genuine political responsibilities. She thought, however, that her long conversations with the King, the ministers and the ambassadors had given her the experience she lacked. With most of the councillors indebted to her, she hoped she could govern with the sovereign in perfect harmony.

The kingdom at that moment needed the competence and skills of a clear-sighted statesman, experienced in the subtleties of politics. The hesitant initiatives of a woman, motivated as much by her love for the monarch as by resentment of her personal enemies, could endanger Louis XV; in addition the Marquise did not fully grasp the magnitude of the problems facing him. She thought the war would be brief and victorious; she was far from suspecting the perils of the Austrian alliance or the weakness of the French high command. She apparently also underestimated the gravity of the domestic crisis. Whereas the parliamentary rebellion had expressed itself in a predictable way, Damiens's assassination attempt pointed to its potentially violent consequences. Madame de Pompadour found it unacceptable that the parliament should have the audacity to go against the King. She was firmly convinced that Louis XV had to end this revolt with a show of authority; the magistrates were simply rebels who had to be punished. Royal power, in her view, had to be absolute and inviolable.

Now that this ongoing conflict had been revived by the *lit de justice* of December 13, it seemed imperative to bring it to an end. Three days after this memorable session, at the King's request, Madame de Pompadour had asked Bernis's advice on how best to deal with the members of the parliament. The Abbé encouraged the sovereign to be firm, but advised him to negotiate; he should summon the first Président, Monsieur de Maupeou, and demand that he bring the members who had resigned back to reason so that justice could be dispensed in a normal fashion. The Abbé also suggested that the sovereign tell Monsieur de Maupeou that he was willing to listen to his parliament's remonstrances, as custom required.

The King could benefit from the assassination attempt, for it had frightened the magistrates. Président Maupeou, as well as several of his colleagues, had rushed to Versailles. They remained there until they were reassured about the sovereign's state of health. Reacting emotionally, several "hotheads" wrote to the Chancellor that they were ready to resume their duties. But one ambitious member of the parliament colluded with a scheming minister and changed the wording in the letter, so that it seemed insolent. The text was examined in a Council meeting. Bernis felt that the equivocal expressions should be ignored and recommended replying favorably to the magistrates, who seemed eager to get into line. The other ministers disagreed. The Chancellor (who was still Machault) answered with "a haughtiness and dryness that dampened the zeal" of the repentant "hotheads." Bernis lamented this decision. It was a sure way of allowing the most unpredictable disturbances to develop in the capital and of fomenting the ire of the parliament members, just when the sovereign needed new appropriations for the war. Each minister now tried to follow his own political line with the parliament.[1]

Madame de Pompadour, for her part, tried to regain control of the situation. It was at this point that some friends thought it might be wise to arrange a discreet meeting between her and Président de Meinières,[2] one of the magistrates who had resigned and whose legal arguments had often prompted the remonstrances of his peers.[3] On January 26, at six o'clock, a valet let the Président in to see the Marquise. Alone, she stood next to the fireplace and eyed him scornfully from head to foot without saying a word. Chilled by this welcome, the Président went up to her timidly, like a schoolboy. "Bring a chair," she said "in an angry voice" to her valet, who didn't know which chair to bring her. Monsieur de Meinières sat opposite her "dying of fear" and delivered a very respectful harangue. He had come to plead the cause of his son whom the King had turned down twice for appointments, once for position as councillor in the parliament and, the second time, for admittance into a regiment.[4]

The Marquise sat "straight as a rod" and listened to him without taking her eyes off him for a second. When he had finished his speech, she told him that his son had been the victim of the rebellious attitude he had adopted in the parliament. "The King is the master, Monsieur; he does not find it appropriate to show you his displeasure personally, but to make you aware of it by depriving your son of a position. . . . He uses the means at his disposal; his will must be respected." On seeing her visitor upset at being responsible for his son's difficulties, the Marquise offered him a deal. "You know, for example, that right now the King would appreciate seeing signs of submission on the part of the gentlemen from the Inquiries and Petitions who have resigned; he has rewarded those who wrote him personal letters with acts of kindness. If you were to write him this kind of letter, and through your example enlist a few other members to write similar ones, you would be helping the government under the present circumstances. I would be able to hold this up in your favor, and then you could expect a change in the King's attitude toward you. But if I have nothing to say to H.M. other than, 'Sire, I saw Monsieur de Meinières today; he assured me of his most respectful attachment to you, etc.,' the King will ask, 'What has he done to prove it? Nothing.' And things will remain as they are and I won't be able to do anything for you."[5]

In reply, Monsieur de Meinières told the Marquise that he could not write such a letter, for he would be discredited with his professional group. "Given the choice between losing my honor or seeing my son deprived of a position, I do not waver. . . ."

"Monsieur de Meinières," she said, "I would like to make you happy, but I see that this will not be possible, for you are not flexible."

"You can see my reasons, Madame."

"They are worthless. . . . You would not be granted your wish for your son at once; hence it would not seem like a reward for your accommodating attitude." And since the Président stressed the dishonor that would befall him if he took this step, the Marquise started laughing. "I am always surprised to hear so-called honor invoked for not doing what the King desires, wants and commands, when it should be clear that true honor lies in carrying out the duties of one's position and in putting a stop, as soon as possible, to the disorder which reigns in all sectors of the administration because of the lack of justice. That, Monsieur, is what honor should consist in—in acknowledging your wrongs, the rashness of an approach so contrary to all rules and decorum; in adopting a different behavior so as to erase, in the minds of the King and his subjects, the negative impression that an action like this inevitably causes. No one is unaware, I think, that I greatly respect the magistracy, and I would give anything not to have to make such a reproach to this august tribunal, the foremost parliament in the kingdom."[6]

Monsieur de Meinières listened to the Marquise, and "marveled" at the ease with which she expressed herself and the aptness of the terms she used. And when he tried to defend himself, she resumed her speech, with greater vehemence: "Let me repeat, it is the King's excessive kindness that has made you all, today, so enterprising and so difficult. In the end, Monsieur, his kindness is wearing thin and he wants to be the master. Don't go attributing the King's particular and personal resentment to the ministers, as you always do. This has nothing to do with them. It is the King who is personally wounded here and who, of himself, without having been roused by anyone, wants to be obeyed.

"And honestly, I ask you, gentlemen of the parliament, who are you to go against the will of your master as you have? Do you think that Louis XV is not as great a king as Louis XIV? Do you think that today's parliament is made up of magistrates who are superior in distinction, capacity and merit than those who were in the parliament then? Oh, I wish it were so!" she exclaimed before reminding the dumbfounded magistrate of the decree of 1667 and the special session of 1673. When Monsieur de Meinières dared to mumble that the magistrates in Louis XIV's day had yielded to the monarch's absolute power, Madame de Pompadour lost her temper. "What a sentiment! What an expression!"[7] she cried out. Experienced in verbal sparring, Monsieur de Meinières found the appropriate rejoinder: Louis XV was not a despot, he respected the laws and was willing to listen to the truths that the magistrates told him. "It's a great misfortune," he said, "when a king does not want to listen to the professionals whose institutional function is to warn him of the possible surprises in store for him. And allow me to say that Louis XV would not at present be burdened by the immense debts contracted by Louis XIV if the members of parliament living at the time of his reign had shown some resistance to the profuse creation of positions and pensions in the city that now oppress the State."[8]

Madame de Pompadour ended the interview, undoubtedly surprised that Monsieur de Meinières had dared to stand his ground. She had no idea that he left "filled with wonder and admiration" for her. The Marquise bore no resemblance to the "sultana" vilified in the satirical pamphlets. They went their separate ways and thought things over. When she learned that Monsieur de Meinières was preparing a compromise, the favorite summoned him again. On February 8, he reappeared in her study and tried to plead the cause of the parliament members who had resigned and whose positions the King had decided to abolish. He pleaded in vain. In the name of the principles of absolute monarchy, which she defended tooth and nail, the Marquise remained inflexible. "The King's honor, which is just as important as yours, must be treated with consideration and spared. He has twice announced his decision to exile certain individuals and to replace them in their posts; do you think he can change his mind in the face of the whole world? . . . For even if you were a common citizen, could you calmly watch a handful of men go against the authority of the King of France? Wouldn't you have a bad opinion of them? Remove your little magistrate's cloak, Monsieur le président, and you'll see all of this the way I see it."[9] Madame de Pompadour was certainly the King's best attorney, but she didn't succeed in making the parliament members budge from their positions.

As the only active parliament, the Great Chamber of the Parlement conducted the investigation for the trial of Damiens, the attempted assassin of the King. It included "a sufficient number of magistrates to conduct a criminal trial."[10] The would-be regicide had been incarcerated in the Conciergerie, in the same Montgomery tower where Ravaillac, Henri IV's assassin, had been imprisoned. The members of his family had also been arrested and imprisoned. It soon became known that this forty-two-year-old man, originally from Artois, had started his career as a valet with the Jesuits and that his last job had been with Madame de Sainte-Reuze, the mistress of the Marquis de Marigny, Jeanne-Antoinette's brother. She had dismissed him at the Marquis's urgings, for he had thought him dangerous. Unstable and violent, he had committed theft in her house. Damiens had not stayed long with any of his other employers, who were almost all members of the legal profession.

Fearing that he was part of a conspiracy, the judges tried to make him name those who had armed him. But Damiens informed against no one. In the hope of discovering his secrets, the magistrates asked the guards, who watched him around the clock, to transcribe his comments into a notebook. He revealed nothing that wasn't already known from the cross-examinations. He asserted that he "had made an attempt on the King's life because H.M. hadn't listened to his parliament's remonstrances." He had not wanted to kill the monarch, but had only "wanted him to think about the poverty of his people." He was also anxious to know whether the parliament had resumed its functions, whether the Archbishop was still in Conflans and whether the sacraments were still being refused. He blamed Monseigneur de Beaumont for causing the religious conflicts and stated that there would be no social peace until the Church obeyed the parliament. He also said that

"God would console him because he was dying for the people, that the King had poor advisers, and that the ministers concealed most political matters from him."[11]

As far as the magistrates were concerned, Damiens was unbalanced and his slender intellect had been "fired up" by his poor grasp of remarks that he had picked up near the Palais de Justice (the Courthouse) and at refreshment counters, as well as in the homes of his former employers. But since they were for the most part advisers to the parliament, his judges stressed the criminal's "insanity." During the ten sessions of the trial, they showed exceptional severity in order to clear the parliament of suspicion. Président Hénault, who sat among them, felt that "this monster was of a unique kind; different from Ravaillac or Jacques Clément; religion had no part in his atrocious act. He had no accomplice; his was a fanaticism motivated only by pity, he said, for the hapless population, who had armed him against the best of our kings. . . . I was one of his judges. I have never seen a more insolent man; he made us lower our eyes as he looked over all the benches. The surprising thing was that when he was questioned concerning his theft he became humbled, whereas on the subject of his hateful deed, he was again audacious. However, he did show repentance, and said that he would have been sorry had he succeeded in his crime."[12] Since Damiens consistently denied having knowledge of the writings justifying regicide, the thesis of the solitary, feebleminded "monster" was never challenged, for it satisfied all sides.

The sentence was handed down on March 26, 1757. Like Ravaillac, Damiens was condemned to be quartered, and his mortal remains burned at the stake and dispersed in the wind. No voices were raised against this barbaric punishment. It was regarded as the proper sentence for regicide. Conceived as a kind of grand spectacle of collective expiation, the execution attracted a large crowd of people on the Place de Grève.[13] Several aristocratic ladies prided themselves on attending, but their presence at this kind of torture session inevitably shocked the Court; it preferred to cast a veil of decency over the dreadful punishment inflicted on the condemned man.

Since the assassination attempt, rumors abounded and the malaise in the kingdom was vividly expressed in countless clandestine writings. The official newspapers made it appear that the tragedy had made everyone in France rally in unison around the *Bien-Aimé*; no words were sufficiently strong to denounce the crime. But in the meanwhile satirical tracts were distributed clandestinely, as well as coded letters and drawings of swords, upside-down lilies and broken crowns. Posters insulting the King continued to appear in the most unexpected places. In the light of these activities, Damiens hardly seemed like an isolated fanatic, or the agent of a political faction, but like the spokesman for the abused lower classes, squeezed for taxes, and eager to find both scapegoats and defenders.

Following the example of Voltaire and most of the *philosophes*,[14] Madame de Pompadour saw Damiens as a figure whose archaic fanaticism dishonored the century of Louis XV. As for the King, he remained convinced that the crime had been instigated by the seditious remarks of the magistrates for whom his assassin had worked. A short time after the execution of the criminal, he said to the Marquise: "If it hadn't been for those councillors and presidents, I wouldn't have been struck by that monsieur" (this was how he always referred to his would-be assassin). "Oh, Sire!" Madame de Pompadour exclaimed. "Read the trial," he replied, "it was those gentlemen's remarks that he describes as unsettling his mind."[15]

The King and his favorite were getting on marvelously. The ambassador from Saxony even claimed that they had resumed intimate relations. Trips and small dinners succeeded one another at the usual pace. The Marquise was dazzlingly elegant and asked Madame de Lutzelbourg to send her lace. However, she also followed Bernis's negotiations with Starhemberg very attentively; these resulted in the signing of a new French-Austrian treaty, on May 1, 1757. Even before the agreement was signed, the French royal forces had crossed the Rhine, for the King was very eager to assure the Empress of his good faith.

Madame de Pompadour wanted Choiseul to be appointed ambassador to Vienna. Success depended on her thwarting Rouillé's plan to get the Comte de Broglie appointed to that post. Though he was Minister of Foreign Affairs, Rouillé was gravely ill and actually had very little authority. Broglie, however, was a serious rival. The King knew him and had appreciated his services. But he had the shortcoming of not supporting the alliance. And therefore it was not very difficult to convince Bernis, who was all-powerful in the Council, to impose Choiseul instead of Broglie. The Abbé "decided to leave this nomination up to the Marquise and to make himself useful to the Comte de Stainville"[16] (this was how the future Duc de Choiseul was still called). The latter was very deferential with Bernis, who professed his friendship to him with great warmth.

Realizing that it would be practically impossible to work under a minister as narrow-minded as Rouillé, who moreover did not approve of the treaty that he would have to uphold, Choiseul decided to get him to resign and be replaced by Bernis. When he told Madame de Pompadour of his intention, she began by protesting. "But Monsieur Rouillé is dying; he sleeps in the Council meetings and in his study. We can simply wait for apoplexy to deliver us of him; the King doesn't want to be responsible for the homicide of a decent man but inept minister by dislodging him; if he were to dislodge himself on his own, the King would be very pleased. But Madame Rouillé, who loves the Court, like a bourgeoise who was not meant to be here, will always stop him. . . ." The Comte de Stainville interrupted her in a lively tone: "Would you like me to bring you Rouillé's resignation in an hour? Would you?"[17] Madame de Pompadour called his plan mad, but consented to it with a laugh.

A short time later, Choiseul returned in triumph. He had asked to be announced at Madame Rouillé's and had convinced her that her husband was endangering his life by taking on such heavy responsibilities. He promised her that if her husband would agree to resign from Foreign Affairs, he would still retain his position as Superintendent of the Postal Services and this would allow him to remain at Court. Madame Rouillé didn't need to be coaxed; she convinced her husband to give up the higher position. Choiseul had won.

The news surprised Madame de Pompadour as much as it left her overjoyed. She was dazzled by her protégé's speediness, boldness and skill. From then on, everything was like child's play for her. Several days later, her dear Bernis succeeded Rouillé. Before taking his oath to the King, the Abbé had the honor of informing him of the Kollin victory—the Austrian forces' defeat of Frederick II on June 19. This was an unhoped-for success. On May 7, the King of Prussia had laid siege outside Prague, where Maria Theresa's troops[18] were deployed with hardly any ammunition. But an unexpected attack, led by the Comte de Daun,[19] had forced the Prussians to end the siege. Within five weeks, the Court of Vienna, which had been on the verge of ruin, regained a clear superiority over the Prussians. This pleased Louis XV immensely.

It was during a trip to Choisy that Choiseul read the clauses of the historic accord that would seal the destiny of France and Austria for several decades. As he handed him the text of the treaty, Bernis seemed to be saying: "Here, once you've read this, you'll have admit that I'm the greatest man in politics there ever was."[20] The Maréchal de Belle-Isle tapped the ground with his cane as a way of showing his approval of the Abbé, and Madame de Pompadour beamed with pleasure. Choiseul spent the night reading the treaty. He was appalled by its content. At least, so he claims in his *Mémoires*. However, he was careful not to let his doubts show in the morning. His career was at stake. As he returned the document to the Marquise, in the presence of the Abbé and the Maréchal, she asked him "what he had thought of the work accomplished." "It's so huge," he replied, "that it would be rash of me to give my opinion after one reading. This treaty has to be studied at length before all its ramifications can be grasped. It is a great, indeed very great, project, but its implementation frightens me, I must admit." Choiseul had mastered the subtleties of diplomatic language to perfection in the days before it had become wooden. "We will reassure you," murmured Belle-Isle. And then they spoke of other matters. Choiseul spent the beginning of the summer at Court and made his entry into Vienna on August 20, 1757.

The treaty certainly contained much for the new ambassador to worry about, since he was "in charge of lifting all the obstacles that could impede its execution."[21] The new accord increased France's responsibilities considerably. Louis XV pledged to support 6,000 German soldiers fighting on the side of Austria, send 105,000 men to assist

Maria Theresa and pay her 12 million florins. He also promised not to lay down arms until Austria had recovered Silesia. In exchange for his help, the Empress promised to give the King several cities in Flanders (Mons, Ypres, Furnes, Ostende, Nieuport) and to hand over the rest of the Netherlands to the Infante of Parma, husband of Madame Elisabeth, provided the duchies of Parma, Piacenza and Guastalla reverted to Austria. In effect, the agreement put France at the service of Austria and committed her to a continental war whose outcome was uncertain—whereas, in fact, her principal enemy was England, against whom she had to wage war on the seas and in the colonies.

Twenty-two

A Perpetual Combat

At Versailles, Compiègne, Choisy and Fontainebleau, all people talked about was the war. Obsessed with diplomacy and strategy, Madame de Pompadour could easily have neglected the pleasures of the King and the Court had she not been afraid of someone replacing her. She seemed "at the helm of government"[1] along with the Abbé de Bernis. The ministers, who suffered this subjugation without complaining, stopped by the favorite's twice a day to bring her up to date. When they were with her, they attended to affairs of State and, given the opportunity, to their own affairs. Her regular visitors grew in number constantly, reaching about forty at that time. "Never was any influence so far-ranging. . . . She did absolutely everything."[2]

The treaty with the Empress guided most of her actions, and she seemed more preoccupied by the continental war than by the operations against England. She followed the army's progress on the maps that were spread out in her study, and grew impatient with the Maréchal d'Estrées's slow advance, which Vienna complained about as well. When her old friend Pâris-Duverney informed her of the troops' situation, she would not rest until she had arranged to get d'Estrées relieved of his command.

The war had further increased the power of the Pâris brothers. Montmartel had been enjoying extraordinary trust in Europe for a long time and he directed all of the kingdom's financial operations. As for

Duverney, he happily resumed his activities as a supplier of food and ammunitions. As someone who had always collaborated with generals and ministers, his experience in all aspects of war was impossible to match. Bernis regarded him as a kind of genius in this field. The Abbé had enjoined the Comte d'Estrées to confer with him at the beginning of the campaign. But they had had a falling out and soon there was a shortage of food and ammunition, and to the Empress's great displeasure, the army did not advance as quickly as planned. At Versailles Duverney made it clear that the Maréchal had shown him contempt and that he held the Maréchal responsible for the breakdown in operations.

He thought that Richelieu was the person who might live up to his expectations and satisfy his desire for revenge. Forever craving glory, Richelieu had been incensed when he heard of d'Estrées's nomination and he dreamed of supplanting him. He confided his ambitions to Duverney, who had held him in high esteem ever since the capture of Minorca. The financier thought he saw in Richelieu—grand-nephew of the famous Cardinal—a leader of men and the worthy successor of the late Maréchal de Saxe. The two comrades reached an agreement and won over the Maréchal de Maillebois[3] and Monsieur de Crémilles,[4] men whom the King trusted. The only person who still had to be persuaded was the favorite, who was always suspicious of Richelieu.

Duverney expounded a plan to the King, in the presence of the Marquise and Monsieur de Paulmy, a minister in name only, who had been reduced to the part of a bit player. Duverney's plan was to attack the King of Prussia from the Elbe and Oder rivers. The French and Austrians were to converge on Magdeburg, with supplies being sent on the Meuse, the Rhine and the Weser. Duverney suggested replacing d'Estrées with Richelieu and giving the Prince de Soubise an army of 25,000 to 30,000 men who were to take action in Saxony immediately "in order to keep the King of Prussia amused, without risking battle, and to give the Austrians time to capture Silesia."[5] The item about Soubise was included in order to get the approval of Madame de Pompadour, who had been very disappointed that her friend had not been appointed commander-in-chief of the royal armies, as she had wished. She wanted him "to win some signal advantage so that she could legitimately request he be given the command of the armies and a position on the Council in his military capacity."[6] She would thereby have had one more loyal person in a key post. "Pâris-Duverney had no trouble convincing Madame de Pompadour that this plan was excellent, for it made Monsieur de Soubise play such an attractive role and removed the Maréchal d'Estrées whom she could no longer stomach." She was convinced that her dear Soubise would win much glory, become Maréchal of France and replace Richelieu in the next campaign. "Friendship prevailed over hatred in her heart."[7] Duverney arranged a meeting between the Marquise and Richelieu, who promised to give the Prince de Soubise excellent troops. They both put on a pretense of mutual friendship.

Ultimately the decision belonged to the King and he was easily convinced by Duverney's arguments. Louis XV informed the Dauphin of the project and he approved of it, to the King's great relief. Indeed, he had begun to doubt whether he had made the right choice in giving the Comte d'Estrées the command of his armies. D'Estrées seemed much more preoccupied with guaranteeing his retreat in case of defeat than driven by the desire to win. Furthermore, he had the reputation of being hostile to the alliance. Once his mind was made up, the King assembled the Council and described the plan that he had decided to implement. His ministers had no choice but to approve it.

Appointed to replace d'Estrées, Richelieu set off for Germany on July 28. To everyone's surprise, the day after his departure, news came of the July 26 victory against the English and Hanoverians in Hastenbeck.[8] The enemy army had withdrawn and the Hanover Electorate, a possession of the King of England, fell to the French. In spite of this dazzling victory, the Maréchal d'Estrées was obliged to deliver his command to his successor. Though he could not collect the laurels for this victory, Richelieu decided to reap its fruits. He pillaged the conquered regions, earning the nickname "*Père la Maraude*" from his own soldiers. He soon advanced in the Electorate, easily subduing the cities of Hanover, Brunswick and Wolfenbuttel. At that point, the Duke of Cumberland, son of the King of England and commander-in-chief of the Anglo-Hanoverian army, wanted to enter into negotiations with him. The Maréchal answered that his only assignment was to fight, and Louis XV congratulated him on his reply.

However, several weeks later, when he and his demoralized troops had taken refuge in the city of Stade,[9] in the extreme north of the country, the Duke of Cumberland made another stab at negotiating with Richelieu. He flattered Richelieu, stressing the glory that would be his if the war were to end without bloodshed thanks to his peace-making gesture. Although Richelieu had just informed Bernis that he had surrounded the Hanoverian army, he agreed to enter into negotiations with Cumberland. And without awaiting orders from Versailles, on September 8, 1757, he concluded the Convention of Closter-Seven, according to which the Anglo-Hanoverians agreed to lay down arms until the end of the conflict. But neither Richelieu nor Cumberland had been given the mandate to make these decisions.

Threatened in the north by a landing of Swedish troops in Pomerania and in the east by the Russians, who were occupying eastern Pomerania, Frederick II was in a desperate position. While he protested vigorously to the English Crown against the Convention of Closter-Seven, the French were already congratulating themselves. They believed in the King of Prussia's impending defeat. Richelieu was thus given the power to ratify the accord, though he was told that capitulation would have been preferable to the convention he had signed. To be valid, the convention still had to be ratified by the British government and depended solely on the good faith of the English. Madame de Pompadour was satisfied, however: "I find the capitulation good and even excellent, though several points should be clarified,"[10] she wrote to Richelieu. Versailles was still ignorant of the fact that William Pitt, who had returned to government in the beginning of June, was opposed to the notorious convention and was busy convincing George II to disavow the Duke of Cumberland.[11] He did so on January 1, 1758.

In the meanwhile, Richelieu, who was convinced that he had won a great victory, allowed his regiments to plunder the country. He was in no hurry to get to Saxony, where Soubise—who had had to be content just harassing the Prussians and avoiding a real battle—was waiting for him. Some people accused Soubise of pusillanimity. When the Court of

Vienna complained, once again, of the French army's sluggishness, Madame de Pompadour wrote several letters to Richelieu asking him to discipline his army and bring aid to Soubise. "I shall not conceal from you that if you do not stop the plundering by your superior officers who are overturning the measures taken by him [Duverney] and causing food shortages where there used to be abundance, it will be impossible for me to stop Duverney from taking action against you."[12] Several days later she brought up the subject again: "I must urge you once again to put an end to the plunder and bad behavior of your army. I realize it is difficult to stop an evil that began with the campaign. But, Monsieur le Maréchal, if you don't put a stop to it now, in six months' time you will no longer be master. Surely you have intelligent people in your midst. Use them to get evidence against the rascals. The higher their rank, the greater the effect their punishment will have on their subordinates. I cannot help reproaching you for your leniency toward evildoers and nuisances. What can you possibly fear since your master supports you? If you don't want to punish them in person, send the evidence to the King. He will dispense justice. But, Monsieur le Maréchal, when one commands men, one must not fear impotent enemies, even if they have the power to harm you. One must be noble enough to sacrifice oneself to the welfare of the State. You will surely find me fierce and courageous. I shall always be so if I feel the King's glory is compromised and I see quite clearly that [if you fail to stop your army's lack of discipline] by the spring the King will be altogether without glory. He will be ruined and everyone else will be handing down orders to him when he should be handing them down to everyone."[13] In all her letters, the Marquise insisted that Richelieu should join Soubise, from whom she had great expectations. "For a week I have been seeing the King's army in danger, and the glory and life of a man whom I hold in the dearest friendship unduly compromised. . . . You're a sensitive person, you know my heart, consider how much I suffer."[14]

Richelieu had no desire to rush to the aid of Madame de Pompadour's great friend. Louis XV had to send Monsieur de Crémilles with his orders. This made Richelieu feel slighted and he suspected a maneuver on the part of the favorite, who thought it wise to justify herself: "I see nothing about the facts or the people that could lead you to believe that we wish to exile you. . . . I have no doubts that you have been given carte blanche concerning your return. Monsieur de Soubise has conveyed his exact situation here. . . . He didn't complain and didn't ask for help. He didn't let it be known to his army or in his letters here, the despair he felt because of his position, which was cruel indeed. I could sense its depth because of my friendship for him. But it was only in reply to my letters that he admitted to me that he had been suffering inwardly for several days."[15]

From Halberstadt, where he now was, Richelieu sent several battalions of reinforcement to Soubise, who had been obliged to merge his troops with those of the imperial army, under the command of the Prince of Saxe-Hildburghausen, and to become his subordinate. When Frederick II set up camp opposite them, the Prince of Saxe-Hildburghausen wanted to attack. Frederick II had only 20,000 men against an allied force of 60,000. Soubise hesitated, but finally consented to give battle, near the village of Rosbach, on November 5. Because of the superior strategies employed by the Prussian army, it was a disaster in spite of the heroism of the French troops.

When she learned of this defeat in a letter from the Prince de Soubise, the Marquise broke down and wept. She was unable to eat or sleep for several days. Louis XV tried to console her, assuring her repeatedly that the Prince de Soubise was not responsible for this fiasco that was so humiliating to French pride. Rage soon replaced despondency. Jeanne-Antoinette saw Richelieu as responsible for this misfortune. She opened her wounded heart to Choiseul: "Allow me, Monsieur l'Ambassadeur, to speak to you very frankly and for the last time about Monsieur de Richelieu. Yawn as you will, I must bore you with something that I did not want to say to anyone, for if I don't I'll die." Whereupon Madame de Pompadour launched into lengthy strategic considerations before coming to the point: "Monsieur de Richelieu is jealous of Monsieur de Soubise. He was very cross that Soubise wasn't under his command. He wanted to have the one hundred and forty thousand men—and, had they existed, five hundred thousand men—under his command and would have been even more distressed if

Soubise had defeated the King of Prussia. Hence he arranged things accordingly and for the capture of Dresden as well. That's the gospel truth. I shall never speak of it again, but not out of ignorance, and I want you to know about it, even if it gives you vapors."[16]

Public opinion raged against the Prince de Soubise and particularly against the favorite, who was held responsible for this defeat. For hadn't she imposed the appointment of an incompetent leader? People demanded Soubise's discharge. "Imagine my pain at the enormous injustice that was done to him in Paris. . . . it drives me to despair,"[17] Jeanne-Antoinette wrote to Madame de Lutzelbourg. She received anonymous letters filled with insults and death threats. "Our friend is very much to be pitied. The public would have forgiven Monsieur de Soubise's appointment only if he'd had a victory,"[18] Bernis wrote to Choiseul. "She gave Monsieur de Soubise the strongest assurances of friendship and so did the King."[19] The Rosbach defeat, followed by the defeat of the imperial troops at Leuthen and their loss of Silesia at the end of the year,[20] the news of the violation of the Convention of Closter-Seven and the recalling of the parliament—all these events shattered the Marquise.

Exhausted, ill and very depressed, she secretly made out her will on November 15, 1757.[21] She designated the Prince de Soubise as her executor and begged him to consider this "assignment as the incontrovertible proof of her trust in his probity and virtue." She bequeathed two rings to him: one with a big aquamarine-colored diamond, the other with a Guay engraving symbolizing friendship. "I flatter myself that he will never part with them," she wrote, "and that they will remind him of the person in the world who had the warmest feelings of friendship for him." It may have been during this painful period that Madame de Pompadour went secretly to see a "witch" to ask her under what circumstances she would meet death and whether it would be soon. "You will have time to know death is near," were the soothsayer's only words.[22]

The Marquise's enemies then tried to give her a rival, one who was particularly dangerous in that she was young, pretty and well born. Marie-Anne de Mailly, a relative of the King's former mistress and the estranged wife of the Marquis de Coislin, yielded to the King's advances without a moment's hesitation—perhaps even a bit too quickly. Titillated by this new romance, the Court distracted itself from the misfortunes of war by watching the duel between the two women. One evening, at Marly, Jeanne-Antoinette returned to her quarters completely exasperated, threw down her coat and muff, undressed in haste and dismissed her chambermaids. When she was alone with the faithful Nicole du Hausset, she exploded. "I never saw such insolence as that of Madame de Coislin. I was at the same table as her for a game of *brelan* this evening and you can't imagine what I suffered. The men and women seemed to take turns looking us over. Once or twice Madame de Coislin looked at me and said, 'I take the lot,' in the most insulting manner. And I thought I would faint when she said triumphantly, 'I have a hand full of kings.' I wish you could have seen her curtsey when she left me." "And the King," asked Madame du Hausset, "did he greet her warmly?" "You do not know him, my dear. If he was going to move her into my apartment tonight, he would treat her coldly in public and be extremely friendly with me. That's how he was educated, for by nature he is kind and open."[23]

Madame de Pompadour wrote to the King asking for permission to leave the Court. But Louis XV was in no hurry to answer her. Seeing her forlorn, Bernis inquired why she was sad. When she told him, the Abbé decided to write to the sovereign himself "to impress on him that a new mistress, paraded in public, would be harmful to his reputation and to governmental affairs, that it would offend the Court of Vienna which had appealed to Madame de Pompadour in its alliance with him."[24] He added that he would refuse to work with another woman and would resign from his ministry if this were to happen. This last statement proves, better than any other, the importance of Madame de Pompadour's role in political life.

Bernis's decision made the Marquise tremble with fear. The Abbé wrote his letter, read it to her, sealed it and gave it to the King in her presence. Her anguish was so great that she burst into tears. The very next day, Louis XV handed his minister a letter that he brought, still sealed, to Jeanne-Antoinette. She opened it, trembling. "The King spoke with great kindness and frankness; he described the Marquise's qualities and faults and promised to discontinue his relationship with her rival, because he realized the danger involved for his governmental affairs and his reputation."[25] Once again, Madame de Pompadour had prevailed, though she triumphed without glory. She had sacrificed everything for a man who stayed with her solely out of habit. Her youth was running out, her beauty was fading. She was probably suffering from both tuberculosis and a heart condition, and she felt frail. Yet she saw herself as indispensable to the King's glory. She still wanted to give him her support, haunted as he was by private torments, and help him surmount the difficulties of war. But could she do so with, as sole helper, a minister almost as depressive as his master? "My life is a perpetual combat,"[26] she said to Madame du Hausset.

Twenty-three

BERNIS'S FALL FROM GRACE

Madame de Pompadour still ruled over a Council the majority of whose members were far from talented or brilliant. Paulmy in the War Ministry and Moras in the Navy were overwhelmed by their duties. Boullongne had no idea what to do about the disastrous financial situation. Saint-Florentin behaved like a courtier. Bernis, who was in charge of Foreign Affairs, as well as relations with the parliament and religious questions,[1] seemed to be at the "pinnacle"[2] of power. But this was an impression that showed an ignorance of the difficulties he was wrestling with. The unhappy Abbé was answerable to an inaccessible and unpredictable sovereign and he tried to govern by taking into account Madame de Pompadour's wishes, which were not necessarily those of the monarch. It was up to him to unravel what Louis XV wanted. The latter "still led the same life and never talked about things that could flatter or rouse his interlocutors. This disgusted many of them. His even-tempered kindness could not make up for this fault, which seemed like a form of insensitivity or indecision; he followed the course of action suggested to him rather than his own, which would have been better. All of this affected subordination in the different orders of the State and put him in a cruel position,"[3] remarked the Duc de Croÿ sadly. During this period of uncertainty, "the Marquise, though she did not have the title, was in effect the King's Prime Minister."[4]

However, in spite of their long-standing friendship and the invaluable help Bernis had just given her, the Marquise had started to cool in her feelings toward him. Their views on foreign policy clashed. The Abbé was frightened by the defeats the allies had suffered. He considered it "madness" to continue a ruinously expensive war. He wanted the King and the Empress to initiate peace negotiations. He reminded Choiseul that the English threatened France on its coasts and in its colonies. The previous summer, the British had almost taken possession of the île de Ré and the île d'Aix. New attacks were expected in the spring. Furthermore, the situation in America was alarming. Was it reasonable to continue to fight for the Empress? "The King will do everything he can to support his allies, but I will never advise him to risk his crown," he wrote to the ambassador. "Since I was initially in charge of this great alliance, I should be believed when I advise peace. . . . The sacrifice of my pride and of an immense amount of work prevent me from being suspect."[5] He added that no French general was capable of conducting a victorious campaign against Frederick II and that bankruptcy threatened.

Bernis explained his arguments to the King and to Madame de Pompadour, but they showed incredible optimism. Encouraged by the Marquise, Louis XV had no intention of putting an end to the war. Besides, Choiseul claimed it would be shameful to abandon Maria Theresa before she had recovered Silesia. Bernis was appalled. "Let's be noble, my dear Comte," he said to Choiseul, "but let's not be taken in; let's be steadfast and faithful, but let's not bring about our downfall; let's start with the safety of the kingdom."[6] The perfect diplomat, and bearing his own future in mind, Choiseul trusted the mood of his master. It was premature and humiliating, he felt, to negotiate with Frederick II. He contended that the allied armies could still win a war that was only just beginning.

The thoughtlessness with which the King, the Marquise and their friends plunged into the days of Carnival further dismayed the Abbé. Madame de Pompadour had recovered her liveliness. "Gaiety suddenly got the upper hand to the point where she became radiantly beautiful once again. She had gained weight. She spoke only of romantic things. She seemed enchanted. The King grew more cheerful. There was no question of devoutness any more."[7] It also seemed as if the demon of politics had loosened its grip. But this was not the case. The Marquise wanted to maintain a distance from a gloomy Abbé who might make the sovereign—who was naturally inclined to skepticism—share his fears. The Carnival arrived just at the right time to tear him away from the inner demons that could make him lose faith in what Madame de Pompadour called his lucky star. The Carnival celebrations were intoxicating and this delighted the favorite. She had spirited Louis XV away from the pressures of his position and prevented him from listening to the despondent Bernis.

Richelieu's disgrace and the return of her dear Soubise had satisfied her. Without having been discharged—like Richelieu—from his command, he was coming to take up winter residence at Versailles. She welcomed her friend in the Château de Champs, which she was renting from the Duc de La Vallière. They returned to Choisy together. The King received the defeated warrior of Rosbach affectionately, whereas the Maréchal-Duc de Richelieu had been given the cold shoulder.

The "revelry" lasted only a week. The King and his favorite were soon summoned back to the realities of alarming events. On February 26, the Marquis de Paulmy resigned without having been asked to do so. In his place, Louis XV appointed the Maréchal de Belle-Isle, aged seventy-four, who as both duke and peer felt he was losing rank and title by accepting a ministerial portfolio. The monarch named a prince of royal blood, the Comte de Clermont, as Richelieu's successor, in the hope that he would succeed in restoring discipline among the French troops in Germany.

Maria Theresa's recriminations, and the fact that she denounced the incompetence of the royal armies, worried Madame de Pompadour more than the dangers facing the kingdom. She feared the breakup of the alliance above all else. Hence she continued to write to the generals, handing down orders or rebuking them, depending on the mood of the day. Outraged that a woman could arrogate to herself such power, when she knew nothing of the military arts and decided on the army's march by moving black patches around a map, the Comte de Clermont wrote her some rather sharp words. "You must let me do things my own way, Madame, and not impede me with ideas that come from too great a distance, or at least share them with me before giving orders; otherwise things will go badly. The Court's way of directing military movements is old-fashioned and ill-considered. It hinders a general who is on the scene, who knows his profession and who has knowledge of political opinions. . . . An army is not led like a finger moving on a map."[8] Unfortunately, Clermont did not distinguish himself; he did not live up to the wording of his message. Versailles soon received news that he had abandoned Hanover. The reaction was one of complete dismay.

Faithful to his agreements with Maria Theresa, Louis XV still refused to initiate peace negotiations with the King of Prussia in spite of Bernis's urgings, urgings that the Marquise considered extremely ill-timed. Giving up the alliance would have been tantamount to disclaiming her own self. Not knowing where to turn, the Abbé found nothing better than to open his heart to Choiseul. The ambassador became the keeper of his minister's complaints and torments. In his long litanies, the Abbé reiterated the same themes. He spoke of the "shameful conduct of the military,"[9] deplored the vast sums that were being spent in ignorance of what they were being used for and denounced, in veiled terms, the embezzlements of the Pâris brothers, who were supported by the Marquise. He preached in favor of peace and was appalled to see that France was not governed. "The government which is too weak, which doesn't even exist, is in good faith, but it doesn't know how to foresee, or remedy or compel recognition.[10] . . . There is no overall plan, nothing concerted, no forethought, no timely expenditure and even less thrift; very little money, very little credit and a deplorable military. The only solution left, therefore, is peace."[11] He was surprised that the King "was not the least bit worried."[12] And in every one of his letters Bernis repeated that the King should appoint a Prime Minister, in spite of his aversion to that office. He denied wanting to exercise that function, but it certainly tempted him. These confidential statements were of the utmost interest to Choiseul. He would use them to serve his ambitions, when the time came.

Bernis should have been more mindful of the Marquise's correspondence with Choiseul. Confident that the ambassador was serving him faithfully, he asked him to intercede with her on his behalf. "The main favor you can do me is to impress on her how sorely misled she would be if anyone persuaded her that my influence would be harmful to her. At this point, only political affairs or the death of the King can bring down Madame de Pompadour. The King is young, and will not die for a while. Political affairs are the only other thing. If everything goes well, then there is nothing else to be said. What else could Madame de Pompadour want but for her friend to be the person in charge? The point here is not the odious title of Prime Minister. The point is the King trusting someone enough to follow his advice and make others follow it."[13]

Choiseul maneuvered skillfully and profited from the tension he saw mounting between the Marquise and Bernis. The Abbé's "whining" exasperated the favorite. He dared tell her truthful things that "distressed her and made her sick."[14] The defeat of Krefeld, which Versailles received news of at the end of June 1758, put them in hopeless conflict. This latest disaster, sustained by the Comte de Clermont, who had been forced to withdraw to the Rhine, put France in danger. More than ever, Bernis advocated a peace agreement that the Marquise refused to consider. The Abbé then wrote to the King asking him to return to the helm of government or to appoint a Prime Minister. The Abbé had his letter dropped off at Madame de Pompadour's and addressed a "more forceful and more detailed letter" to her. He urged her to take into account the serious arguments he was putting forward in the letter. When he went to see her, several hours later, he found her "cold and cutting." She refused to show the letter to Louis XV, "because she was sure he would not like it."[15] Bernis admitted defeat and tore up his memorandum to the King in her presence.

However, the minister did get Louis XV and the Marquise to accept a "plan of government" that in effect created a kind of coordinating commission at the head of the State. "To spare the King the long discussions that are necessary to the running of government, I suggested," he said, "that all the affairs of State be discussed in committees composed of the *Conseil d'En Haut* [the Council at the Top][16] and, when necessary, of the entire Council, and at which the Comptroller General would always be present." The meetings were to take place three times a week. The decisions, based on a majority vote, were to be handed to

Madame de Pompadour, who would submit them to the King. He would then approve or reject them. This was a way of giving the Council the role of Prime Minister. This system, which functioned, for better or for worse, until the Abbé's fall from grace, resulted in all the ministers becoming aware of the government's dire financial straits and the confusion reigning in all the governmental departments.

It was at the close of a particularly turbulent committee meeting that the Minister of the Navy was forced to resign. Madame de Pompadour imposed Berryer as his replacement, after a stormy discussion with the Abbé, who suggested reappointing Maurepas. The Marquise never forgot offenses! As former Police Lieutenant, the new minister was better acquainted with Paris's lower depths than with the affairs of the Navy, for which he had no competence. But the favorite trusted him. . . .

As Bernis had predicted, the situation in America was worsening. On July 28, the fall of Louisburg, at the mouth of the Saint Lawrence River, opened Canada to the English. The English were also on the verge of obtaining the capitulation of Guadeloupe, and seizing Marie Galante and La Désirade. Worse still, British squadrons attacked the French coasts. Admiral Anson blockaded the port of Brest with twenty vessels, while Lord Marlborough sailed with the rest of the fleet to Cancale, where he disembarked on June 7. He then captured Saint-Servan, and marched on Saint-Malo. In his wake, he burned rope factories, stores and nearly eighty merchant and corsair vessels. When he heard that troops were coming to the rescue of Saint-Malo, Lord Marlborough returned to his ship on June 10. But only to strike again. The same fleet left England and blockaded the port of Brest once again, on July 30. Admiral Howe dropped anchor off Cherbourg. He bombarded the city and landed his men under the command of Bligh, who behaved like a ruffian and in defiance of all the rules of warfare. He removed all the cannons, set fire to the vessels, ravaged the surrounding countryside and enforced unbearable taxes on the population. Thanks to the resistance organized by the Duc d'Aiguillon[17] with Breton volunteers and coast guard militia, the English took flight.

These "victories," if they can be called victories under the circumstances, had lifted the Marquise's spirits. Yet in Vienna, Maria Theresa grumbled that "the French were invincible only when they fought against her."[18] Bernis found it mad "to perish without glory in the service of the Empress." He begged Choiseul "to demonstrate the uselessness of a war that would be increasingly badly conducted and unfortunate. . . . I am of the opinion," he said, "that we make sacrifices to England in order to have peace and I think the Court of Vienna should make some as well . . . by giving up most of its expansionist ideas."[19]

The Austrian armies and Soubise's army had finally just won a few victories, which led the King and the Marquise to favor the continuation of operations in Germany. Moreover, Choiseul was not urging Kaunitz to consider peace. Imperceptibly, the ambassador was conducting his own personal policy in Vienna, without listening to his minister. He flattered the Marquise, who was in power since she had the ear of the master. Choiseul hinted to her that Bernis's nerves were frayed by too many worries and that his melancholic state might be harmful to the good progress of governmental affairs. Why was Bernis allowing himself to get discouraged when the situation was not so desperate?[20]

The Marquise felt the need to lean on someone strong and, above all, not depressive. For a long time she had wanted Choiseul by her side—this seemed like the opportune moment to do something about it. She still had to get Bernis to leave and Louis XV to agree to summon Choiseul to the ministry. She cajoled the Abbé and secured a cardinalship for him, thanks to Choiseul, who had remained on the best of terms with the Court of Rome. Bernis was jubilant and already envisioned a career for himself as a Cardinal–Prime Minister. He thanked his protector, Pompadour, and his benefactor, Choiseul, effusively, but they alone knew that this was a severance gift. Choiseul was also incredibly pleased: Louis XV had just made him duke.[21] The two noblemen congratulated each other. In a moment of euphoria, Bernis naïvely suggested to Choiseul that he could succeed him at the Ministry of Foreign Affairs. "We will act in complete concert, and thank God, with no professional jealousy. We would assure the fate of our friend. Her happiness and health depend on the state of governmental affairs."[22]

Was Bernis sincere or did he want to make Choiseul into an assistant and give himself the role of Prime Minister without the title?

Exhausted by the duties that had been assigned to him, he needed to govern with a minister worthy of the name. He probably thought that Choiseul would be just that kind of devoted collaborator. He wanted to give him the management of Foreign Affairs under his own supervision. But the new Duc would never have agreed to be supervised by a priest—even a cardinal—whose abilities he regarded as far inferior to his own. Furthermore, he would not hear of immediate peace. A harmonious relationship was therefore impossible. Choiseul, however, pretended to play the game and accepted the position of Secretary of State of Foreign Affairs.

Bernis immediately moved into one of the most beautiful apartments at Versailles, and the Court assumed that the era of the Cardinal–Prime Minister had begun. They were forgetting the Pompadour factor. The Marquise had no intention of allowing Bernis to supplant her in a role that she felt she was fulfilling faultlessly. She hoped to govern with Choiseul, who exercised a kind of attraction over her. She had no great difficulty in convincing Louis XV of the danger the new Cardinal now represented. On December 13, 1758, in a very dry letter, the King thanked Bernis for services rendered and exiled him to the abbey of his choice.

Choiseul and the favorite won the day. Madame de Pompadour sacrificed Bernis because he no longer served her in the way she wanted. The Cardinal was too sensitive, too pessimistic and too fragile, and she couldn't tolerate him anymore. What difference did it make if he still sent her dignified and moving letters? She wanted to forget him, along with his thin-skinned politics that she saw as unworthy of royal grandeur. Her mind was at rest. The Duc de Choiseul was by her side, and he now shared the burden of government with the person who was still for her—in spite of everyone and everything—the *Bien-Aimé*. Her possessive love for Louis XV, which was draining all her strength, had allowed her to develop the cynicism required for her survival.

Twenty-four

THE KING, THE MINISTER
AND THE MARQUISE

With his turned-up nose, his fleshy, sensual lips and his air of a bright, overgrown child, Choiseul personified gaiety and joie de vivre. "Very pleasantly ugly,"[1] he exerted an irresistible charm on everyone he met, collected mistresses galore and had captivated the Marquise. His intelligence, his biting wit and his appetite for pleasure fascinated her. Malicious gossips claimed that she had yielded to his charms—a claim that shows an ignorance of both, for they needed each other in order to remain in the good graces of the King. Madame de Pompadour certainly enjoyed the minister's discreet wooing of her. She might have felt the need for someone to comfort her, but she would never have committed the folly of surrendering to this Don Juan whom she had sought out so he would govern with the monarch. He was really the only great politician that she had singled out and she had been preparing his rise to power for a long time.

Choiseul knew exactly what the King and his favorite expected of him. Thanks to his clear, methodical mind and his ability to present a complicated dossier succinctly and effectively, he immediately impressed his difficult master. He also maintained the habit of sharing State secrets with the Marquise, and he used her to influence the monarch when needed. He had been able to prove to her, on many occasions, that he knew how to get to the bottom of intrigues and find political solutions in the most complicated instances.

The Marquise immediately welcomed him, as well as his wife and sister, into her circle of intimates. The Duchesse de Choiseul was very refined, and at twenty-four, she looked like a Tanagra figurine. As the granddaughter of the financier Crozat, she provided her husband with an enormous fortune that he spent cheerfully. Reserved, intelligent and sensitive, Madame de Choiseul impressed people and attracted much praise, without seeming aware of it. She remained incredibly faithful to her libertine husband, while he paraded his liaisons shamelessly. She loved him silently, to the great despair of her many suitors. Horace Walpole did not conceal the tender admiration this inaccessible woman inspired in him. He described her as gay, modest and very attentive, as expressing herself with propriety and as having good judgment and a vivacious mind. He thought she looked like the queen in an Allegory. A lover, had she been the kind of woman to have one, might have wanted the Allegory to end, but he and her other admirers hoped otherwise.[2]

The Duchesse was strikingly unlike her sister-in-law, the imperious Béatrix de Choiseul, who was four years her elder. Though tall and rather brusque, domineering and not very feminine, Béatrix was nonetheless attractive. Having no personal fortune, she lived from her prebend as canoness of the Remiremont chapter (a secular order whose members took no vows) until her brother arranged for her to be married to the Duc de Gramont, who was wealthy but had a ruined reputation. The aim was to give the young woman a station; she quickly separated from her husband and moved in with her brother, whom she adored and whom people took to be her lover.

In spite of how different they were, both Madame de Choiseul and Madame de Gramont captivated Madame de Pompadour. Jeanne-Antoinette did not even seem worried by the interest the King showed in Béatrix. The newly elected pair got on marvelously with the Duchesses de Mirepoix and de Brancas, the Marquise's closest friends, and with Mesdames d'Esparbès[3] and d'Amblimont, whom she called her "little kittens." Among the men, the Prince de Soubise was still one of Jeanne-Antoinette's favorites, as were the Duc de Gontaut, Choiseul's brother-in-law, and the Prince de Beauvau,[4] Madame de Mirepoix's brother. Playful and considerate, the Choiseuls injected new life into this little circle that sometimes bored the favorite. She never left them, invited them to her suppers, where she now chose to have fewer guests, and went to Monsieur de Choiseul's for dinner two or three times a week.

The Court changed completely. There were more receptions and they were more dazzling. The princes of royal blood and the noblemen became more assiduous, for it was finally possible to see the King. The Marquise organized balls in which the entire Court participated. The costumed evenings were immensely successful. There was a memorable quadrille danced by the "monstrously fat" Duc d'Orléans and the imposing Duchesse de Mazarin in costumes from the period of Louis XIV. These balls started at midnight. Louis XV, the Queen and their retinue would take their places in a grandstand erected inside a hall that had been specially built for these entertainments. "The King sat in the center box where there was also Madame de Pompadour, Madame de Brancas and Madame d'Esparbès, the Duc de Choiseul, the Duc de Gontaut and the Prince de Beauvau. Madame de Pompadour sat in the armchair on the right; the two ladies, one in back of the other, were on the opposite side; the King was in the middle, and the three men behind him." One night, the monarch stood up after a half hour, asked Choiseul to take his seat, sat behind him, played familiarly with his hair and joked, "Everyone could infer the great favor he had risen to, for the King, in public, usually acted with much self-respect."[5]

The Marquise felt great joy on receiving from Maria Theresa a lacquer writing desk with, in the center, a portrait of the Empress set in diamonds.[6] The Empress wanted to show her gratitude to Louis XV's great friend, for her past and present support of the alliance. The gift was so valuable that Madame de Pompadour chose to hide it, fearing nasty comments. Touched that the austere Empress had made this gesture to show her regard for his favorite, the King allowed Jeanne-Antoinette to answer her in her own hand, a signal honor that was a significant breach of protocol. We can imagine how many drafts the Marquise must have scribbled before finding phrases worthy of the great Maria Theresa, who had honored her with a glance:

"Madame, may I be allowed to hope that Your Imperial Majesty will kindly accept my very humble thanks and the expressions of the respectful gratitude I feel for the inestimable portrait she presented me with. If to be worthy, Madame, of this precious gift required the most profound and enthusiastic admiration for Your Imperial Majesty's graceful charms and heroic virtues, then no one, without exception, could be worthier than I. I dare add that Your Imperial Majesty has no subject who could be more sincere than I in paying homage to her rare and sublime qualities. You are accustomed, Madame, to seeing sentiments like the ones I have the honor of expressing to you in everyone who is fortunate enough to approach you; but I hope that Your Imperial Majesty will deign to single mine out and regard them as the consequence of the very deep respect with which I am, Madame, Your Imperial Majesty's very humble and obedient servant. Jeanne de Pompadour."[7]

The King reread the letter and gave permission to send it. Contrary to the nasty rumors instigated by Frederick II, Madame de Pompadour only wrote to the Empress once. Frederick, nicknamed the "Solomon of the North," had concocted a so-called correspondence between the two women, in which Maria Theresa, whom Jeanne-Antoinette called "my beautiful Queen," replied by addressing her as "cousin" or "good friend." His contemptuous anger at Louis XV and the Marquise led him to send Voltaire—along with some doggerel verses that he asked him to correct—an *Epistle* that denigrated France, "mad and vain nation," and insulted her King:

> *What, your weak monarch,*
> *Plaything of Pompadour,*
> *Branded by more than one mark*
> *With the opprobrium of love,*
> *Who, hating effort,*
> *Gives to chance the reins*
> *Of his empire in desperate straits,*
> *This slave speaks as a master!*
> *This Céladon[8] under a beech tree*
> *Thinks he is dictating the fate of kings.*

When he received the unsealed package at Les Délices, where he had been living for four years, Voltaire was very alarmed. He knew

Postal Services[9] and its affiliated police department were very vigilant. He could be suspected of treason if he did not take precautions. So he wrote to Choiseul immediately expressing indignation at Frederick's verses, which he included in his letter. He assured the Minister of his loyalty to Louis XV and of his rejection of the King of Prussia's "favors."[10] Choiseul calmed him; he had not shown the *Epistle* to the King. But he had commissioned a scathing reply from Palissot denouncing the Prussian King's homosexuality. He instructed Voltaire to warn Frederick that this poem would be made public if the verses incriminating Louis XV were published. Choiseul thought he could use Voltaire as a secret intermediary between the Court of Berlin and Versailles, since the *philosophe* maintained lively epistolary relationships not just with Frederick II, but also with the Palatine Elector, the Duke of Württemberg and the princes of the House of Saxe-Gotha. However, the writer's attempts did not meet with success. His actions allowed him to get back in the good graces of Madame de Pompadour, and he requested her permission to dedicate his latest tragedy, *Tancrède*, to her. The wording of the dedication was balm to the Marquise's heart. "Madame," said Voltaire, "I have seen your charms and talents develop since your childhood; I have received tokens of unparalleled kindness from you. . . . I venture to thank you publicly for the help you have given to a great many genuine writers, great artists, and people of merit. . . . You have shown discernment in your good deeds because you have relied on your own judgment. I have not known a single man of letters, or other unbiased person, who has not done justice to your character, not only in public, but also in private conversations, when people usually blame much more than they praise. Believe me, Madame, it is quite an accomplishment to receive the approval of those who know how to think."

It was around that time that Marmontel went to visit the *philosophe*. Voltaire reminisced about Versailles and spoke about how kind the Marquise had been to him. "'She is still fond of you,' said Marmontel. 'But she is weak. She cannot and dares not do whatever she wants.' On a sudden inspiration, Voltaire told Marmontel to invite her for a stay at Les Délices. 'She should come here,' he said with enthusiasm, 'and perform tragedies with us. I will write parts for her, parts of queens. She is beautiful; she must know the effects of passion.' 'She has also known profound grief and bitter tears.' 'That's wonderful, that's what we need,' he cried out, apparently enchanted at having a new actress. You might think he believed she would be coming."[11]

The war did not put a damper on the Marquise's activities as an art patron or on her passion for buildings. She sold Bellevue to the King in 1757,[12] Crécy to the Duc de Penthièvre[13] and the marquisate of Pompadour to Choiseul in 1760. But in March 1757, she acquired the usufruct of the château of Saint-Ouen from the Duc de Tresmes for 170,000 livres with the right to make whatever renovations she wished.[14] On June 30, 1760, she purchased the seventeenth-century Château de Ménars,[15] between Orléans and Blois, and in March 1761, the château of Auvilliers,[16] near Artenay, which she would use for stopovers on her way to Touraine. The Marquise undertook major renovations at Ménars, under the aegis of Gabriel. She became accustomed to spending time there every three months or so. Given the financial crisis, the expense of renovating this residence and the cost of her travels gave rise to vicious comments.

The war had had no effect on the style of life of the Court over which the Marquise still ruled. In spite of his high spirits, Choiseul was perfectly aware of the dangers facing France. The war had emptied the State coffers, and bankruptcy was still to be feared. Receipts remained well below expenses. Taxes were not being collected, and foreign trade was in serious deficit. Montmartel had just retired, to Madame de Pompadour's great fury. The banker was criticized for having imposed exorbitant rates on the loans he had approved. In the circumstances, the Minister of Foreign Affairs inevitably turned his attention to making peace. However, it had to be an honorable peace for France.

Choiseul wanted to make it clear to Maria Theresa that Louis XV would meet all his commitments, but he would not continue to weaken his kingdom much longer for the sole purpose of reconquering Silesia, which seemed lost for good. His instructions to Choiseul-Praslin,[17] the new ambassador to Vienna, could not have been more explicit on the subject. But Kaunitz turned a deaf ear, in spite of the detailed report

Choiseul had sent to him on the state of France. Maria Theresa made only two concessions to him—France could provide her with only 24,000 men and cut her subsidies by about a third. In exchange France had to relinquish the Netherlands. The public wondered why this war, which had been lost before it had begun, was still being waged. There seemed to be no reason for it.

Supported by the Marquise, Choiseul justified the continuation of the conflict by the need to keep the country's allies. He was afraid that Austria might turn against France if Louis XV were to sign a separate peace with the King of Prussia in order to fight the British more effectively. Therefore, military objectives had to be set for the next campaign. The Versailles cabinet hoped to reconquer Hanover and safeguard part of the colonial empire. Meanwhile, Frederick II, for his part, was getting ready to resume hostilities against the "three illustrious whores"—the Empress, the Czarina and the Marquise—vowing that all three would be "screwed."[18] Most execrated of the three was Madame de Pompadour, whom he thought of as the person most responsible for the reversal of alliances and the outbreak of war.

After the victory of Bergen, for which a *Te Deum* was immediately sung at Versailles, the new German campaign ended in ghastly defeats. The French army, placed under the command of the Maréchal de Contades, was literally slaughtered on April 13, 1759, at Minden, on the bank of the Weser River. In Canada, where only scant reinforcements had been sent, Montcalm was killed on September 12 defending Quebec, and shortly thereafter Montreal fell to the British. In India, ever since Lally had replaced Dupleix, the situation was hardly any brighter. Finally, the plan of landing the French fleet on the British coast collapsed when the Royal French Navy, after it left Toulon on its way to Brest, was defeated by Admiral Boscawen off Portugal on August 7, 1759. Eleven days later, the Brest squadron suffered the same fate at the hands of Admiral Hawke at the Cardinaux Islands off the coast of Quiberon. Masters of the seas, the British seized Belle-Isle. In the period of one year, France had lost sixty-four warships and was no longer in a position to defend her colonies. Public opinion raged against a deadly and ruinously expensive conflict for which there seemed to be no solution in sight. "It was still the Marquise and the Duc de Choiseul who were in charge of everything. . . . Since we could not make peace, we continued a war that was going badly,"[19] sighed the Prince de Croÿ.

By October the situation was so serious that Louis XV, following the example of Louis XIV during the War of Spanish Succession, asked the French population to bring their silverware and jewelry to the Mint in order to bail out the Treasury. The Marquise set the example. She had originally participated in the war effort financially, by equipping twenty-three high-speed ships. But in spite of these displays of goodwill, the financial situation remained disastrous. Comptroller General Silhouette had resigned and his successor, Bertin, found himself in what was undeniably the most awkward predicament of anyone in the kingdom—even with the help of the new Court Banker, Laborde, Choiseul's protégé, who, like his predecessor, enjoyed immense prestige in Europe.

Occasionally, matters were so urgent that the Marquise used her personal contacts, like the banker Beaujon, who had advised her on some good investments. The following short memo addressed to the Comptroller General offers a glimpse into her activity in the course of those difficult months: "Monsieur Berryer just brought me Monsieur Beaujon," she wrote to Bertin. "He is ready to give the Navy a million as special money, otherwise the necessary event will not take place. Now it's only a matter of his making arrangements with you. I am certain that you will do everything possible given the need for such an important thing to work out. Please send for Beaujon at once."[20]

By the end of 1759, the atmosphere at Court was gloomy. With increasing frequency, Madame de Pompadour was ill with bronchitis and fever, and coughing blood. She spent much of her time in bed, though this did not prevent her from receiving the King, his friends, the ministers and supplicants. Oppressed by terrible palpitations, she realized she was dying. Yet the Duchess of Parma preceded her and was buried first. She had been living at Versailles since 1757 in order to look after the interests of her husband. In December the Duchess fell ill with what was diagnosed as smallpox. She died on the sixth day of her illness, December 6, 1759. "My brother, cousin, and son-in-law, you are now suffering the greatest anxieties, and I suffer them for you, my dear son, if I may still call you by that name. I promise to give you news often, since I now have no one through whom I can send news to you. My tears compel me to end," the King wrote to the Infante Don Philippe to inform him of the royal family's bereavement.[21] After the death of this princess whom he loved most dearly, he found comfort, once again with his incomparable friend Jeanne-Antoinette. And she felt herself revive . . .

The new year was full of bad omens. The peace negotiations with England at The Hague, under Spain's aegis, failed. Pitt wanted to crush France in order to seize her colonial empire. It was therefore necessary to continue fighting. In Germany the French won two victories, at Korbach near Kassel, and then at Klostercamp. This brought glory to the Maréchal de Broglie and the Marquis de Castries, whose troops showed great heroism. But it did nothing to change the fate of the armies; the allies still never managed to carry out a common military action against the King of Prussia. Though Frederick II had come within a hairsbreadth of catastrophe in several instances, he had still not been defeated.

As Pitt predicted, the French possessions in America finally fell to the British. Worse still, the British were threatening the French coastline, occupying Belle-Isle as well as Houat and Houëdic. Still hard at work and more dictatorial than ever, Madame de Pompadour sent threatening letters to the Duc d'Aiguillon, whom she had nickname "Monsieur Cavendish" since his victory at Saint-Cast. "You will admit, later, Monsieur, that I'm quite insufferable in being always right," she said. "What? I dared tell you that even with your great, outstanding qualities, you're dim-witted and get worked up too quickly, and at this moment here you are proving it to me once again. It is true, I'm odious, and I cannot conceive how you had the kindness to answer me given this fault. . . . You want to leave Brittany. That's real madness you've come up with. . . . You are angered; tell me, who wouldn't be if they let themselves go? Oh, *bah! I blush for you when I see that you have less courage than I. You have the annoyances of your small command, and me those of all the administrations, for there isn't a single minister who doesn't come to me to tell me his troubles.*

Pray, may I not hear about yours anymore. I would like to extend my friend-ship to Monsieur Cavendish without reservations. Whereas his soul seems wor-thy of it, I would like his mind to be so too. I will judge from your behavior whether you take notice of this."[22]

Other letters followed, all written in the same imperious tone. However, when the Duc d'Aiguillon saw he could not recapture Belle-Isle, he chose to resign, thereby bringing the favorite's wrath upon him. "It can only be fitting for ordinary souls to resign over a difficulty; the soul of Monsieur d'Aiguillon should be above such troubles and his only aim should be whether he can be useful to his master. You cast your bad cause in the best possible light; but please don't think I am fool enough to accept it. Probe your conscience, and you will find everything I tell you. . . . I am angry, indeed very angry, with you. The dimwit I mentioned to you on the day of your departure has played too big a part. I don't know when I'll forgive you. You deserve that I show no more interest in you. Good evening, Monsieur, with great rancor."[23]

In January 1761, when the Maréchal de Belle-Isle died, Choiseul took over the War portfolio and asked for the Navy portfolio after getting Berryer dismissed and giving Foreign Affairs to his cousin Choiseul-Praslin, who always worked under his supervision. Though he did not have the title, Choiseul actually exercised the functions of a Prime Minister. Given the gravity of the situation, Madame de Pom-padour was forced to stay in the background. Yet she continued to have daily conversations about State matters with the King and his principal minister. She still supervised the work of the other ministers. She turned against the members of the parliament who refused to adopt the fiscal edicts needed to finance the war. "Probity is often taken in; this is what is happening to you right now, Monsieur," she wrote to Bertin. "I told you it would be so, because sixteen years in this country are worth a hundred years of experience. . . . I would call these men unworthy citizens and much greater enemies of the State than the King of Prussia and the English. If peace is not made, or if it is a bad peace, they alone will be to blame and I would like the whole world to be informed of this fact."[24] And when the magistrates wanted to inspect the King's per-sonal expenses, as well as all the expenses authorized by a simple signed bond or cash voucher signed by His Majesty, she gave vent to her anger: "Oh! Concerning the small proposition of being accountable, I can't control myself," she cried out, "and I can't conceive how you had the patience not to spit in their faces. The King has read your letter. So we must patiently wait for the answer from those charming creatures. The horror! I'll keep quiet; but I have my thoughts nonetheless."[25]

While she fumed against the parliament, Choiseul carried out the plan that he had been nurturing since he had taken office—an alliance between France and Spain, called *Pacte de famille* (family pact). The Bourbons of Parma and of Naples were to adhere to it. Though Austria was not part of this league of Catholic States that was opposed to the Protestant powers, she remained France's ally. This rapprochement strengthened Louis XV's diplomatic position, but could no longer be of any great help to him at this stage of the war. This became clear in August 1762, when the Spanish fleet, incapable of helping Martinique, was defeated by the English, who seized Havana and occupied Cuba, a Spanish colony. In Germany Frederick signed an attractive peace with Czar Peter III, confirmed by the Czarina Catherine II, and could turn against the French and the Austrians. He defeated the French in Kassel and in Hesse, and the Austrians in Feidberg, Saxony. It was feared that in 1763 he would invade Austria and cross the Rhine.

There was no choice but to conclude a peace and agree to many losses. At the Peace of Paris, signed with England on February 10, 1763, France ceded Canada, Saint Vincent, Tobago, Dominica and Grenada. In order to retain Guadeloupe and Martinique, center of the spice trade, Louis XV ceded the left bank of the Mississippi to the British. He also had to cede the right bank of the Mississippi to Spain, in compensation for its losing Cuba and Florida. France retained its trading posts in India, and returned Minorca to the English in exchange for Belle-Isle. Five days after the signing of the Peace of Paris, the Treaty of Hubertsburg was signed with Frederick II, by which he kept possession of Silesia, but had to restore his States to the Elector of Saxony. The prestige of the "Solomon of the North" was at its zenith; that of the Empress, even though she had failed to reach any of her objectives, was more or less intact. Britain had asserted its supremacy throughout the world. As for Louis XV, he was the humiliated monarch of Europe. "The peace we have made is neither good, nor glorious," he admitted after ratifying the treaty. Public opinion put the blame for this shameful peace on the sovereign and his favorite. Yet Louis XV, Madame de Pompadour and Choiseul did not see the loss of a colonial empire—difficult to defend and costing more than it brought in—as disastrous. After all, France had retained the islands needed for its commerce. However, France's armies, hitherto reputed to be the best in Europe, had been defeated; the Navy had to be rebuilt; France no longer exercised leadership in Europe; and the State coffers were hopelessly empty. Louis XV had lost the affection and respect of his subjects. As for the favorite, she was quite simply detested.

However, the city of Paris organized festivities to celebrate the peace. On June 20, 1763, after the sovereign had assembled his Court at Choisy, where the Marquise had presided over every imaginable kind of entertainment, they went to the capital. The three days of celebration planned by the aldermen were supposed to start with the inauguration of Bouchardon's equestrian statue of the King, erected in his honor on the new Place Louis XV, facing the Tuileries gardens. At the four corners of the pedestal were Pigalle's statues representing Strength, Prudence, Justice and Love. They had attracted scathing epigrams. On the pedestal itself, there were graffiti like the following: "Grotesque monument, loathsome pedestal/Virtues go on foot, vice on horseback." Or: "He is here as at Versailles/Without heart or entrails." Nor was the favorite spared. The crowd milling in front of the four allegorical figures yelled out, "Mailly, Vintimille, Châteauroux, Pompadour," and booed loudly after her name.

On June 20, however, the first ceremony, which entailed going around the square and greeting each statue, took place without incident. Nothing could have kept the Parisians away from such a spectacle. In the evening, they went in large crowds to the illuminated Tuileries, where refreshments were distributed to the sound of an orchestra until a violent storm shortened the festivities. On the following day, they could admire the cavalcade of heralds moving through the city for nine hours to proclaim the peace. Everybody looked forward impatiently to June 23. On that evening there was to be a great bonfire on the Seine, followed by fireworks and the illumination of the square. Nineteen boxes covered with crimson damask had been set up in front of the Palais-Bourbon for the King, his family and some of his friends. The Marquise, who had her own box, hurried to her mansion as soon as the spectacle was over, in order to give the signal for lighting her gardens, scheduled to follow the lighting of the square. Princes and spectators all rushed to her gardens, causing the first memorable traffic jam in the history of the Champs-Elysées. It lasted until dawn. The unanimous opinion was that the favorite's illuminations surpassed those of the city. Always royal, "Madame de Pompadour told the Provost of Merchants that she was furious that the city ceremony, which, she said, might have been the most august of all, had not been more dazzling."[26]

Twenty-five

"ONE MOMENT,
MONSIEUR LE CURÉ"

Madame de Pompadour had changed considerably since the beginning of the war, both physically and mentally. Now over forty, she was no longer the appetizing young woman painted by Boucher. If we can trust the portrait painted by Drouais in 1764, several weeks before her death, the Marquise had become a woman who still showed traces of her lost youth, but could now be classed in the category of pretty dowagers. Indeed, she still has considerable grace and elegance in her satin brocade dress with a leaf pattern, but the lace headscarf tied under her slightly fleshy chin is that of a woman who has given up on the seductions of youth. We might see wisdom in the eyes of this mature beauty, if we were ignorant of the endless dramas and conflicts being played out in the innermost depths of her anxious soul.

Despite the many ailments that overwhelmed and prematurely aged her, Madame de Pompadour remained just as strongly attached to the King as she had been in the summer of Fontenoy. Louis XV belonged to her. She still intended to run his life down to the very last detail. She still lived with the obsessive fear of a usurper appearing on the scene and relegating her to the Queen's inner circle, where she was a kind of trespasser. She would choose exile rather than face a semblance of disgrace. The role she played in politics and the fact that she had Louis XV's trust should have set her mind at rest, but Madame de Pompadour was a perpetually troubled person, in spite of her calm, self-confident appearance.

After several years of being demoted to the role of the "necessary friend," the Marquise was not displeased, secretly, to see the King grow gradually older. Would her beloved not grow weary in his quest for sensual pleasures? She and he could then form the ideal couple, sobered by the years. Who knows if, in her innermost self, the Marquise did not wish for the death of the harmless Marie Leczinska in the hope that she could become the *Bien-Aimé*'s secret wife and queen? After all, Louis XIV had married Madame de Maintenon! "My heart and mind are constantly busy with the King's affairs," she wrote to the Duc d'Aiguillon. "But were I not so inexpressibly attached to his glory and person, I would often be disheartened by the constant obstacles I meet in trying to do good. I would have preferred the big niche, but I must be content with the small one; it does not suit my temperament at all."[1] What "niche" is she alluding to if not the throne?

To get rid of any potential rivals, Madame de Pompadour resolved to play on the King's religious scruples. Louis XV kept away from the sacraments for the reasons we know. She thought that perhaps the pope's intervention could make him return to the fold. This was her hope, and she counted on the skill of Choiseul, who was familiar with the mysteries of the Vatican and could intercede with the Holy Father. The promise of absolution for his dissolute private life would put an end to the monarch's amorous escapades. If the Holy Father agreed to be lenient and allowed her to stay with her former lover, she would now be ready to adopt the appearance of piety once and for all. She wrote a long report to Clement XIII. In it, she described her problems with the Court's Jesuit confessors, who denied her the sacraments so long as she remained at Versailles, even though her relations with Louis XV had been completely chaste for a long time. Fortunately, an understanding priest had agreed to absolve her of her sins and, since then, she had been reconciled with God in her everyday life. However, she was worried about Louis XV's salvation and was certain that the Holy Father "would lift the obstacles that prevented the King from fulfilling a duty that was holy for him and edifying for the people."[2]

Choiseul's initiatives in Rome on behalf of Louis XV and his favorite did not meet with success. Besides, the King had no desire to

mend his ways just then. He had fallen in love with a statuesque beauty
and was intoxicated by her charm. Casanova had been dazzled by her
luminous pale complexion set off by abundant, long black hair, her oval
face, regular features, small pink mouth and perfect white teeth. Of
much taller than average height and with an ample bosom, she looked
like a goddess. The daughter of a bourgeois from Grenoble, Anne
Coupier, who went by the name of Mademoiselle de Romans,[3] had
been brought to Paris by her sister, Madame Varnier, who owned a
drinking establishment in the Palais-Royal. It is not known exactly
how the King had become acquainted with this beautiful young
woman. His procurers, who were perpetually on the lookout, scoured
all the pleasure spots in the capital and knew all the procuresses.
Madame Varnier knew what she could ask in return for this imposing
virgin, who was probably around twenty when she was introduced to
Louis XV in 1759. She got what she wanted.

Whereas the female boarders the King kept in the Parc-aux-Cerfs
were under the illusion that he was a great Polish nobleman, Mademoiselle de Romans knew that she was the mistress of the King. Furthermore, the King did not move her into his small house in the
Parc-aux-Cerfs, like the others; he rented a house for her alone, on the
main street of the village of Passy. When he wanted to see her at Versailles, he sent a six-horse carriage to pick her up. At Court the King's
new beloved was the only subject of conversation, and Madame de
Pompadour was so alarmed that political affairs failed to provide a dis-
traction for her. Her spies kept her informed of the two lovers' comings
and goings, and the Duchesse de Mirepoix tried to reassure her.
"Princes are above all creatures of habit. The King's friendship for you
includes your apartment and your surroundings. You are used to his
ways and his stories; with you he is not embarrassed, he's not afraid of
boring you. Where would he find the courage to uproot himself from all
this from one day to the next, to create another environment, and to
make a spectacle of himself to the public by a change in décor?"[4]

The Marquise knew the King all too well not to be aware that he was
very much in love. When she learned that Mademoiselle de Romans
was pregnant, her fears deepened. Might not the sovereign recognize the

child and make the child's mother his official mistress? "This was Louis XIV's way; such grand manners are not those of our master," the Duchesse de Mirepoix kept repeating.[5] But this did not reassure Jeanne-Antoinette. Though Madame du Hausset denies it, it was probably the Marquise who ordered a search of the beautiful Romans's house in order to remove the papers proving Louis XV's paternity. This served no purpose. On January 13, 1762, the young woman gave birth to a child who was baptized the following day at the church of Chaillot. The boy was given the name Louis-Aimé de Bourbon, and recognized as the son of Louis de Bourbon and Mademoiselle Anne Coupier de Romans, a lady from Meilly-Coullonge. The King even signed the certificate that the priest presented him. This quasi-legal recognition caused a great to-do. Some people claimed that the child would be a future Duc du Maine, like the son of Louis XIV and Madame de Montespan.

Intoxicated by this exalting motherhood, Mademoiselle de Romans soon got into the habit of taking the child to the Bois de Boulogne. Dressed in the latest fashion, her bosom covered with expensive lace, she would sit on the grass and breast-feed her child, in full view of everyone. Madame de Pompadour had an irrepressible desire to see the mother and child. Accompanied by Madame du Hausset, the Marquise—her face concealed in a headdress and a handkerchief held over her mouth—walked to the clearing where she knew she would find the lucky young mother. "She stared at us," recounts Madame du Hausset. "Madame greeted her and nudged me with her elbow, saying, 'Talk to her.' I went up to her and said, 'That's a very beautiful child.' 'Yes,' she said, 'I agree, even though I'm the mother.' Madame, who was holding my arm, was trembling, and I didn't feel very confident. Mademoiselle de Romans asked, 'Are you from around here?' 'Yes, Madame,' I said, 'I live in Auteuil with this lady who is suffering from a dreadful toothache at the moment.' 'My heart goes out to her, for I know what it's like. I've often suffered from that sort of ache.' I looked all around, worried that someone might recognize us. Then I asked her boldly if the father was a handsome man. 'Very handsome,' she said, 'and if I named him, you would say the same.' 'Then I have the honor of knowing him, Madame?' 'It is very likely.'"[6]

The Marquise and her companion brought the conversation to a close and returned to their carriage. "'There is no denying that the mother and child are beautiful creatures,' said Madame, 'and let's not forget the father; the child has his eyes. If the King had come while we were there, do you think he would have recognized us?' 'Without a doubt, Madame. And I would have been so embarrassed! And what a scene for those present to see the two of us! But what a surprise for her!'"[7] That evening, Madame de Pompadour told the King only that she had been to the Sèvres factory to buy cups—which was also true.

Louis XV's relationship with Mademoiselle de Romans lasted five years, but he never presented her at Court. He eventually grew weary of her demands and sent her into exile at the convent of the Ursulines in Saint-Denis. He took away their son, but refused to make him legitimate. The Marquise died too soon to have witnessed her rival's disgrace.[8] The liaison the King struck up in 1762 with Mademoiselle de Tiercelin, a completely different kind of young woman, probably reassured Jeanne-Antoinette: the sovereign was clearly indulging in a flirtation. When he grew tired of Mademoiselle de Romans, he went "slumming" with the young Tiercelin. Neither one nor the other could replace the true favorite. News of Mademoiselle de Tiercelin's pregnancy probably distressed her less than Mademoiselle de Romans's had. By now she knew that the King would not recognize his illegitimate children[9] and would not make their mothers "official." In 1766, Tiercelin, whose child was also a boy, was to experience the same fate as Mademoiselle de Romans.[10]

In the summer following the Peace of Paris, the Marquise seemed very tired. In Compiègne, where she continued to receive the usual personalities, she appeared in public less often than in previous years. In the morning, she spent considerable time at her toilette trying to cover up the ravages of time, which were more visible on her than on others due to her poor state of health. But she "continued to run everything,"[11] and had daily conversations with Choiseul, Madame de Gramont and, of course, the King. At Fontainebleau she still prepared all the season's entertainments. But at the beginning of 1764, she looked like a specter. In January she hosted the young Mozart and listened to

him play the harpsichord. A short time later, her joy was sincere on seeing the Abbé de Bernis again; Louis XV had lifted his exile and
appointed him ambassador to Rome. On this occasion, she also received the Marquise de La Ferté-Imbault, a fake prude who had
snubbed the former Madame d'Etiolles as well as the Marquise de Pompadour. This lady deigned to visit the sultana now that her days were
numbered. She left a perfidious and cruel account of her visit: "I found
her beautiful and grave," she writes. "She seemed in good health,
though she complained of insomnia, bad digestion and shortness of
breath whenever she had to climb stairs. She began by saying that I was
undoubtedly pleased with her, since she had arranged for my friend
[Bernis] to return in such illustrious fashion. She added, moreover, that
he had always behaved like a gentleman, but that political misfortunes
had made him so somber and sad that it had become nerve-racking for
the King and herself. . . . She then went on to tell me, with the warmth
and feeling of an actress who is good at playing her part, how distressed
she was by the deplorable state of the kingdom, the parliament's rebellion and the things going on up there (pointing to the King's apartment, with tears in her eyes). She assured me that her staying with the
King was a great token of her affection for him; that she would have
been a thousand times happier living alone and quietly in Ménars, but
that the King would not know what to do if she left him; and in open-
ing her heart to me—which, she said, she could open to no one—she
depicted her torments for me with an eloquence and energy that I had
never seen in her before. . . . In sum, she seemed demented and raving,
and I never heard a more convincing sermon proving the misfortunes
tied to ambition; and at the same time, I saw her in turn so miserable,
so insolent, so violently agitated and so uncomfortable with her
supreme power that I came away from her, after an hour of conversation, struck by the thought that she had no refuge left but death."[12]

During the Court's stay at Choisy, in February 1764, the Marquise's
health suddenly deteriorated. For the first time, she did not attend the
informal suppers and she let the Duchesse de Gramont fill in for her
with the King. On the twenty-ninth, she was in the large formal drawing room when she suddenly felt so unwell that she had to ask a valet to

help her back to her room. She went to bed immediately. Her ailment was diagnosed as pneumonia, which worsened in the days that followed. The King came to see her several times a day. However, he soon had to return to Versailles, after which couriers went back and forth from Choisy to Versailles with news of the Marquise. The monarch curtailed his activities and rushed to Jeanne-Antoinette's bedside whenever he found time. "Madame de Pompadour's illness put a stop to everything and was quite an event. . . . The entire Court, and all of Paris, sent for word or went to Choisy constantly. Everybody indulged in speculations." Some people thought the King would turn to religion, others that Madame de Gramont would succeed the Marquise. "In sum, people went to extremes about everything and as might be expected, this created quite a sensation."[13]

However, unexpectedly, the Marquise's condition improved at the end of March. A thanksgiving mass was celebrated at the Madeleine church of La Ville-l'Evêque, the Marquise's Parisian parish. Dr. Quesnay allowed his patient to drive around the grounds in a carriage, but his prognosis was guarded. "People find Madame de Pompadour much improved, but her illness is far from over and I dare not have much hope," wrote Madame du Deffand. However, Favart and Palissot were already writing odes to celebrate her recovery. Cochin and Boucher took up their pencils and set to work finding appropriate allegories. Madame de Pompadour was recovering her taste for life so well that she was allowed to return to Versailles. On April 7, as soon as she had moved back into her quarters, she fell violently ill again. Her condition worsened every day. To relieve her difficulty in breathing, she sat in an armchair all the time. The King came to see her often in her apartment. "My anxieties do not diminish," he wrote to the Infante of Parma. "And I must say I have very little hope of a complete recovery, and fear that the end may be all too imminent. An acquaintance of over twenty years and an unshakable friendship! Of course, God is the master. We must bow to all his wishes. Monsieur de Rochechouart learned of his wife's death after much suffering; I am sorry for him, if he loved her."[14]

It was the King, her former lover, who begged the Marquise to take the sacraments. With this, they bade each other farewell. Propriety required that she ask her husband to come assist her in her final moments, but he replied that he was unable to make the trip at that time. Before rectifying her position in the eyes of God, she summoned her lawyer and reread her will; it made her brother Abel Poisson, Marquis de Marigny, her sole heir.[15] Not having the strength to hold a pen, she dictated a codicil stipulating additional bequests to some dear friends, and to all those who had cared for her.

On the night of April 14 to 15, the priest from the Madeleine of La Ville-l'Evêque heard the Marquise's confession and administered Extreme Unction, which she took with resignation. "She is dying with a courage that is rare for any sex," the Dauphin wrote to the Bishop of Verdun. "Every time she breathes, she thinks it is her last breath. It is one of the most painful and cruel deaths imaginable. . . . The King has not seen her since yesterday. The priest from the Madeleine of La Ville-l'Evêque never leaves her. These are grounds for hope and her receiving mercy. However, I think this event will cause much fuss but have little effect. You can sense everything I mean by this, both for morality and politics."[16] In the priest's presence, Madame de Pompadour spoke firmly with her brother, and with Messieurs de Choiseul, de Soubise and de Gontaut. When she knew the end was near, she said to them: "It will be soon, leave me to my confessor and my ladies." Then calling de Soubise back, she gave him the keys to her writing desk; she still had the strength to indicate which carriage should take her mortal remains to her house, her Versailles mansion that communicated with the château. She gently refused to be changed by her ladies: "I know that you are very dexterous; but I am so weak that you could not help but make me suffer, and it is not necessary for the short time I have left to live."[17] And since the priest wanted to take his leave, she murmured with a smile: "One moment, Monsieur le Curé, we'll go together."[18] At seven-thirty at night the Marquise drew her last breath. It was Palm Sunday and she was forty-two years old.

A few minutes later, the Duchesse de Praslin saw a stretcher go by, carrying a woman's body covered in a simple shroud.[19] It was the Marquise, being carried to her house without even waiting for the carriage. Madame de Pompadour had benefited from a princely prerogative by dying of illness at Versailles.

As soon as he learned of her death, the King cancelled the formal dinner and retired to his chambers with Jeanne-Antoinette's friends. The devout Marie-Josèphe expressed the hope that on leaving for the hereafter, the favorite "had sincerely acknowledged and detested the evil she had done." She nevertheless had to admit that the King "was extremely distressed and had to control himself with everyone including his family."[20] On the day after his friend's death, Louis XV wrote to the Infante: "All my anxieties are gone, in the most cruel manner, you can guess what I mean!"[21]

On April 17 at six in the evening, in the midst of a violent storm, the funeral procession of the very lofty and very powerful lady, Madame la Marquise-Duchesse de Pompadour, left the church of Notre-Dame at Versailles, where the first funeral service had taken place. It crossed the Place d'Armes, before heading up the avenue de Paris and bringing the Marquise to the church of the Capuchins. "The King takes Champlost by the arm; when he reaches the mirrored door of his private study, giving out on the balcony facing the avenue, on the courtyard, he tells him to shut the entrance door and goes out on the balcony with him. He keeps a religious silence, looks at the procession drive into the avenue and keeps watching it until it is entirely out of sight, in spite of the bad weather and the cold wind to which he seems impervious. He goes back inside the apartment. Two large tears are still running down his cheeks and he says to Champlost: 'These are the only respects I can pay her!'"[22]

Notes

The following abbreviations are used throughout the Notes:

A.N.: Archives Nationales de France
B.N.: Bibliothèque Nationale de France
A.A.E.: Archives du Ministère des Affaires Etrangères de France

1. Death of a Favorite

1. Louis de Noailles, Duc d'Ayen (1713–1793), Sergeant in the King's army in 1740, Lieutenant General in 1748, Maréchal of France in 1775, married Catherine de Cossé-Brissac in 1737.
2. Charles-Louis de Montmorency, Duc de Luxembourg, Captain of the King's Bodyguards, Maréchal of France.
3. Charles-Antoine de Gontaut, Comte de Biron and later Duc de Gontaut (1708–1800), younger brother of Louis-Antoine, Maréchal-Duc de Biron (1700–1788). Charles-Antoine had married Antoinette-Eustachie Crozat du Châtel, the granddaughter of Crozat du Châtel, Treasurer General of the Clergy, called "the poor one" in contrast to her uncle Crozat, Collector General of Finances in Bordeaux, called "the rich one." The celebrated Duc de Lauzun was the son of this union.
4. In 1711, the Grand Dauphin, Louis XIV's only son, died of smallpox. The following year, his oldest son, the Duc de Bourgogne, who had in turn become Dauphin, died of measles as had his wife from whom he doubtless contracted the disease. They left two male children: the first soon followed his parents to the grave; the second was the future Louis XV. His life was saved by his governess, Madame de Ventadour, who removed him from the care of physicians.
5. Duc de Richelieu, *Mémoires*, ed. Barrière, vol. I, p. 331.

6. Duc de Croÿ, *Journal inédit*, vol. I, p. 51.

7. Duc de Luynes, *Mémoires*, vol. VI, pp. 188–89.

8. Twins, born on August 14, 1727, Louise-Elisabeth, future Duchess of Parma, called Madame Première, and Anne-Henriette, called Madame Seconde; Marie-Adelaide, born March 23, 1732; Marie-Louise-Thérèse-Victoire, born May 11, 1733; Sophie-Elisabeth-Justine, born July 17, 1734; Louise-Marie, born July 15, 1737.

9. Duchesse de Brancas, *Mémoires*, pp. 64–65.

10. Luynes, op. cit., vol. IV, p. 267.

11. Duchesse de Brancas, op. cit., p. 71.

12. Duclos, *Mémoires secrets*, vol. II, p. 38.

13. Marquis de Valfons, *Souvenirs*, p. 130.

14. Ibid.

2 . M A D A M E   D ' E T I O L L E S

1. Dufort de Cheverny, *Mémoires*, ed. Guicciardi, p. 97.

2. Madame du Deffand, *Correspondance complète*, vol. I, p. 70. Président Hénault's letter to Madame du Deffand, dated July 18 [1742?].

3. She had given birth to a boy on December 26, 1741, who lived only a few months. Her daughter Alexandrine was born three years later, on August 10, 1744, and was baptized at the church of Saint-Roch.

4. Cf. P. A. Leroi, "Curiosités historiques," p. 222, "Relevé des dépenses de Mme de Pompadour . . . ," *Mémoires de la Société des Sciences morales, des lettres et des arts de Seine-et-Oise*: "Pension de 600 livres faite à Mme Lebon, pour avoir prédit à Mme de Pompadour qu'elle serait un jour la maîtresse de Louis XV." ["Six hundred livre pension given to Mme. Lebon, for having predicted to Mme. de Pompadour that she would one day be Louis XV's mistress."]

5. Luynes, op. cit., vol. VI, p. 302.

6. Ibid., p. 288.

7. Cf. The title of the engraving is: Decoration for the masked ball given by the King in the great gallery of the Château de Versailles, on the occasion of the wedding of Louis, Dauphin of France, with Marie-Thérèse, Infanta of Spain, on the night of February 25 to 26, 1745. . . . C. N. Cochin filius delineavit, C. N. Cochin, sculpsit.

8. Cardinal de Bernis, *Mémoires et Lettres*, vol. I, p. 109.

9. Luynes, op. cit., vol. VI, p. 341.

10. Bernis, op. cit., vol. I, p. 109.

11. Valfons, op. cit., p. 132.

12. Luynes, op. cit., vol. VI, p. 354.

13. Ibid., p. 393.

14. Ibid., p. 396.

15. Ibid., p. 418.
16. Claude-Henri Feydeau de Marville, *Lettres . . . au ministre Maurepas*, vol. II (1742–1747), p. 65.

3 . A S t e a d y R i s e t o t h e T o p

1. Lapeyre, *Les Moeurs de Paris*, Amsterdam, 1747, p. 32.
2. Claude-Henri Feydeau de Marville, op. cit., vol. II, pp. 70–71.
3. He showed courage under the circumstances, and his behavior on this occasion was specifically mentioned in the letters of ennoblement he received in 1747.
4. Previously unpublished letters of the mother superior of the Ursulines convent in Poissy, published by M. Fromageot: "L'enfance de Madame de Pompadour d'après des documents inédits" [Madame de Pompadour's childhood according to unpublished documents], in *Revue de l'histoire de Versailles*, 1902.
5. Ibid.
6. Marie-Anne Thiercelin, Madame Poisson's sister, had married Laurent Deblois, head of the Dauphine's fruit supplies, in 1708.
7. Previously unpublished letters of the mother superior of the Ursulines convent in Poissy, published by M. Fromageot, op. cit.
8. Prosper Jolyot Crébillon (1674–1762), author of tragedies and royal censor.
9. Born Marie-Anne de Maupeou, wife of Prosper Bauyn d'Angervillers, Secretary of State in the War Office.
10. Cited by René Pomeau, *Voltaire*, vol. I, p. 456; according to J. Sareil, pp. 104–05.
11. Pierre de Ségur, *Le royaume de la rue Saint-Honoré*, p. 158. Pierre de Ségur worked on the manuscripts of Madame de La Ferté-Imbault, daughter of Madame Geoffrin. Submitted to the National Archives around ten years ago, these papers are still unavailable for consultation.
12. Born Jeanne-Thérèse d'Albert de Luynes.
13. Luynes, op. cit., vol. VII, pp. 68–69.
14. Deed drawn up by Maître Melin, January 8, 1738. A.N., M.C., Et. CVII, 450.
15. Holograph will dated December 15, 1740. A.N., Y 351.
16. Contract drawn up by Perret and Marchand, March 4, 1741. A.N., M.C., Et. XCV, 155.
17. The young bride was only entitled to the rents, which came to 3,000 livres per year. Monsieur Poisson had kept the right to sell the property in case of need.
18. Elisabeth-Charlotte Huguet de Sémonville had married the Comte d'Estrades, who would die at the battle of Dettinghen, on July 9, 1743. He was the son of Charlotte Le Normant, Le Normant de Tournehem's sister.
19. Pierre de Ségur, op.cit., p. 159.
20. Louis-Jules Mancini-Mazarini, Duc de Nivernais (1716–1798), Corporal in the Infantry, Ambassador to Rome, member of the French Academy. In 1730, he had married Hélène Phélypeaux de Pontchartrain, Maurepas's sister.

21. See Chapter 4.
22. Pierre-Joseph-Justin Bernard, called Gentil-Bernard (1708–1775), military man and poet. Madame de Pompadour would arrange to have him appointed Royal Librarian, at Choisy.
23. Pierre de Ségur, op. cit., p. 159.
24. Bertin de Blagny, Master of petitions and Treasurer of commission money, was the squire of Coudray-sur-Etiolles.
25. Paul-Maurice Masson, *Madame de Tencin*, Paris, 1909. The quotation comes from the *Correspondance de Madame de Tencin et le duc de Richelieu*.

4 . T H E   S U M M E R   O F   F O N T E N O Y

1. D'Argenson, *Mémoires et Journal inédit du marquis d'Argenson*, ed. Elzévirienne, Paris, 1857, vol. II, pp. 341–42.
2. Voltaire, *Mémoires*, p. 105.
3. Casanova, *Histoire de ma vie*, vol. I, pp. 557–58.
4. Feydeau de Marville, op. cit., vol. II, p. 73, letter dated May 6, 1745.
5. Ibid., p. 73, letter dated May 9, 1745.
6. Ibid., p. 75, letter dated May 10, 1745.
7. Ibid., p. 76, letter dated May 13, 1745.
8. Ibid., p. 81, letter dated May 18, 1745.
9. Bernis, op. cit., vol. I, pp. 110–11.
10. Ibid., p. 114.
11. Ibid.
12. In 1740, Cardinal Fleury had made France enter into a coalition that included Prussia, several German princes, Spain and the two Sicilies. These governments refused to recognize Maria Theresa as the heir to the imperial crown. Frederick II retired from combat in June 1742 after she had been forced to yield Silesia to him. The Empress, supported by the Anglo-Hanoverians, regrouped troops against her other enemies and threatened Alsace in 1744. The resumption of war by Frederick II had saved France from a critical situation. The Fontenoy victory would allow the invasion of the Austrian Netherlands, followed by that of the United Provinces.
13. The appointment dated from April 1, 1745.
14. Voltaire, *Correspondance*, ed. de la Pléiade, vol. II, p. 965.
15. Luynes, op. cit., vol. VI, p. 469.
16. Bernis, op. cit., vol. I, p. 114.
17. Voltaire, *Oeuvres complètes*, ed. Besterman, letter dated June 10, 1745.
18. Voltaire, *Correspondance*, ed. de la Pléiade, vol. II, p. 986, letter dated June 20, 1745, and p. 1016, letter written around August 25.
19. It would be *Le Temple de la Gloire*.
20. A.N., Archives Privées 463.
21. Feydeau de Marville, op. cit., vol. II, p. 104, letter dated June 30, 1745.

22. Luynes, op. cit., vol. VI, pp. 492–93.
23. Luynes, op. cit., vol. VII, p. 49.
24. Ibid., p. 55.

5. The Court

1. The King had exempted these courtiers from producing proof of nobility. The French Court therefore included many descendants of lawyers who had bought their positions in the sixteenth and seventeenth centuries, and even at the beginning of the eighteenth. Under Louis XV's reign, the old nobility, the noblesse de robe and the grandsons of royal financiers were related by many intermarriages.
2. Louise-Elisabeth de Bourbon-Condé (1693–1775), daughter of Louis, Prince de Condé, and Mademoiselle de Nantes, Louis XIV's legitimatized daughter; and widow of Louis-Armand III, Prince de Conti. In 1743, her daughter Louise-Henriette had married the Duc de Chartres, who would become Duc d'Orléans in 1752.
3. The Queen, the Dauphine and the princesses each had a lady-in-waiting called "dame d'honneur" and a wardrobe lady. The Queen's other lady companions were called "dames du palais."
4. "ce pays-ci" was the time-honored expression used to refer to the Court.
5. Luynes, op. cit., vol. VII, p. 60.
6. Ibid.
7. Ibid.
8. The incident had been noticed of course. A singer-songwriter, informed by someone present (probably Maurepas), composed some satirical couplets. (Cf. Lettres de M. de Marville, vol. II, pp. 154–55.)
9. Political writings of the Comte de Sade, "Le courtisan," in Maurice Lever, Sade et la Révolution, Que suis-je à présent?, p. 40.
10. Bernis, op. cit., vol. I, p. 104.
11. Ibid.
12. Dufort de Cheverny, Mémoires, ed. Guicciardi, vol. I, pp. 100–01.
13. D'Argenson, op. cit., vol. II, p. 321.
14. Luynes, op. cit., vol. VII, p. 64.
15. Ibid., p. 65. The Duc de Luynes gives a rather detailed description of them.
16. Ibid., p. 110.
17. Feydeau de Marville, op. cit., vol. II, p. 172.
18. Luynes, op. cit., vol. VII, p. 126.
19. Feydeau de Marville, op. cit., vol. II, p. 173.

6. Debut in "This Country"

1. Soulavie, Mémoires historiques et anecdotes de la cour de France pendant la faveur de la marquise de Pompadour, p. 362.

2. Feydeau de Marville, op. cit., vol. II, p. 197.

3. Soulavie, op. cit., p. 44.

4. Bernis, op. cit., vol. II, p. 115.

5. Feydeau de Marville, op. cit., vol. II, pp. 72, 73, 137, 150–51.

6. Ibid., p. 197, letter dated December 4, 1745.

7. Cf. Luynes, op. cit., vol. VII, p. 136; d'Argenson, op. cit., vol. II, p. 361; Barbier, op. cit., vol. IV, pp. 105–06.

8. He would succeed Tournehem. This practice of inherited positions was relatively widespread in the ministries.

9. A cruel epitaph that translates as follows made the rounds in Paris at the time: "Here lies the one who came from manure,/Who wanting to make a great fortune,/Sold her honor to the *Fermier*/And her daughter to the owner." It is found in Marville, op. cit., vol. II, p. 216, and in Barbier, *Journal*, vol. IV, p. 115.

10. Marie-Antoinette Victoire de Gontaut, daughter of the Maréchal-Duc de Biron, married on July 16, 1721, to Louis-Claude-Scipion de Grimoard de Beauvoir, Comte du Roure. The Dauphine's Lady-in-Waiting, she dined often in the private chambers.

11. Louis-César Le Blanc de La Baume (1708–1780), Duc de La Vallière since 1739, Hunting Captain and Grand Falconer of France since 1748. He had married Anne de Crussol in 1742. He made a name for himself as a bibliophile. His collections, bought by the Comte d'Artois, are now in the Bibliothèque de l'Arsenal.

12. Charles de Rohan, Prince de Soubise (1715–1787), Brigadier in 1748, Maréchal of France in 1758. His third wife was Anne-Victoire, Princesse de Hesse-Rheinfels.

13. Jean-Baptiste Colbert de Torcy, Marquis de Croissy (1703–1777), Lieutenant General in 1744, had married Henriette de Franquetot de Coigny, the Maréchal's daughter.

14. Jean-Antoine-François de Franquetot, Comte de Coigny (1702–1748), the Maréchal's son, Governor of Choisy in 1739.

15. Louis-François de Bourbon, Prince de Conti (1717–1776), Peer of France, Governor and Lieutenant General of the Hainaut and the Bas Poitou, Generalissimo of the Armies of France and Spain in Italy in 1744. He had married the Regent's daughter, Louise-Diane d'Orléans, called Mademoiselle de Chartres, in 1732. She had died in 1736.

16. Croÿ, op. cit., vol. I, p. 71.

17. Ibid., pp. 71–73.

18. Ibid., p. 56.

19. Ibid., p. 62.

20. Soulavie, *Mémoires historiques et anecdotes* . . . , pp. 80–81.

21. "Apartment days" was the term used for those evenings when the King received the entire Court in the Hall of Mirrors and the drawing rooms.

22. Croÿ, op. cit., vol. I, p. 59.

23. *Renaud et Armide*, a five-act opera, libretto by Quinault and music by Lulli, had been performed at the Opera for the first time on February 15, 1686. It had just been performed again on the occasion of the victories of the Maréchal de Saxe.
24. Louise-Elisabeth, Duchess of Parma, called Madame Première (1727–1759).
25. Anne-Henriette, called Madame Seconde (1727–1752).
26. Marie-Adélaide, called Madame Troisième (1732–1800).
27. Richelieu, *Mémoires*, vol. VIII, p. 150.

7 . " T H E   O R A C L E   O F   T H E   C O U R T "

1. Marc-Pierre de Voyer de Paulmy, Comte d'Argenson (1696–1764), Lieutenant General of the Police for two terms (January–July 1720 and 1722–1724), *Intendant* of Paris (1740–1743), Secretary of State in the War Office (1743–1757).
2. The relations between the Comte d'Argenson and the Pâris brothers were complex. It is thought that in 1723 d'Argenson avoided taking the ministry because he feared being "governed" by the two financiers. On the other hand, in 1745, he was pleased that Pâris-Duverney obtained Orry's dismissal, thanks to Madame de Pompadour. (Cf. Yves Combeau, *Le comte d'Argenson*, pp. 8 and 136.)
3. René-Louis de Voyer de Paulmy, Marquis d'Argenson (1694–1757), Secretary of State in Foreign Affairs (1744–1747).
4. The Marquis d'Argenson's *Mémoires* have benefited from several editions, the most important being: (1) *Mémoires et Journal inédit du marquis d'Argenson*, ed. Elzévirienne, Paris, 1857, 5 vols.; (2) *Journal et Mémoires du marquis d'Argenson . . .* , Paris, 1859–1867, 9 vols. This second edition, called édition Rathery, is more complete than the previous one.
5. Jérome Phélypeaux (1674–1747), son of the Chancellor of Pontchartrain.
6. Président Hénault, *Mémoires*, p. 203.
7. Richelieu, op. cit., vol. VIII, p. 160.
8. The Marquis de Brunoy, who was famous for his extravagance, was born of this union.
9. Feydeau de Marville, op. cit., vol. II, p. 263.
10. August II, Elector of Saxony, was the King of Poland.
11. Feydeau de Marville, op. cit., vol. II, p. 169.
12. Luynes, op. cit., vol. VII, p. 300.
13. The château and estate of Crécy, which yielded a revenue of 25,000 livres a year, were purchased for 300,000 livres from Louis Verjus de Crécy, who had spent 1.5 million livres to build it. In order to make it seem like the Marquise was buying the estate, Montmartel advanced, once again, the necessary funds, which the King reimbursed by creating and selling a new official position (cf. Luynes, op. cit., vol. VII, p. 303). The château was destroyed during the Revolution.
14. Lassurance was Comptroller General of Buildings in Marly.

15. Born Duc d'Anjou, Philippe V, Louis XIV's second grandson, mounted the throne of Spain in November 1700, after the death of Charles II, who had designated him as his successor. The Infanta Marie-Thérèse Raphaëlle was born of his marriage to Elisabeth Farnese.
16. Luynes, op. cit., vol. Vll, pp. 351–52.
17. Ibid., p. 363.
18. Quoted by Vitzhum d'Eckstaedt, in *Maurice, comte de Saxe et Marie Josèphe de Saxe, d'après les Archives de Dresde*, p. 37.
19. Ibid., p. 53, letter dated October 3, 1746.
20. Eléonore Marie Thérèse was eighteen years old, Marie-Louise Gabrielle, seventeen, and Marie Félicité, sixteen. They were the daughters of Charles-Emmanuel I of Piedmont and Christine de Hesse-Rheinfels.
21. As Dauphine, Marie-Josèphe de Saxe would be the mother of, among other children, the future Louis XVI, Louis XVIII and Charles X.
22. Valfons was Captain in the Piedmont regiment and Assistant Major General of the army of Flanders.
23. Valfons, op. cit., p. 191.
24. Ibid., p. 193.
25. The italics are mine.
26. Dresden Archives, 789, letter dated October 26, 1746, in Stryienski, *La mère des trois derniers Bourbons*, p. 22.
27. Valfons, op. cit., pp. 201–02.
28. Luynes, op. cit., vol. VIII, p. 27.
29. Dresden Archives, 2738, vol. XII, fol. 188, in Stryienski, *Mesdames de France, filles de Louis XV*, p. 72.
30. Croÿ, op. cit., vol. I, p. 62.
31. Ibid.
32. First Gentleman of the Chamber at that time, he was in charge of the organization of the Menus-Plaisirs (Entertainments), in this instance the festivities planned for the marriage.
33. Soulavie, op. cit., p. 47.

8. THEATER IN THE PRIVATE APARTMENTS

1. Charlotte-Victoire Le Normant (1712–1786), daughter of Hervé-Guillaume Le Normant and Elisabeth de Francine, wife of François de Baschi. (Cf. Chapter 3.)
2. Luynes, op. cit., vol. VIII, p. 105.
3. Ibid.
4. Croÿ, op. cit., vol. I, p. 81.
5. Maurice de Saxe's letter to his brother, King August III of Poland, dated February 12, 1747, in Stryienski, *La mère des trois derniers Bourbons*, p. 63.

6. Marie-Françoise Renée de Carbonnel de Canisy, widow of the Marquis d'Antin, had married the Comte de Forcalquier, Lieutenant General of the Provence Government, in 1742.

7. Croÿ, op. cit., vol. I, p. 78.

8. D'Argenson, op. cit., vol. III, p. 173.

9. Ibid., p. 174.

10. Maurice de Saxe's letter to August III, dated March 6, 1747, in Stryienski, *La mère des trois derniers Bourbons*, p. 81.

11. Dresden Archives, 2738, vol. XII, in *La mère des trois derniers Bourbons*, p. 82.

12. Croÿ, op. cit., vol. I, p. 81.

13. Feydeau de Marville, op. cit., vol. II, p. 190, letter dated November 10, 1745.

14. Ibid.

15. Philippe Beaussant counted 626 in the period between 1740 and 1750, which comes to more than one performance a week. (Cf. Philippe Beaussant, *Les Plaisirs de Versailles*, p. 180.)

16. The only plays performed were *La Surprise de l'Amour* and *Le Legs*. (Cf. *Les Plaisirs de Versailles*, p. 181.)

17. Luynes, op. cit., vol. VII, p. 132.

18. Marmontel and Madame de Campan were full of praise for this young woman who, when widowed, married the Comte d'Angivillers. She was still alive at the beginning of the Empire.

19. The Regent's grandson, Louis-Philippe, Duc de Chartres (1725–1785), was the son of Louis, Duc d'Orléans (1703–1752), and Marie-Jeanne de Bade. The husband of Henriette de Bourbon-Conti, he was the father of Louis-Philippe-Joseph, Duc d'Orléans, better known in history as Philippe-Egalité.

20. Of all the services of his Household, the Administration de l'Argenterie, Menus-Plaisirs et les Affaires de la Chambre du Roi was the one most closely concerned with the sovereign's personal well-being. Its responsibilities included the renewal of the King's wardrobe, as well as his wife's and the royal children's, the Court carriages, trips to the royal châteaux, the upkeep of the shops and entertainments, including stage spectacles. The Menus-Plaisirs also organized Court mourning arrangements, royal weddings and exceptional public festivities.

21. According to the Duc de Luynes (vol. VIII, p. 87), the Buildings service, which Tournehem headed, replaced the Menus-Plaisirs on this occasion. Pierre de Nolhac (*Louis XV et Madame de Pompadour*) followed Luynes, but Emile Campardon (*Madame de Pompadour et la cour de Louis XV*), Adolphe Jullien (*Histoire du théâtre de Madame de Pompadour*) and, more recently, Philippe Beaussant (op. cit.) believe that the Menus-Plaisirs provided for the little theater's needs.

22. Luynes, op. cit., vol. VIII, p. 91.

23. Ibid., p. 147. In *Les Plaisirs de Versailles* (pp. 171–72), Philippe Beaussant analyzes these remarks. He feels that the terms used by the Duc de Luynes, which seem

imprecise to us today, were not so in the eighteenth century: "'She does not have a very full-bodied voice,' is rather comprehensible. . . . This refers not just to the register but the quality of the timbre; if it lacks body this does not just mean that it is 'light,' nor even that it lacks volume, it means that the timbre favors the higher register to the detriment of the lower ones. . . . Nowadays, 'having taste' does not mean much. . . . In the eighteenth century, on the contrary, with regard to music, it had a very specific meaning. 'Taste in singing' was then the supreme art of controlling expression and placing ornaments appropriately, in a word it was style."

9. PLEASURES AND DAYS

1. Each royal or princely residence called for a different outfit.
2. The Marquise's Lady of the Bedchamber and confidante, Madame du Hausset, gave the manuscript of her memoirs to the Marquis de Marigny. Quentin Crawfurd probably made a fair copy of her text in the beginning of the nineteenth century; it went through several editions, some of which were expurgated.
3. Originally physician and surgeon to the Duc de Villeroy, François Quesnay subsequently became Madame de Pompadour's physician. He lived at Versailles in a small apartment beneath hers, followed her on her trips and became Louis XV's consulting physician. Passionately interested in economics, Quesnay received many *philosophes* and hosted a true coterie representing the beginnings of the Physiocratic School.
4. Madame du Hausset, *Mémoires sur Louis XV et Mme de Pompadour*, pp. 50–52.
5. Lazare Duvaux left a journal-book that remains a first-rate document for the history of the arts during Louis XV's reign. It was published in 1873.
6. D'Argenson, ed. Rathery, vol. V, p. 81.
7. Luynes, op. cit., vol. VIII, p. 368.
8. Luynes, op. cit., vol. XI, p. 86.
9. Luynes, op. cit., vol. VIII, p. 139, and vol. IX, p. 437.
10. Reputed to be impregnable, the city of Berg-op-Zoom had surrendered on September 16.
11. Croÿ, op. cit., vol. I, p. 93.
12. Ibid., p. 91.
13. Ibid., p. 93.
14. Ibid., p. 92.
15. The play was given its first performance in 1721 by the actors of the Comédie Française.
16. Verses cited by Adolphe Jullien, in *Histoire du théâtre de Madame de Pompadour*, p. 18.
17. Cited by Laujon, in *Avertissement d'Eglé*.
18. The play was given its first performance on October 10, 1736, at the Comédie Française.

19. Cf. Preface to *L'Enfant prodigue*.
20. Voltaire, *Correspondance*, ed. de la Pléiade, vol. II, pp. 1195–96, Voltaire's letter to Cideville dated January 2, 1748.
21. Barbier, *Journal*, vol. IV, p. 280.
22. Pierre Laujon, *Oeuvres choisies*, Paris, 1811, vol. I, pp. 87–88.
23. Barbier, op. cit., vol. IV, pp. 280–81.
24. Croÿ, op. cit., vol. I, pp. 105–06.
25. D'Argenson, op. cit., vol. V, p. 132.
26. Ibid., p. 182.
27. This small opera in one act, with a libretto by Moncrif and music by Royer, was performed at the Paris Opera on August 28 and had no success at all.
28. Libretto by Néricault-Destouches and music by Mouret.
29. Luynes, op. cit., vol. IX, p. 461.
30. Antoine-François, Comte de Coigny (1702–1748), was the son of the first Maréchal by the same name.
31. Letter cited in a footnote by Rathery, in *Mémoires et Journal du marquis d'Argenson*, vol. V, p. 217.
32. The Prince de Dombes was the son of the Duc du Maine, the legitimized son of Louis XIV and Madame de Montespan.
33. Louis XV's letter to the Maréchal de Richelieu, dated April 16, 1748. Bibliothèque Victor Cousin, Fonds Richelieu, ms. 2, unpublished.
34. By Fuzelier and Colin de Blamont.
35. Luynes, op. cit., vol. X, p. 2.

1 0 . " A W e l l - T r a i n e d O d a l i s q u e "

1. D'Argenson, op. cit., vol. V, p. 185.
2. Choiseul, *Mémoires*, p. 369.
3. The Infante Don Philippe, son of Philippe V and Elisabeth Farnese, had married Madame Henriette's twin sister, Louise-Elisabeth, called Madame Infante.
4. Barbier, op. cit., vol. IV, p. 310.
5. The Duchesse de Luynes was the Queen's intimate friend.
6. Luynes, op. cit, vol. IX, p. 44.
7. Ibid., p. 43.
8. Ibid., p. 44.
9. D'Argenson, op. cit., vol. V, p. 242.
10. Montretout is near Saint-Cloud.
11. D'Argenson, op. cit., vol. III, ed. Elzévirienne, p. 189.
12. The King bought Saint-Cloud from Bachelier for 260,000 livres.
13. D'Argenson, op. cit., vol. V, p. 253.
14. Ibid., p. 274.
15. Louis XV, in recognizing the legitimacy of the Hanovers on the British throne,

had committed himself to driving out of France Prince Charles Edward, the Stuart pretender, who had fought on the side of the French against the English. He was very popular in Paris, where he led a merry life. His arrest at the door of the Opera, on December 10, 1748, contributed greatly to the King's unpopularity.

16. D'Argenson, op. cit., vol. V, p. 291.
17. Ibid., p. 308.
18. Grimm, *Correspondance*, vol. II, p. 348.
19. Marmontel, *Mémoires*, ed. Renwick, vol. I, p. 122.
20. Ibid.
21. Ibid., p. 123.
22. Ibid.
23. Letter dated March 18, 1749, Voltaire, in *Correspondance*, ed. de la Pléiade, vol. III, p. 37.
24. Letter to Louise Denis dated August 12, 1749, ibid., p. 76.
25. A reference to the "poissonades"; see Chapter 11. (So-called because of the Marquise's maiden name, Poisson, meaning fish.)
26. Dated letter written around September 5, 1749, cited by R. Pomeau, op. cit., vol. I, p. 605.
27. Cf. R. Pomeau, op. cit., vol. I, p. 626. Voltaire crossed the frontier on June 30, 1750. However, it should be noted that Louis XV maintained his title of *gentilhomme ordinaire*, as well as the honors pertaining to it. Furthermore, he allowed him to sell his office of historiographer, which he did. The transaction earned him 60,000 livres, and the person who succeeded him was Duclos.
28. Voltaire never forgave Jeanne-Antoinette for what he considered a betrayal. At his former benefactress's death, fifteen years later, he could not refrain from writing: "Though Madame de Pompadour defended the detestable play *Catilina*, I still liked her, that's how good-natured I am; she had even done me some small favors. . . ." (Voltaire, *Correspondance*, letter to the Comte d'Argental, dated April 23, 1764, vol. VII, p. 669.)

11. THE "POISSONADES"

1. *Recueil Clairambault-Maurepas, chansonnier historique du XVIIIe siècle*, "La Cour et les courtisans," vol. VII, p. 119ff.
2. Ibid., "La paix d'Aix-la-Chapelle," p. 127.
3. D'Argenson, op. cit., vol. V, p. 338.
4. Ibid., p. 414.
5. Ibid., p. 94.
6. Ibid., p. 119.
7. Ibid., p. 329.
8. Ibid., pp. 211–12.

9. Ibid., p. 350.

10. Ibid., p. 355.

11. Ibid., p. 362.

12. Ibid., p. 361.

13. Ibid., p. 391.

14. *Recueil Clairambault-Maurepas, chansonnier historique du XVIIIe siècle*, "Imprécations contre le roi," vol. VII, pp. 144–45.

15. Letter to Madame de Lutzelbourg, dated February 27, 1749, in Pompadour, *Correspondance*, pub. Poulet-Malassis. (*Toise* = 6½ feet.)

16. *Recueil Clairambault-Maurepas, chansonnier historique du XVIIIe siècle*, "L'Etat de la France," vol. VII, p. 142.

17. The expression comes from the Marquis d'Argenson, op. cit., vol. V, p. 406.

18. Luynes, op. cit., vol. X, p. 110.

19. D'Argenson, op. cit., vol. V, p. 462.

20. Ibid., p. 470.

21. D'Argenson, op. cit., vol. V, p. 456.

22. It was by consulting a list of trusted persons left by his father, the Dauphin, Louis XV's son, that Louis XVI made this decision.

23. D'Argenson, op. cit., vol. V, p. 462.

24. Letter of Madame de Pompadour to the Duc de Nivernais, cited by Lucien Perey, in *Un petit-neveu de Mazarin, Louis Mancini-Mazarini, duc de Nivernais*, p. 170.

25. D'Argenson, op. cit., vol. V, p. 467.

26. A.N. O1, 1192–127.

27. D'Argenson, op. cit., vol. VI, p. 20.

28. Ibid., p. 43.

29. Anne-Louise de Bourbon-Condé (1676–1753) had married the Duc de Maine, the illegitimate son of Louis XIV and Madame de Montespan. During the Regency, she held a genuine court at Sceaux where the intellectual elite of the period met. She had also inspired the famous Cellamare conspiracy whose aim was to place Philippe V on the French throne. This affair cost her several months' detention.

30. Built by Jules Hardouin-Mansart, the château belonged to the Duc de Bouillon, the King's great chamberlain. The drawing room where the supper was served resembled the one at Marly.

31. Letter of Madame de Pompadour, cited by Perey, op. cit., pp. 162–63.

32. *Relation de l'arrivée du roi au Havre de Grâce, le 19 septembre 1749, et des fêtes qui se sont données à cette occasion* was printed in 1753. The six prints, engraved by Jean-Philippe Lebas (1707–1783), are the work of Jean-Baptiste Descamps (1714–1791). Madame de Pompadour owned a set, bound in red morocco leather, in her library. (Cf. the article by Danielle Gallet, in *Madame de Pompadour et la floraison des arts*, Montreal, Musée David M. Stewart, 1988.)

12. "The Life I Lead Is Dreadful"

1. The Marquise's letter to her brother, dated December 28, 1749, in Pompadour, *Correspondance*, p. 30.
2. Letter to her brother, dated May 19, 1750, ibid., p. 47.
3. This is the word she uses in a letter to the Duc de Nivernais, written shortly after her return from Le Havre, cited by Perey, op. cit., p. 162.
4. Ibid., p. 163.
5. The Marquise's letter to her brother, dated March 25, 1750, in Pompadour, *Correspondance*, p. 41.
6. This is a reference to the gardening of flowers and rare plants, an occupation the Marquise enjoyed.
7. Letter to the Duc de Nivernais, written shortly after the return to Le Havre, cited by Perey, op. cit., p. 162.
8. Kaunitz-Rietberg (Comte de, then Prince de), "Mémoires sur la cour de France, 1752," p. 452.
9. Alexandrine entered the convent in June 1750.
10. Kaunitz-Rietberg, op. cit., p. 453.
11. The Marquise's letter to her brother, dated December 28, 1749, in Pompadour, *Correspondance*, p. 29.
12. The Marquise's letter to her brother, dated June 13, 1750, ibid., p. 41.
13. Madame Elisabeth, called Madame Infante, and her daughter Isabelle were at Versailles at the time.
14. The Marquise's letter to Madame de Lutzelbourg, dated 1749, in Pompadour, *Correspondance*, p. 103. The small château she mentions is La Celle.
15. He was to die there on November 30, 1750.
16. Madame du Hausset, *Mémoires*, p. 59.
17. Ibid.
18. Ibid.
19. Ibid., pp. 59–60.
20. D'Argenson, op. cit., vol. VI, p. 126.
21. Cf. Madame de Pompadour's letter to Madame de Lutzelbourg, dated January 22, 1750, in Pompadour, *Correspondance*, p. 104.
22. D'Argenson, op. cit., vol. VI, p. 113.
23. Luynes, op. cit., vol. X, p. 173.
24. First performed at the Opera in 1698, the music was by Destouches and the libretto by La Mothe.
25. Music by Colin de Balmont and de Bury, libretto by Roy.
26. The Marquise performed *Alzire* on February 28, 1750, and Voltaire left France the following June 30. (Cf. Chapter 10.)
27. Madame de Pompadour's letter to her father, dated 1750, in Pompadour, *Correspondance*, p. 10.

28. The Marquis de Beringhen, First Equerry of the King and Governor of the Château de La Muette.
29. Croÿ, op. cit., pp. 152–53.
30. Ibid., p. 149.
31. Kaunitz-Rietberg, op. cit., p. 846.
32. D'Argenson, op. cit., vol. VI, p. 87.
33. Kaunitz-Rietberg, op. cit., p. 446.
34. Barbier, op. cit., vol. IV, pp. 422–38.
35. Madame de Pompadour's letter to her brother, dated June 13, 1750, in Pompadour, *Correspondance*, p. 55.
36. D'Argenson, op. cit., vol. VI, p. 219.
37. Ibid., p. 213.
38. Madame de Pompadour's letter to her brother, dated June 15, 1750, in Pompadour, *Correspondance*, p. 58.
39. Louis XV later had a road built from Versailles to Saint-Denis that bypassed Paris. It led to the Porte Maillot and was called "the road of the Rebellion."
40. D'Argenson, op. cit., vol. VI, p. 206.

13. THE SHADOW OF MADAME DE MAINTENON

1. Lassurance was the project manager, and for his work he réceived the decoration of the Order of the Saint-Esprit from the King.
2. Madame de Pompadour's letter to Madame de Lutzelbourg, dated January 3, 1751, in Pompadour, *Correspondance*, p. 106.
3. A statue by Falconet presently at the Musée de Louvre.
4. The work of Lambert Sigisbert Adam.
5. Now at the Metropolitan Museum of Art in New York.
6. Now at the National Gallery of Art in Washington.
7. Now in the Lyon Museum.
8. Cf. Danielle Gallet, *Madame de Pompadour et la floraison des arts*, pp. 94–95.
9. Madame de Pompadour's letter to Madame de Lutzelbourg, dated January 3, 1751, in Pompadour, *Correspondance*, p. 106.
10. D'Argenson, op. cit., vol. VI, p. 342.
11. Kaunitz-Rietberg, op. cit., p. 448.
12. Ibid.
13. Baron Le Chambrier's report to Frederick II, dated March 15, 1751, in Flammermont, *Correspondance des agents diplomatiques . . .* , p. 21.
14. The italics are mine.
15. Flammermont, op. cit., p. 21.
16. A.N. K 149 no. 17, letter published by Poulet-Malassis, op. cit., p. 122.
17. Ibid., p. 124.
18. Ibid., p. 129.

19. Ibid., p. 130.

20. D'Argenson, op. cit., vol. VI, p. 355.

21. Ibid., p. 365.

22. Ibid., p. 387.

23. "Instructions rédigées au nom de Madame de Pompadour et relatives à la négociation entamée en cour de Rome pour vaincre l'opposition des confesseurs qui refusent de laisser approcher Louis XV des sacrements tant qu'il gardera près de lui Madame de Pompadour," in Choiseul, *Mémoires*, pp. 376–79.

24. Cf. Bernis, *Mémoires et Lettres*, vol. II, p. 70.

25. Kaunitz-Rietberg, op. cit. p. 454.

26. The Marquise de Pompadour used to give nicknames to her correspondents. Madame de Lutzelbourg was *grand-femme* (big woman); the Duc de Nivernais, *petit-époux* (little husband); Pâris-Duverney, *nigaud* (simpleton); Vandières, *frérot* (little brother); etc.

27. Madame de Pompadour's letter to Madame de Lutzelbourg, dated September 29, 1751, in Pompadour, *Correspondance*, pp. 108–09.

28. D'Argenson, op. cit., vol. VII, p. 29.

14. 1752: The Year of Living Dangerously

1. The Comte de Sade's letter, dated October 15, 1751, in *Bibliothèque Sade, Papiers de famille, Le règne du père*, ed. Maurice Lever, vol. I, pp. 532–33.

2. Letter to Madame de Lutzelbourg, dated December 5, 1751, Pompadour, *Correspondance*, p. 110.

3. Cf. d'Argenson, op. cit., vol. VII; Barbier, op. cit., vol. V, pp. 114–15; Luynes, op. cit., vol. XI, p. 264ff.

4. Madame Sauvé remained in the Bastille until 1757. Upon her release, she was prohibited from living in Paris or the Paris area.

5. D'Argenson, op. cit., vol. VII, p. 38.

6. The most recent wing of the Grand Trianon, which is now made available to the French Président.

7. D'Argenson, op. cit., vol. VII, p. 117.

8. Madame Infante was not taken into account, as she was considered a foreign princess since her marriage to the Infante of Parma.

9. D'Argenson, op. cit., vol. VII, p. 118.

10. Cf. Croÿ, op. cit., vol. I, p. 173.

11. Ibid., pp. 185–86.

12. D'Argenson, op. cit., vol. VII, pp. 305–06.

13. Charlotte Rosalie de Romanet was the daughter of Pierre-Jean de Romanet, Président of the Grand Conseil, and Marie-Charlotte d'Estrades. She was the niece of Madame d'Estrades, who was herself Madame de Pompadour's cousin by marriage.

14. D'Argenson, op. cit., vol. VI, p. 409.
15. Ibid., p. 33.
16. Kaunitz-Rietberg, op. cit., p. 454.
17. Marmontel, *Mémoires*, p. 173. Marmontel, who was protected by Madame de Pompadour, got this account from Dubois, the Comte d'Argenson's secretary.
18. Choiseul, *Mémoires*, p. 83.
19. Madame de Choiseul-Beaupré died on June 2, 1753, after giving birth to a daughter.

1 5 .   A   D U C H E S S   H I G H   A N D   L O W

1. Royal warrant dated October 12, 1752. A.N. O1, 96, fol. 313.
2. Dufort de Cheverney, op. cit., vol. I, p. 272.
3. Croÿ, op. cit., vol. I, p. 190.
4. Dufort de Cheverny, op. cit., vol. I, p. 274.
5. It seems that Casanova had her painted nude and lying on her stomach by a German artist who, according to experts, was the Swede Gustave Lundberg. D'Argenson claims that she posed for Boucher (op. cit., vol. VII, p. 436). But, according to the same experts, she was not the model for the famous Boucher painting entitled *L'Odalisque*. (Cf. Casanova, *Histoire de ma vie*, pub. F. Lacassin, vol. I, book 3, p. 622, n. 1.)
6. This unobtrusive house was located at numbers 2 and 4 in the rue Saint-Médéric in Versailles. It was rented by the bailiff Vallet on behalf of the King, on November 25, 1755, but it is probable that this house or some other house in the neighborhood had been used earlier for Louis XV's trysts.
7. D'Argenson, op. cit., vol. VII, p. 439; Barbier, op. cit., vol. V, p. 372.
8. Croÿ, op. cit., vol. I, p. 200.
9. Ibid., p. 189.
10. D'Argenson, op. cit., vol. VII, p. 282.
11. Madame du Hausset, op. cit., p. 61.
12. This manuscript would remain unpublished until 1756.
13. Charles-Emmanuel de Vintimille, Marquis du Luc, born in 1742, was successively called Monsieur de Savigny, Comte de Marseille and Marquis du Luc. He was Captain in the Bourbon-Cavalrie regiment, Colonel in the Royal-Corse and Brigadier in the King's armies. He married Marie-Madeleine de Castellane-Esparron in 1764, emigrated at the Revolution and became the princes' representative in Turin. He died in 1814.
14. Cf. Chapter 1.
15. Madame du Hausset, op. cit., pp. 66–67. Louis XIV had wanted his legitimized son, the Duc de Maine, to play a prominent political role and even succeed him, if need be.
16. D'Argenson, op. cit., vol. VII, p. 3.
17. Sophie de Lorraine de Guise, who had died in 1740 and with whom he had had Louis-Antoine, Duc de Fronsac, later Duc de Richelieu (1736–1791).

18. Anne-Josèphe Bonnier de La Mosson, who had married the Duc de Chaulnes, Lieutenant General since 1748. In 1752, he obtained the position of Governor and Lieutenant General of the provinces of Picardie and Artois.

19. Marie-Joseph-Louis d'Albert d'Ailly, born in 1741, Vidame of Amiens, then Duc de Picquigny and finally Duc de Chaulnes after his father's death, married Marie-Paule-Angélique d'Albert, daughter of the Duc de Chevreuse, in 1758.

20. The Marquise's letter to Monsieur Poisson, dated December 7, 1752, in Pompadour, *Correspondance*, p. 17.

21. Partisans of Luis de Molina's views on grace and free will generally adopted by the Jesuits.

22. Fulminated by Pope Clement XI on September 8, 1713, it condemned Jansenism. It aroused very bitter polemics and divided the Church of France. It was imposed as the law of the kingdom by a royal declaration on March 24, 1730.

23. Catherine Maire, *De la cause de Dieu à la cause de la nation*, pp. 442–43.

24. The members of parliament.

25. Pierre-Augustin-Robert de Saint-Vincent (1725–1799), counselor in the Chamber of Inquiries, known for his aggressive Jansenism.

26. Monseigneur de Beaumont.

27. Madame du Hausset, op. cit., p. 60.

28. Ibid., p. 61.

29. D'Argenson, op. cit., vol. VIII, p. 20.

30. Four among them were prisoners of the State. Most of the Councillors in Inquests and Petitions were banished to Bourges, and the magistrates of the Grand Chamber to Pontoise.

31. Croÿ, op. cit., vol. I, p. 192.

32. Ibid.

33. Ibid., p. 202.

16. PATRONESS OF THE ARTS

1. Luynes, op. cit., vol. XIII, p. 442.

2. In Levron, *Louis XV, Un moment de perfection de l'art français*, p. 40.

3. Cf. Chapter 13.

4. These were the tradesmen from the corporations considered most prestigious since the fifteenth century: haberdashers, drapers, hosiers, grocers, silversmiths and furriers; they were the spokesmen for the shopkeeping bourgeoisie and occupied important positions in the administration of the city.

5. Croÿ, op. cit., vol. I, pp. 230–31.

6. *Portrait de la marquise de Pompadour*, 1756, oil on paper, affixed to canvas (0.60 m. high by 0.45 m. wide), Paris, Musée du Louvre.

7. *Portrait de Madame de Pompadour*, 1756, oil on canvas (2.01 m. high by 1.57 m. wide), Munich, Pinakothek.

8. *Madame de Pompadour à sa toilette*, 1758, Cambridge, Mass., Fogg Art Museum.

9. *Madame de Pompadour lisant dans un sous-bois*, 1758, London, Victoria and Albert Museum.

10. *La Marquise de Pompadour devant le groupe de Pigalle, L'Amour et L'Amitié, dans les jardins de Bellevue*, 1759, London, Wallace Collection.

11. This pastoral by Guarini (1589) rivaled Tasso's *Aminta*. A model of Baroque poetry, it was still appreciated in the eighteenth century.

12. Jacques Guay (1705–1787) had been Boucher's student before specializing in engraving. He was Barrier's successor as Official Engraver.

13. October 18 and 24, 1752.

14. Rousseau, *Correspondance complète*, vol. II, p. 212.

15. Diderot, *Oeuvres complètes*, ed. Lewinter, vol. II, p. 895, according to a ms. copy. B.N. Mss. Fs. Na.fr. 13781.

16. Diderot would not overflow with gratitude toward Madame de Pompadour. "What has remained of that woman who drained us of men and money, left us without honor or energy, and completely upset the system of Europe? The Treaty of Versailles, which will last as long as it can; Bouchardon's *Amour*, which will be admired forever; some stones engraved by Guay, which will astonish future antique dealers; a good little painting by Van Loo that people will look at occasionally; and a handful of ashes . . . ," in Diderot, *Oeuvres complètes*, vol. VI, p. 29, "Salon de 1765."

17. D'Argenson, op. cit., vol. VII, p. 224.

18. Marmontel, op. cit., p. 151.

19. Ibid., p. 129.

20. Ibid.

21. Cf. Chapter 25.

22. The publication was limited to 2,500 copies. Louis XV ordered 200 and Madame de Pompadour, 50.

17. THE TEMPTATION OF POLITICS

1. D'Argenson, op. cit., vol. VIII, p. 280.

2. Ibid., p. 266.

3. Ibid., p. 297.

4. Morphise remarried two years later with a Le Normant, a tax collector in Riom and distant cousin of Le Normant d'Etiolles.

5. The autopsy report suggests that Alexandrine had come down with acute peritonitis but, as in all violent and unexplained deaths, there was talk of poison.

6. On October 19, 1754, Alexandrine's mortal remains were exhumed from the choir of the Ladies of the Assomption and taken to the family burial place, in the chapel of the church of the Capuchins, a sepulchre that the Duc de La Tremoille had sold to Madame de Pompadour. Madame Poisson, mother of the Marquise, already rested there.

7. Croÿ, op. cit., vol. I, p. 282.

8. Madame de Pompadour's letter to the Duc de Richelieu, Bibliothèque Victor Cousin, Fonds Richelieu, ms. 24, fol. 130, unpublished.

9. Text cited by Barbier, op. cit., vol. VI, p. 82.

10. Ibid., p. 84.

11. "Lettres de madame de Pompadour à Choiseul," edited by General de Piépape, *Revue de l'Histoire de Versailles*, 19e année, 1917, pp. 13, 17.

12. Rouillé, the Minister of Foreign Affairs, wrote to Choiseul at the time: "You can assure the pope that the King is extremely displeased by this new initiative of his parliament and that very shortly H.M. will be taking the necessary measures to allay the concerns that might conceivably exist in the country where you are as a result of what just took place." (A.A.E. Corresp. Pol. Rome t. DCCCXVII, fol. 301, quoted by Maurice Boutry, in *Choiseul à Rome*, p. 44.)

13. "Lettres de madame de Pompadour à Choiseul," pp. 18, 19.

14. Ibid., letter dated May 12, 1755.

15. Ibid., letter dated June 28, 1755, p. 21.

16. Ibid., letter dated December 1, 1755, p. 22.

17. See Chapter 19.

18. Bernis, op. cit., vol. I, p. 208.

19. Ibid.

20. Ibid., p. 209.

21. It was this policy conducted by Louis XV, aimed at placing the Prince de Conti on the Polish throne, that was commonly called "the King's secret." The project never succeeded, but the Comte de Broglie, Louis XV's main agent, succeeded—not without difficulty—in establishing relations of trust between the King and Czarina Elizabeth. (Cf. Michel Antoine, *Louis XV*, pp. 729–31; and especially the Duc de Broglie, *Le secret du roi*.)

22. Bernis, op. cit., vol. I, p. 208.

23. The Duke of Newcastle had succeeded Walpole and become George II's main adviser.

18. Secret Negotiations

1. Croÿ, op. cit., vol. I, p. 305.

2. D'Argenson, op. cit., vol. IX, p. 47.

3. The Chancellor was like the Minister of Foreign Affairs.

4. *Correspondance secrète entre le comte A. W. Kaunitz-Rietberg et le baron Ignaz de Koch, 1750–1752*, pub. Hans Schlitter, letter dated November 7, 1750, p. 22.

5. Ibid., letter dated February 12, 1752, p. 167.

6. Ibid., letter dated August 22, 1751, pp. 113–14.

7. Bernis, op. cit., vol. I, p. 227.

8. *Correspondance secrète entre le comte A. W. Kaunitz-Rietberg et le baron Ignaz de Koch, 1750–1752*, pub. Hans Schlitter, letter dated June 23, 1752, p. 239.

9. Bernis, op. cit., vol. I, p. 227.

10. George Adam, Count Starhemberg (1724–1807). After being plenipotentiary minister at the Court of Louis XV from 1753 to 1756, he would be accredited as ambassador in September 1756. He would remain at Versailles until 1766.

11. Quoted by Nolhac, in *Madame de Pompadour et la politique*, p. 131, based on *Politische Correspondenz Friederich des Grossen* (vols. XI to XXIV) and Alfred Ritter von Arneth, *Geschichte Maria Theresia's*.

12. Quoted by Nolhac, op. cit., p. 132.

13. Arneth, op. cit., vol. V, p. 550, n. 482.

14. Bernis, op. cit., vol. I, p. 225.

15. Ibid., p. 227.

16. D'Argenson, op. cit., vol. IX, p. 136.

17. Arneth, op. cit., vol. IV, p. 561.

18. Ibid.

19. Starhemberg's correspondence, written in French, has been preserved in Vienna, Staatsarchiv Frankreich 93–95, Berichte (cf. Victor-Lucien Tapié, *L'Europe de Marie-Thérèse*, p. 358, n. 26).

20. See Chapter 19.

21. Bernis, op. cit., vol. I, p. 274.

22. Arneth, op. cit., vol. V.

23. Ibid.

24. Duclos, *Mémoires*, vol. I, pp. 121–22.

25. Letter to Choiseul, op. cit., p. 25.

19. ARRANGEMENTS WITH THE POWERS ON HIGH

1. Madame du Hausset, op. cit., p. 88.

2. A.N., M.C., Et. LVI, 111.

3. Luynes, op. cit., vol. XV, p. 322.

4. Croÿ, op. cit., vol. I, p. 337.

5. Luynes, op. cit., vol. XV, p. 324.

6. Letter quoted by Pomeau, op. cit., vol. I, p. 853.

7. Madame de Pompadour to Choiseul, op. cit., pp. 22–23.

8. Bernis, op. cit., vol. II, pp. 74–75.

9. Croÿ, op. cit., vol. I, p. 358.

10. Ibid., p. 354.

11. Bibliothèque Victor Cousin, Fonds Richelieu, ms. 27, fol. 182, unpublished.

12. Madame de Pompadour to Choiseul, op. cit., p. 25.

13. King of Saxony and Poland, he was the father of the Dauphine Marie-Josèphe.

14. Quoted by Jacques Levron, based on the Vienna Archives, in *Secrète Madame de Pompadour*, p. 192.

15. The Abbey of Saint-Denis is where the French kings were buried.

2 0 . T H E   A S S A S S I N A T I O N   A T T E M P T

1. All the accounts of the assassination attempt are consistent with one another. Essentially we have used the Duc de Croÿ's *Journal*; the *Mémoires* of Bernis, Luynes and d'Argenson; as well as letters published by Maurice Lever in *Bibliothèque Sade, Papiers de famille, Le règne du père*, vol. I, pp. 726–31.

2. Bernis, op. cit., vol. I, p. 354.

3. Ibid., p. 355.

4. Dufort de Cheverny, op. cit., p. 202.

5. Madame du Hausset, op. cit., p. 100.

6. Bernis, op. cit., vol. I, p. 363.

7. Madame du Hausset, op. cit., pp. 101–02.

8. Ibid., p. 102.

9. Bernis, op. cit., vol. I, p. 364.

10. Choiseul, *Mémoires*, p. 132.

11. Madame de Pompadour to Choiseul, op. cit., pp. 181–82.

12. Bernis, op. cit., vol. I, p. 367.

13. Berryer was then Lieutenant General of the Paris police.

14. Valfons, op. cit., pp. 254–55.

15. Madame du Hausset, op. cit., p. 103.

16. Antoine-René de Voyer, Marquis de Paulmy, was the son of the author of the *Mémoires*. He headed the Ministry of War only from February 1757 to March 1758. Governor of the Arsenal, he left a very large library, which makes up the basic collection of what is now the Bibliothèque de l'Arsenal.

17. Président Hénault, *Mémoires*, p. 244.

18. Choiseul, *Mémoires*, p. 141.

19. Bernis, op. cit., vol. I, p. 372.

20. Jean-Baptiste, Comte de Sade (1702–1767), father of the famous Marquis, friend and correspondent of Voltaire.

21. Letter from the Comte de Sade to Madame de Pompadour, in *Bibliothèque Sade*, vol. I, pp. 731–33.

22. Ibid., p. 733.

23. Marmontel, op. cit., p. 144.

21. THE GIDDINESS OF POWER

1. Bernis, op. cit., vol. I, p. 333.
2. J.B.F. Durey de Meinières (1705–1785) had been Président at the second Chamber of Inquiries since 1731.
3. The quotations that follow are taken from the "Première conversation" and the "Seconde conversation de la marquise de Pompadour avec le président de Meinières," published by Jérôme Pichon in *Mélanges des Bibliophiles français*, 1856, according to the autograph manuscript of Président de Meinières. These two texts, which are also included in the Duc de Richelieu's *Mémoires*, vol. VIII, p. 386ff, have been republished by Poulet-Malassis in his edition of Pompadour, *Correspondance*, pp. 173–214. Our endnotes refer to that edition.
4. Ibid., pp. 181–83.
5. Ibid., pp. 186–87.
6. Ibid., p. 193.
7. Ibid., pp. 202–05.
8. Ibid., p. 206.
9. Ibid., pp. 211–12.
10. Luynes, op. cit., vol. XV, p. 361.
11. "Extrait de ce que le prisonnier à dit et qui à paru mériter attention aux douze sergents des régiments des gardes-françaises chargés de le garder à vue," B.N., Mss. Fonds Joly de Fleury, ms. 2070, fol. 158–62, quoted by Pierre Rétat in *L'attentat de Damiens*.
12. Hénault, op. cit., pp. 243–44. (Jacques Clément was Henri III's assassin.)
13. Cf. the account of it given by the lawyer Barbier, op. cit., vol. VI, pp. 505–08.
14. Diderot alone would express indignation in a letter to Sophie Volland in October 1760, and would compare Damiens to Regulus.
15. Madame du Hausset, op. cit., p. 127.
16. Bernis, op. cit., vol. I, p. 383.
17. Ibid., p. 387.
18. These troops were under the command of Charles-Alexandre, Prince of Lorraine (1705–1766), brother of Emperor Francis I.
19. Léopold-Joseph-Marie, Comte de Daun (1712–1780), Field Marshal and intimate adviser since the peace of Aix-la-Chapelle.
20. Choiseul, op. cit., p. 145.
21. Filon, *L'ambassade de Choiseul à Vienne*, "Instructions données à Choiseul, ambassadeur à Vienne, pièces justificatives," vol. I, pp. 79–86.

22. A PERPETUAL COMBAT

1. Croÿ, op. cit., vol. I, p. 411.
2. Ibid., p. 415.

3. Jean-Baptiste-François Desmarets, Marquis de Maillebois (1682–1762), was the son of General Inspector Desmarets and Colbert's grand-nephew. He began his military career under Villars and received his marshal's baton in 1741. He received the government of Alsace in 1748. His son, Comte de Maillebois, was Lieutenant General in Minorca in 1756, and army Sergeant in Germany in 1757.

4. Louis-Hyacinthe Boyer de Crémilles (1700–1768), Lieutenant General in 1748, would be summoned in 1758 to help the Maréchal de Belle-Isle, Secretary of State in the Ministry of War.

5. Bernis, op. cit., vol. I, p. 392.

6. Ibid.

7. Ibid., p. 396.

8. This victory of the French army under the command of the Maréchal d'Estrées was mainly due to the actions of Chevert and the Marquis de Bréhan.

9. Principal city in the Duchy of Bremen, in the Hanover Electorate, located fifteen leagues northeast of the city of Bremen.

10. Bibliothèque Victor Cousin, Fonds Richelieu, ms. 27, fol. 189, Madame de Pompadour's letter to Richelieu, dated October 2, 1757, unpublished.

11. Cumberland resigned as soon as he learned that his father had disavowed him.

12. Bibliothèque Victor Cousin, Fonds Richelieu, ms. 27, fol, 189, Madame de Pompadour's letter to Richelieu, dated October 2, 1757, unpublished.

13. Ibid., no date, fol. 161, unpublished.

14. Ibid., no date, fol. 153, unpublished.

15. Ibid., no date, fol. 159, unpublished.

16. Madame de Pompadour to Choiseul, op. cit., p. 183.

17. Madame de Pompadour's letter to Madame de Lutzelbourg, dated November 28, 1757, in Pompadour, Correspondance, p. 114.

18. Bernis, op. cit., vol. I, p. 138, letter to Choiseul, dated November 14, 1757.

19. Ibid., p. 142, letter to Choiseul, dated November 22, 1757.

20. Leuthen was Frederick II's most surprising victory. On December 5, he attacked the imperial forces, under the command of Charles of Lorraine, who had just captured Breslau. He took 22,000 prisoners. Two weeks later, he marched into Breslau and proceeded to reconquer Silesia.

21. Madame de Pompadour's last will and testament, in Pompadour, Correspondance, pp. 216–22.

22. Madame du Hausset, op. cit., p. 160.

23. Ibid., p. 78.

24. Bernis, op. cit., vol, II, p. 72.

25. Ibid., p. 73.

26. Madame du Hausset, op. cit., p. 82.

23. BERNIS'S FALL FROM GRACE

1. The King had created a new department of religious and parliamentary affairs for Bernis (cf. Bernis, op. cit., vol. II, p. 95).
2. Croÿ, op. cit., vol. I, p. 416.
3. Ibid., p. 417.
4. Bernis, op. cit., vol. II, p. 47.
5. Ibid., p. 162, letter to Choiseul, dated January 14, 1758.
6. Ibid., p. 169, letter to Choiseul, dated January 19, 1758.
7. Croÿ, op. cit., vol. I, p. 420.
8. The Comte de Clermont's letter to the Marquise, quoted by Pierre de Nolhac, in *Madame de Pompadour et la politique*, pp. 252–53.
9. Bernis, op. cit., vol. II, p. 201, letter to Choiseul, dated April 7, 1758.
10. Ibid., p. 206, letter to Choiseul, dated April 16, 1758.
11. Ibid., p. 214, letter to Choiseul, dated April 21, 1758.
12. Ibid., p. 228, letter to Choiseul, dated May 13, 1758.
13. Ibid., p. 210, letter to Choiseul, dated April 21, 1758.
14. Ibid., p. 244, letter to Choiseul, dated June 22, 1758.
15. Ibid., p. 67.
16. The *Conseil d'En Haut* included, in principle, the King, the Dauphin, the Maréchal de Belle-Isle, Monsieur de Saint-Florentin, the Maréchal d'Estrées, Monsieur de Puysieulx, the Abbé de Bernis and Monsieur Berryer.
17. The Duc d'Agenois, become Duc d'Aiguillon, had been Governor of Brittany since 1753.
18. Duclos, *Mémoires secrets*, vol. II, p. 163.
19. Bernis, op. cit., vol. II, p. 261, letter to Choiseul, dated August 20, 1758.
20. Duclos, op. cit., vol. II, p. 167.
21. On August 25, 1758, Louis XV made the Comte de Stainville a hereditary duke. From then on he went by the name Duc de Choiseul. The letters of patent were given at Versailles in November and registered at Parlement on November 29, 1758.
22. Bernis, op. cit., vol. II, p. 265, letter to Choiseul, dated August 26, 1758.

24. THE KING, THE MINISTER AND THE MARQUISE

1. Gleichen, *Souvenirs*, p. 17.
2. Sainte-Beuve, *Causeries du lundi*, vol. VII, p. 198.
3. Ann Thoinard de Jouy (1739–1825) had married Jean-Jacques-Pierre d'Esparbès de Lussan in 1758. She was a relative of the Le Normants.
4. Charles Just de Beauvau (1720–1793), Lieutenant General at thirty-eight, became Governor of Languedoc and Maréchal in 1783.

5. Dufort de Cheverny, op. cit., p. 255.

6. The gift had been ordered by the Empress in 1756. It had cost 77,278 livres and 19 sols, or 39,911 florins, according to the invoice published in the Vienna Archives, in Arneth, op. cit., vol. V, pp. 538–39.

7. Letter dated January 28, 1759, quoted by V.-L. Tapié, op. cit., p. 360.

8. Céladon is the languishing, love-struck hero in *Astrée*, the seventeenth-century pastoral novel by Honoré d'Urfé.

9. Choiseul had just been appointed Superintendent of the Postal Services.

10. Letter dated April 6, 1759, quoted by Pomeau, op. cit., vol. I, p. 901.

11. Marmontel, op. cit., p. 205.

12. She sold Bellevue to Louis XV for 350,000 livres, though she had spent over 2,600,000 livres on it, not counting the furniture. This could be considered as restitution to the Royal Treasury.

13. She resold Crécy for 1,000,000 livres and a life income of 100,000 livres a year, whereas she had spent 4,112,000 livres on it.

14. She would spend 500,000 livres on it over a four-year period. At her death in 1764, the château would be returned to the Gesvres.

15. She purchased it for 880,000 livres. Her brother, Marigny, inherited it and took the title Marquis de Ménars.

16. She sold it in 1763, but continued to enjoy its use until her death.

17. César Gabriel, Comte de Choiseul-Chevigny, later Duc de Praslin (1712–1785), was Choiseul-Stainville's distant cousin. After a brilliant military career, he was appointed ambassador to Vienna (1758–1761), Minister of State (1761), Secretary of State in Foreign Affairs (1761–1766) and finally Secretary of State in the Navy (1766–1770).

18. Letter dated April 11, 1759, in Pomeau, op. cit., vol. II, p. 5.

19. Croÿ, op. cit., vol. I, p. 480.

20. B.N. Mss. Nouv. Acq. Fses. 6498.

21. Parma archives, *Lettere dei principi*, in Stryienski, *Mesdames de France*, p. 115.

22. Letter to the Duc d'Aiguillon, dated the evening of the 8th [*sic*], 1760, in Pompadour, *Correspondance*, pp. 146–47. The italics are ours.

23. Letter to the Duc d'Aiguillon, dated August 20 (probably 1760), ibid., pp. 154–55.

24. B.N., Mss. Nouv. Acq. Fses. 6498.

25. Ibid.

26. Croÿ, op. cit., vol. II, p. 93.

25. "ONE MOMENT, MONSIEUR LE CURÉ"

1. Letter to the Duc d'Aiguillon, undated, but probably from 1759 or 1760, in Pompadour, *Correspondance*, p. 137.

2. "Instructions rédigées au nom de Madame de Pompadour et relatives à la négociation entamée en cour de Rome pour vaincre l'opposition des confesseurs qui lui refusent de laisser approcher Louis XV des sacrements tant qu'il gardera près de lui Madame de Pompadour," in Choiseul, op. cit., pp. 376–79.

3. Eugène Welvert, "Le vrai nom de Mlle de Romans," in *Revue Historique*, 1886.

4. Madame du Hausset, op. cit., pp. 167–68.

5. Ibid., p. 168.

6. Ibid., p. 169.

7. Ibid., pp. 169–70.

8. Several years later, Louis XV allowed his former mistress to marry the Marquis de Cavagnac. As for their son, Louis de Bourbon, he became Abbé de Bourbon and died in Rome in 1787 without having the kind of career that might have been expected from his background.

9. Mademoiselle de Tiercelin's child was born on February 7, 1764, several weeks before the Marquise's death.

10. Her son became known in history as Abbé Le Duc. He played a role in helping the royal family during the Revolution and the period of emigration. He probably died around 1829. Mademoiselle de Tiercelin died in 1779 after leading a rather unsettled life.

11. Croÿ, op. cit., vol. II, p. 96.

12. Ségur, *Le royaume de la rue Saint-Honoré*, pp. 164–65.

13. Croÿ, op. cit., vol. II, p. 133.

14. Parma Archives, *Lettere dei principi*, quoted by Pierre de Nolhac, in *Madame de Pompadour et la politique*, pp. 338–39.

15. Madame de Pompadour's immense fortune went to her brother. A short time after her death, he sold her library, which totaled 3,525 books, and received 41,940 livres. (Cf. *Catalogue des livres de la bibliothèque de feu Mme la marquise de Pompadour, dame du palais de la reine*). Marigny also sold part of his sister's paintings and furniture: the sale lasted a year. The Marquise also left jewels in the amount of 284,059 livres, which included 22 white diamond jewels (154,040 livres), 7 jewels with white and yellow diamonds and rubies (40,800 livres), 41 rings (18,676 livres) and 55 jewels with gems of various colors (70,543 livres). (Cf. *Inventaire après décès de la marquise de Pompadour, dressé par le notaire Dutartre le 27 juin 1764, A.N., M.C., Et. LVI, 113–14.*) Let us recall that Madame de Pompadour had bequeathed the Hôtel d'Evreux to Louis XV, who sold it to the financier Beaujon, who sold it back to Louis XVI.

16. The Dauphin's letter to the Bishop of Verdun, quoted in the Archives Nicolaï, in Boislisle, *La Maison de Nicolaï*, p. 590.

17. Dresden Archives, 2744, IX, April 18, in Stryienski, op. cit., p. 317.

18. Bachaumont, *Mémoires secrets pour servir à l'histoire de la République des Lettres en France*, vol. II, p. 49.

19. Dufort de Cheverny, op. cit., p. 335.
20. Boislisle, op. cit., p. 590.
21. Parma Archives, *Lettere dei principi*, quoted by Pierre de Nolhac, in *Madame de Pompadour et la politique*, p. 344.
22. Dufort de Cheverny, op. cit., p. 335.

BIBLIOGRAPHY*

I. PUBLISHED SOURCES

Bachaumont, Louis Petit de, *Mémoires secrets pour servir à l'histoire de la République des Lettres en France*, London, 1762–1789, 36 vols.

Barbier, *Chronique de la Régence et du règne de Louis XV 1718–1763, ou Journal de Barbier*, Paris, 1866, 8 vols.

Bernis, François-Joachim de Pierre, Cardinal de, *Mémoires et Lettres*, published by F. Masson, Paris, 1878, 2 vols.

Besenval, Baron de, *Mémoires*, published by Ghislain de Diesbach, Paris, 1987.

Casanova, Jacques, *Histoire de ma vie*, published by F. Lacassin, Paris, 1993, 3 vols.

Catalogue des tableaux originaux de différents maîtres, miniatures, dessins et estampes sous verre de feu Mme la marquise de Pompadour, dame du palais de la reine, dressé par Jean-Thomas Hérissant fils en 1765, sur les notices de l'abbé Bridard de La Garde.

Choiseul, Duc de, *Mémoires*, published by F. Calmettes, Paris, 1904.

Croÿ, Duc de, *Journal inédit*, published by the Vicomte de Grouchy and P. Cottin, Paris, 1906–1907, 4 vols.

D'Argenson, Marquis, *Journal et Mémoires*, published by J. B. Rathery, Paris, 1859–1867, 9 vols.

———. *Autour d'un ministre de Louis XV, Lettres intimes inédites*, Paris, 1923.

Diderot, Denis, *Oeuvres complètes*, ed. Roger Lewinter, Paris, 1969, 15 vols.

Du Deffand, Madame, *Correspondance complète avec ses amis*, published by A. de Lescure, Paris, 1865, 2 vols.

Du Hausset, Madame, *Mémoires sur Louis XV et Mme de Pompadour*, published by J.-P. Guicciardi, Paris, 1985.

*The references for the archival sources are given in the Notes.

Duclos, Charles Pinot, *Mémoires secrets sur les règnes de Louis XIV et de Louis XV*, published by Petitot and Monmerqué, Paris, 1829, 2 vols.

Dufort de Cheverny, *Mémoires*, published by J.-P. Guicciardi, Paris, 1990.

Favier, *Doutes et questions sur le traité du 1er mai 1756 entre la France et l'Autriche*, London, 1778.

Flammermont, Jules, *Correspondance des agents diplomatiques étrangers en France avant la Révolution*, Paris, 1896.

Gleichen, Baron de, *Souvenirs*, Paris, 1868.

Grimm, Frédéric Melchior, *Correspondance littéraire, philosophique et critique par Grimm, Diderot, Raynal, Meister . . .* , published by M. Tourneux, Paris, 1877–1882.

Hénault, Président, *Mémoires*, published by the Baron de Vigan, Paris, 1855.

Kaunitz-Rietberg, Wenceslas-Antoine-Dominique, Comte, then Prince de, *Correspondance secrète entre le comte A. W. Kaunitz-Rietberg et le baron Ignaz de Koch, 1750–1752*, published by Hans Schlitter, Paris, 1899.

———, "Mémoires sur la cour de France, 1752," published by the Vicomte du Dresnay, *Revue de Paris*, 11ème année, vol. IV, pp. 441–54 and 827–47.

Laujon, Pierre, *Oeuvres choisies*, Paris, 1811, 4 vols.

Lever, Maurice, ed., *Bibliothèque Sade, Papiers de famille, Le règne du père*, vol. I, Paris, 1993.

———, *Louis XV, Libertin malgré lui*, Paris, 2001.

———, *Théâtre et Lumières, Les spectacles de Paris au XVIIIème siècle*, Paris, 2001.

Louis XV, *Lettres à son petit-fils, l'infant de Parme*, published by Ph. Amiguet, Paris, 1938.

Luynes, Charles Philippe d'Albert, Duc de, *Mémoires sur la cour de Louis XV, 1735–1758*, published by L. Dussieux and E. Soulié, Paris, 1860–1865, 17 vols.

Marais, Mathieu, *Journal et Mémoires . . . sur la Régence et le règne de Louis XV*, published by M. de Lescure, Paris, 1863–1868.

Marville, Claude-Henri Feydeau de, *Lettres de M. de Marville au ministre Maurepas*, published by A. de Boislisle, Paris, 1896, 3 vols.

Marmontel, Jean-François, *Mémoires*, published by J. Renwick, Paris, 1972, 2 vols.

Montbarrey, Alexandre de Saint-Maurice, Prince de, *Mémoires autographes*, Paris, 1826–1827, 3 vols.

Moreau, Jacob-Nicolas, *Mes souvenirs*, published by C. Hermelin, Paris, 1898–1901, 2 vols.

Mouffle d'Angerville, *Vie privée de Louis XV*, Paris, 1781, 4 vols.

Papillon de la Ferté, Denis-Pierre-Jean, *Journal, 1756–1780*, published by E. Boyse, Paris, 1887.

Pompadour, Madame de, *Correspondance*, published by Poulet-Malassis, Paris, 1888.

———, "Lettres à Choiseul," published by Général de Piépape, *Revue de Versailles*, 19ème année, 1917.

Richelieu, Maréchal-Duc de, *Mémoires*, 1790, 9 vols.

———, *Mémoires du Maréchal-duc de Richelieu*, ed. Barrière, Paris, 1889, 2 vols.

Saint-Priest, Comte de, *Mémoires*, published by the Baron de Barante, Paris, 1929, 2 vols.

Soulavie (attributed to), *Mémoires historiques et anecdotes de la cour de France pendant la faveur de la marquise de Pompadour*, Paris, 1802.

Toussaint, François-Vincent, *Anecdotes curieuses de la cour de France*, Paris, 1908.

Valfons, Marquis de, *Souvenirs*, Paris, 1860.

Véri, Abbé de, *Journal*, published by the Baron J. de Witte, Paris, 1928–1930, 2 vols.

Villars-Brancas, Marie-Angélique Fremyn de Moras, Duchesse de, *Mémoires*, published by E. Asse, Paris, 1890.

Voltaire, *Correspondance*, published by Théodore Besterman, ed. de la Pléiade, Paris, 1977–1992, 13 vols.

————. *Mémoires*, published by J. Hellegouarc'h, Paris, 1998.

II. OTHER WORKS

Abensour, Léon, *La femme et le féminisme avant la Révolution*, Paris, 1923.

Antoine, Michel, *Louis XV*, Paris, 1989.

Antoine, Michel, and Didier Ozanam, *Correspondance secrète du comte de Broglie avec Louis XV*, Paris, 1956.

Arneth, Alfred Ritter von, *Geschichte Maria Theresia's*, Vienna, 1863–1879, 10 vols.

Beaussant, Philippe, *Les Plaisirs de Versailles, Théâtre et Musique*, Paris, 1996.

Bély, Lucien, *Les Relations internationales en Europe, XVIIème-XVIIIème siècle*, Paris, 1992.

Bertout, A., *Les Ursulines de Paris sous l'Ancien Régime*, Paris, 1936.

Bois, Jean-Pierre, *Maurice de Saxe*, Paris, 1998.

Boutaric, E. *Correspondance secrète inédite de Louis XV*, Paris, 1866.

Boutry, Maurice, *Choiseul à Rome*, Paris, undated.

Broglie, Duc de, *Le secret du roi, correspondance secrète de Louis XV avec ses agents diplomatique (1752–1774)*, Paris, 1878, 2 vols.

Butler, Rohan, *Choiseul, Father and Son*, Oxford, 1980.

Campardon, Emile, *Madame de Pompadour et la cour de Louis XV*, Paris, 1983.

Castries, Duc de, *La Pompadour*, Paris, 1983.

Chaunu, Pierre, Madeleine Foisil, and Françoise de Noirfontaine, *Le basculement religieux de Paris au XVIIIème siècle*, Paris, 1990.

Chaussinand-Nogaret, Guy, *Choiseul*, Paris, 1998.

————, *La vie quotidienne des femmes du roi*, Paris, 1990.

Combeau, Yves, *Le comte d'Argenson, ministre de Louis XV*, Paris, 1999.

Cordey, J., *Inventaire des biens de Mme de Pompadour, rédigés après son décès*, Paris, 1939.

Cottret, Monique, *Jansénisme et Lumières*, Paris, 1998.

Courajod, L., *Le Livre-Journal de Lazare Duvaux*, Paris, 1873, 2 vols.

D'Estrée, Paul, *Le Maréchal de Richelieu*, Paris, 1917.

Darnton, Robert, *L'aventure de l'Encyclopédie*, Paris, 1982.

Dubois-Corneau, *Pâris de Montmartel*, Paris, 1917.

Durand, Yves, *Les fermiers-généraux au XVIIIème siècle*, Paris, 1996.

Égret, Jean, *Louis XV et l'opposition parlementaire*, Paris, 1970.

Faur, *Vie privée du maréchal de Richelieu*, Paris, 1912.

Filon, M., *L'ambassade de Choiseul à Vienne*, Paris, 1872.

Fleury, Comte M., *Louis XV intime et les petites maîtresses*, Paris, 1899.

Fromageot, Paul, "La jeunesse de Mme de Pompadour" and "La mort et les obsèques de Mme de Pompadour," *Revue de l'histoire de Versailles*, 1902.

Gallet, Danielle, *Madame de Pompadour ou le pouvoir féminin*, Paris, 1985.

————, "Madame de Pompadour et l'appartement d'en bas au château de Versailles," *La Gazette des Beaux-Arts*, Paris, 1991.

————, *Madame Pompadour et la floraison des arts*, Montreal, Musée David M. Stewart, 1988.

Gaxotte, Pierre, *Le Siècle de Louis XV*, Paris, 1998.

Goncourt, Edmond and Jules de, *Les Maîtresses de Louis XV*, Paris, 1860.

Grosclaude, Pierre, *Malesherbes, témoin et interprète de son temps*, Paris, 1961, 2 vols.

Jullien, Adolphe, *Histoire du théâtre de Madame de Pompadour*, Minkoff reprint, Geneva, 1978.

La Barre de Raillicourt, *Richelieu, le maréchal libertin*, Paris, 1991.

La Rochefoucauld, Gabriel de, *Marie Lesczinska, femme de Louis XV*, Paris, 1943.

Lacour-Gayet, G., *Histoire de la Marine*, Paris, 1902.

Laugier, Lucien, *Le duc d'Aiguillon*, Paris, 1984.

Laulan, R., "La fondation de l'Ecole militaire et Mme de Pompadour," *Revue d'histoire moderne et contemporaine*, 1974.

Le Roy Ladurie, Emmanuel, *Saint-Simon ou le système de la cour*, Paris, 1997.

Leroi, P.-A., "Relevé des dépenses de Mme de Pompadour depuis la première année de sa faveur jusqu'à sa mort," *Mémoires de la Société des Sciences morales, des lettres et des arts de Seine-et-Oise*, vol. III, pp. 113–52.

Leroy, Alfred, *Madame de Pompadour et son temps*, Paris, 1936.

Lesueur, F., *Ménars, le château et les collections de Mme de Pompadour et du marquis de Marigny*, Blois, 1912.

Lever, Maurice, *Sade et la Révolution, Que suis-je à présent?*, Paris, 1998.

————, *Pierre-Augustin Caron de Beaumarchais*, Paris, 1999.

Levron, Jacques, *Choiseul, un sceptique au pouvoir*, Paris, 1972.

————, *Secrète Madame de Pompadour*, Paris, 1961.

————, *Louis XV, Un moment de perfection de l'art français*, Paris, 1974.

Luchet, M. de, *Histoire de Messieurs Pâris*, Lausanne, 1790.

Maire, Catherine, *De la cause de Dieu à la cause de la nation, Le jansénisme au XVIIIe siècle*, Paris, 1998.

Marie, Alfred and Jeanne, *Versailles au temps de Louis XV*, Paris, 1984.

Marquiset, A., *Le Marquis de Marigny*, Paris, 1918.

Masson, Frédéric, *Le Cardinal de Bernis depuis son ministère, 1758–1794*, Paris, 1877.

Maugras, Gaston, *Le Duc et la Duchesse de Choiseul, leur vie intime, leurs amis et leur temps*, Paris, 1924.

Maurepas, Arnaud de, and A. Boulant, *Les Ministres et les Ministères, au siècle des lumières*, Paris, 1996.

Mauzi, Robert, *L'idée du bonheur au XVIIIème siècle*, Paris, 1960.

Meyer, Jean, *La Chalotais, affaires de femmes et affaires d'Etat sous l'Ancien Régime*, Paris, 1995.

Mitford, Nancy, *Madame de Pompadour*, London, 1954.

Nicolle, Jean, *Madame de Pompadour et la société de son temps*, Paris, 1980.

Nolhac, Pierre de, *Louis XV et Madame de Pompadour*, Paris, 1903, 2 vols.

———, *Le château de Versailles sous Louis XV*, Paris, 1898.

———, *Madame de Pompadour et la politique*, Paris, 1928.

Perey, Lucien, *Un petit-neveu de Mazarin, Louis Mancini-Mazarini, duc de Nivernais*, Paris, 1890.

———, *La fin du XVIIIème siècle, le duc de Nivernais, 1754–1798*, Paris, 1891.

Picciola, André, *Le comte de Maurepas*, Paris, 1999.

Pomeau, René, *Voltaire en son temps*, Paris, 1985–1995, 2 vols.

Reiset, Comte de, *Le château de Crécy et Mme de Pompadour*, Chartres, 1876.

Retat, Pierre, and his collaborators, *L'attentat de Damiens, discours sur l'événement au XVIIIème siècle*, Lyons, 1979.

Rogister, John, *Louis XV and the "Parlement" of Paris, 1737–1755*, Cambridge University Press, 1995.

Rouart, Jean-Marie, *Bernis le cardinal des plaisirs*, Paris, 1998.

Rousset, Camille, *Le Comte de Gisors*, Paris, 1868.

Saintville, G., *Une confidente de Mme de Pompadour, Madame du Hausset de Demaines, d'après des documents authentiques*, Paris, 1937.

Ségur, Pierre de, *Le royaume de la rue Saint-Honoré*, Paris, 1897.

Solnon, Jean-François, *La cour de France*, Paris, 1987.

Stryienski, Casimir, *Le gendre de Louis XV, don Philippe*, Paris, 1904.

———, *La mère des trois derniers Bourbons, Marie-Josèphe de Saxe et la cour de Louis XV*, Paris, 1903.

———, *Mesdames de France, filles de Louis XV*, Paris, 1911.

Tapié, Victor-Lucien, *L'Europe de Marie-Thérèse, du baroque aux Lumières*, Paris, 1973.

Vaille, E., *Le Cabinet noir*, Paris, 1950.

Vaillot, René, *Le cardinal de Bernis*, Paris, 1985.

Verlet, Pierre, *Le château de Versailles*, Paris, 1961 and 1985.

Vitzhum d'Eckstaedt, Comte de, *Maurice, comte de Saxe et Marie-Josèphe de Saxe*, Leipzig, 1867.

Waddington, Richard, *La Guerre de sept ans*, Paris, 1904, 5 vols.

Zevort, Edgar, *Le Marquis d'Argenson et le ministère des affaires étrangères*, Slatkine reprints, Geneva, 1976.

INDEX